Understanding Paranoia

Understanding Paranoia

A GUIDE FOR PROFESSIONALS, FAMILIES, AND SUFFERERS

Martin Kantor

Westport, Connecticut
London

Library of Congress has cataloged the hardcover edition as follows:

Kantor, Martin.
   Understanding paranoia : a guide for professionals, families,
and sufferers / Martin Kantor.
      p. cm.
   Includes bibliographical references and index.
   ISBN 0–275–98152–5 (alk. paper)
   1. Paranoia. I. Title.
RC520.K36 2004
616.89′7—dc22   2004042205

British Library Cataloguing in Publication Data is available.

Library of Congress Catalog Card Number: 2004042205
ISBN: 978–0–313–36319–1

First published in 2004

Praeger Publishers, 88 Post Road West, Westport, CT 06881
An imprint of Greenwood Publishing Group, Inc.
www.praeger.com

Printed in the United States of America

The paper used in this book complies with the
Permanent Paper Standard issued by the National
Information Standards Organization (Z39.48–1984).

10 9 8 7 6 5 4 3 2 1

Copyright Acknowledgments

The author and publisher gratefully acknowledge permission to reprint the following material:

Excerpts from *Disorders of Personality: DSM–IV and Beyond, 2e.* Theodore Million and Roger
Davis. Copyright © by Theodore Million. This material is used by permission of John Wiley
& Sons, Inc.

Excerpts from an Associated Press article. 10 July 2003. Reprinted with permission of The
Associated Press.

To M. E. C.

Contents

Introduction

Paranoia is a surprisingly common and widespread disorder that takes many forms, benign as well as malignant, covert as well as overt. Yet few of us spot paranoia and fewer still understand it through and through. Instead, glossing over paranoia is the rule, and mishandling paranoia the result. While most of us recognize when someone does not have the physical stamina or strength to run and do not expect them to win a race, most of us fail to recognize when someone is paranoid and does not have the full ability to reason, and we instead expect them to correctly perceive reality and to make free-will choices. When we should be attempting to explain the deviant behavior of paranoid individuals as the product of pathological forces creating a recognizable syndrome, we instead attempt to understand the unfamiliar forces of paranoia solely in familiar terms. So when a criminal kills in response to voices, a reporter writes with a straight face that "his motivation remains unknown." We think behavior that is irrational is rational and respond accordingly. When driving, if we find ourselves followed too closely from behind by another driver who is honking the horn and flashing headlights, we respond by giving the finger instead of just pulling over into the right lane after shrugging off the behavior as crazy. Wives of paranoid men who should be treating their highly sensitive, overly thin-skinned, hyperreactive husbands with kid gloves instead cavalierly cross, humiliate, reject, or embarrass them. Gay men throw caution to the wind and seduce rough trade—latent homosexuals just looking for a blank screen onto which they can project their own homosexual desires, then, finding one, killing their unacceptable self-image as externalized and reflected in their victim. Teachers unthinkingly criticize, or diss, potentially or actually paranoid students, making them angry and possibly violent. Bosses play favorites, oblivious to the serious negative effect their game is having on those who are currently out of favor, or fire their workers cavalierly without recognizing that firing a potentially paranoid worker in an insensitive manner increases the likelihood that one day he or she will come back dressed in army fatigues to return the fire. Employees, viewing their place of work in an adversarial "me-against-them" light, instead of working cooperatively and productively, take advantage of the system by putting in a half-day's work for a full-day's pay or call in sick, in typical paranoid fashion, to take a so-called preventive mental health day to "get them before they get me."

Too many of us, suffering from the paranoia of everyday life, view ourselves as always and entirely the innocent victims of our fate. As drivers, spouses, or authority figures, we make an art form out of disavowing personal responsibility and blaming others entirely for everything bad that happens in our lives. As the comedian Flip Wilson might have said if he were discussing paranoia, whenever we do something wrong we blame it on the devil. We conjure up a history of childhood trauma out of the normative interpersonal negativity that occurs in all families, then for the rest of our lives blame everything evil that befalls us, no matter how much of a hand we had in provoking it, on having been kicked around when we were young. We condemn others for their misdeeds in order to deflect attention from our own, similar transgressions—viewing others as sinners the better to view ourselves as saints. Or we blame society entirely for our own negative thoughts and actions. In effect we buy into the kind of reasoning Richard Rhodes (1999) uses to effectively deny that "violent acts erupt unbidden from pathological mental states" when he notes that it is mainly the social development of violence, which he calls "violentization," not an individual's own emotional problems, that "demonstrably shadows every episode of serious private violence, from school shootings to killings for hire."

An important goal of this book is to place paranoia in all of its forms—mild to severe, covert to overt—center stage, where it belongs, providing information about paranoia to anyone who seeks the utility, comfort, and protection of knowledge and understanding. That would include the following people.

Paranoid individuals themselves. Paranoid individuals can likely benefit from learning all they can about paranoia. I believe that they can benefit the same way patients with an obsessive-compulsive disorder benefited from all the attention paid in recent years to that disorder. Obsessive-compulsive disorder is a not uncommon condition, but until recently many suffered in silence, thinking that they were becoming insane, going to great efforts to conceal their shame because they did not know that many people shared their anxieties, fears, and preoccupations. My hope is that a generation of newly emboldened, better informed paranoid individuals will now come forward, ask questions, seek professional care, and help each other in support groups.

A related goal of my book is to help improve the paranoid patient's image with mental health professionals. Paranoid patients have gotten a bad repu-tation within the mental health community, where they are generally viewed as undesirables and incurables. Therapists (and society at large) think that all paranoid individuals are incurable because the patients rarely know that they are paranoid and, if they do know it, are mostly uninterested in doing anything about it. Of course, some paranoid individuals do seem to be unreachable. In particular, some individuals with delusional disorders seem to be impervious to reason. But the picture of the patient with a delusional disorder who is convinced, and does not want to hear arguments to the contrary, that the CIA has him or her in its sights, is an extreme one—paranoid of paranoids itself, because it does not reflect the true nature of all individuals suffering from paranoia. I discovered that this portrait of the recidivistic, monomaniacal par-anoid individual as typical is a myth when I entered the word *paranoia* on search sites for discussion groups on the Web and learned that there are many individuals suffering from paranoia, including delusional paranoia, who are virtually begging for information about what ails them. The hits that came up fell into two groups. As one would expect, there were those who thought that someone in their immediate environment, like a wife or boss, might be paranoid, wanted to know if that was the case, and, if so, wanted to know what to do about it in order to help the person and to protect themselves from the person. For example, a son attempting to deal with his mother who falsely thought he was a greedy so-and-so stealing all her money wanted in-formation to be able to decide, "Should I try to reason with her, overlook the problem as just the way mother is—a woman with harmless little preoccu-pations and eccentricities, or recognize that mother is suffering from a serious illness, not just a little personality quirk, and insist that she get treatment, and do so immediately?" But, perhaps surprisingly, there were also many individ-uals who were themselves involved with worlds populated by all sorts of imagi-nary unwelcome characters, individuals who wanted help in reality testing and detaching themselves from their fantasies and delusions. Significantly, the first item in one support group was the question, "How do I know if I am paranoid or just sensitive?"

Here are some brief clinical vignettes of people struggling with paranoia who knew that they were paranoid and asked me for my help:

A friend who learned that I was writing this book asked me, "What's the distinction between *suspicion* or *precaution* and *paranoia*? Is it a matter of the degree of fear? I envision grisly scenarios (I watch a lot of forensic television) involving meeting my current pen pal —anywhere to the tune of installing hook-and-eye on my bedroom door when I visit to chickening out altogether and not going. I wonder, is it a fantasy or a fear of something that just hasn't happened yet? I have become like my long-time friend—my first boyfriend, known him since I was fifteen, who interprets almost everything in terms of design against himself. He mentions paranoia frequently, and when I men-tioned your endeavor he said I should tell you about him."

An individual fearing that Bill Gates could read his electronic brain and make trouble, found himself hesitating to install a bootleg copy of a word-processing program on a computer that linked up to the Internet because he feared going to jail. He wanted to know how he should view himself, and what he could do about his "Bill Gates paranoia," if indeed paranoia were his problem.

A friend called me up to tell me that, after she had a few drinks with friends the night before, she woke up the next morning with a headache, felt extremely fatigued and not with it, and became dizzy and unable to regain her balance. She wasn't sure, but she thought that someone put something in her drink. "You know all the drugs, that's why I am asking you if such a thing were possible, and if so, what did they use?" She then asked me to help explain a mysterious occurrence that happened the night of the day her Polish father died. Her clock radio awoke her in the middle of the night. It was tuned to a Polish radio station playing Polish music. She felt that that was strange because she knew that there were no Polish stations in the area. She moved the dial to another station, only it was playing exactly the same music, then to another, and another, all to no avail. The only way she could get the clock radio to stop the racket was to pull out the plug and smash the radio against the wall.

A patient wanted to know, in essence, "do I as a gay man who thinks that the only thing holding me back is other peoples' bad attitudes about and bad behavior towards me deserve to be called paranoid, or am I simply, attitudinally speaking, insightful, up-to-date, politically astute, as well as factually correct? That is, am I right and troubled by the truth, or wrong and bothered by seriously distortive and distractive ideas that are more like delusions than creative, prescient beliefs for the moment merely incomprehensible to, or unaccepted by, the general public?"

While many people like these individuals deal with their worries through the Web, most cannot discover everything they need to know this way, and what they do discover is not always reliable. I hope this book satisfies their curiosity and rewards their interest with useful, accurate information that helps them answer important questions about themselves, such as, "What is and what is not paranoid about me, and how paranoid can I be and still not be diagnosably ill? That is, what admixture of traits defines the paranoid syndrome, and do I fit the category?"

Given the state of our art there are no perfect answers to these and similar big questions about paranoia. But there is enough information available to at least help make paranoia less of an enigma, which will in turn help paranoid individuals themselves find better ways to cope with what can be a serious and pervasive disorder.

Psychotherapists. To date, most psychotherapists have shown little interest in, and not always a great deal of talent for, treating individuals who are paranoid. This is unfortunate because many of these individuals are interesting, valuable people who, if treated correctly and sensitively, respond positively to an offer of help, especially because that offer is sometimes the very first one that they ever had.

Pharmacotherapists. In my opinion many pharmacotherapists have shown a dangerous tendency to misdiagnose paranoid individuals as having another disorder. My goal is to emphasize the importance of treating a paranoid disorder with medication for paranoia, not with medication for depression or social phobia—for these can either do no good or do a great deal of harm. In particular I emphasize throughout the dangers of treating so-called depressed patients who are in fact significantly or mainly paranoid with antidepressants alone—risky business that is likely to be responsible for at least some of the violence in the news these days, violence generally attributed to patient proclivity or social causes, when the real reason is to be found not in the nature of the beast or in violent computer games watched and emulated but, at least in part, in psychological misdiagnosis leading to pharmacotherapeutic mistreatment.

Nonparanoid individuals. There are many people who know or suspect that they are not paranoid but nevertheless think that they might be because of what others, who *are* paranoid, are accusing them of.

The general public. The general public can benefit in at least two ways from becoming better informed about paranoia. First, those who fully understand how the paranoid people in their lives work will be in a far better position than formerly to cope with and offer assistance to some of the difficult people they face every day. Caretakers of paranoid individuals who understand paranoia through and through will know more precisely how, when, and where their friends and family go astray, and so be better positioned to help both those they love and those who victimize them. Second, a general public that understands paranoia will be better positioned to create a less paranoid society by throwing out the old and joining in new and better social rallying cries— not "I am not to blame; you made me do it" and "if I am this way, it is because of what you did to me," but "we all make our own fate, and that is the good news, because it means that the power to change our luck to a great extent resides in the power we already have inside of us to change our minds."

To date, what little material on paranoia that is both available to and suitable for the general public has been mainly confined to the self-help section of the bookstore, where it is to be found in books on difficult people. Many of the difficult people described in those books have in fact been angry and suspicious paranoid individuals ranging from those suffering from the paranoia of everyday life to those with severe and unremitting delusional disorders. Generally these books overlook that people who are difficult because they are paranoid are different and have to be handled differently from people who are difficult for other reasons, for example, because they are unpredictable impulsives or hostile manics, to name just two other possibilities. To illustrate, individuals who are difficult because they are paranoid need help with reality testing, while individuals who are difficult because they are impulsive or manic know the reality but need to learn how to act based on what they have already learned. Handling a difficult person without recognizing that he or she is paranoid is at best ineffective and at worst dangerous. Therefore my book specifically addresses the issue of difficult *paranoid* people, and suggests remedies that are appropriate for and specific to their special needs and often unique emotional problems.

I derive the material in my book from my case files, from the classic and current literature, from personal communications from colleagues and teachers, from secondary sources such as newspapers and television, and from my own everyday personal encounters with paranoid individuals who, thinking that their paranoia goes unnoticed because they are not in formal psychotherapy or part of a large academic study, let their paranoid beliefs roam free, so that they speak and behave spontaneously and therefore without all the inhibitions that appear when people are aware that they are being observed. I spy, but then I expunge and alter the particulars, disguising the individuals I write about in composite cases that retain my core lessons without publicly exposing and embarrassing those who have taught them. Clearly I have not personally studied in depth some of the people I am discussing, because they were not patients but friends, or were acquaintances or strangers whom I have merely encountered in a superficial fashion, or were public or historical figures who should be analyzed with extreme caution, since it is an ethical violation to make a diagnosis without an examination. (For stylistic purposes and purposes of convenience, in this book I sometimes refer to the paranoid person as a paranoid *patient* when the individual is not actually my patient in the sense that I have seen him or her in formal therapy.) But I believe that for those willing to accept surmise, opinion, and speculation about motivation not based on thorough psychoanalyses backed up by therapy notes, the psychohistory, psychobiography, and subway diagnoses (snap opinions derived from cursory inspection leading to conclusions that are good guesses but hardly scientifically validated formulations) that I offer have their usefulness, however limited, if only as anecdotes that illustrate some salient points I wish to make.

Therefore, I include a number of formulations that some, soured by glib, fantastic-sounding explanations based on little evidence, will find merely conjectural. That they are. However, I view these conjectures as untested hypotheses, the validity of which the reader can determine by confirming or denying them within his or her own field of experience. My hope is that my ideas will not be simply condemned as unscientific because they have not been the subject of formal research. Rather my hope is that my ideas will be a springboard for the reader's own research into their ultimate truth and value. Those who demand incontrovertible scientific proof of all contentions, as well as those who believe that personal conflicts do not exist since you cannot see them under the microscope or subject them conveniently to controlled studies, as well as those who believe (and treat accordingly) that if phenothiazines cure paranoia it must mean that paranoia is not an emotional problem but is the product of something like a phenothiazine deficiency will probably be disappointed and displeased with my book; and perhaps, before they waste their money on buying it and their time on reading it, they should look elsewhere.

In this book I use the term *paranoia* in several different ways. I sometimes use it in the lay sense, as a synonym for feeling persecuted. This usage accords with the usage in the DSM-III (American Psychiatric Association, 1987), where the stress in the definition of paranoid schizophrenia was on prominent persecutory (and grandiose) delusions or hallucinations.

But in accordance with current usage, I do not insist on persecutory ideas being present before I call an individual paranoid. I use the term *paranoia* to refer to all forms of delusions and hallucinations. This usage accords with the usage in the DSM-IV (American Psychiatric Association, 1994), where the criterion for making the diagnosis of *paranoid* schizophrenia is simply the presence of prominent "delusions or auditory hallucinations . . . related to the content of the delusional theme" (p. 287). These delusions and hallucinations may be persecutory, or they may be grandiose, erotomanic, somatic (hypochondriacal), jealous, or litigious. This makes sense if only because most if not all delusions are at bottom persecutory. Thus the grandiose idea that "I am the center of attention" goes hand in hand with feeling victimized and persecuted for one's importance and centrality; the erotomanic belief that "I love someone who doesn't love me" makes one soon enough likely to feel either persecuted or disdained and rejected by a lover; the hypochondriacal belief that there is something wrong with me that no doctor can properly diagnose goes hand in hand with the belief that "I am being misdiagnosed and ill-treated by the entire medical profession"; the somatic delusion (supposedly suffered by a famous pianist) that my left hand has turned to stone is conceptually close to a writer's persecutory delusion (mislabeled as a writer's cramp) that "my rivals are causing my hands to malfunction"; and the jealous fear that a faithful wife is cheating goes hand in hand with the husband's conviction that she and the man she is cheating with are going to get him out of the way by killing him.

I also use the term *paranoia* to describe a characterological frame of mind. The term *characterological* defines little more than a sensed unity of what, at least at first, appear to be disparate elements. In the case of the entity *paranoid personality disorder* the elements that congeal into the disorder include suspiciousness, hypersensitivity, extreme vigilance, simmering anger, and a tendency to blame others for and absolve oneself of almost everything, accompanied by a grandiose readiness to feel completely blameless in all things, one that in turn leads to feeling unjustly criticized or unfairly persecuted by one or by a group of blameworthy individuals—the usual culprits, ranging from the Jews to the FBI.

Of course, I never use the term as laypeople often use it, as a hurtful epithet.

That usage is especially prevalent with individuals who are paranoid themselves, and are striving to further their own, often hostile ends by putting others down. This usage of the term *paranoia* as a term of disapprobation is to a great extent responsible for paranoid people, already highly sensitive to being criticized, not coming forward, admitting how paranoid they actually are, and seeking help. In fact, I emphasize repeatedly that paranoid individuals are no more or less evil than persons with any other emotional disorder, or for that matter persons with a physical disorder. We must always remember that: paranoia is disorder of the mind, not a flaw of the character.

I strongly believe that paranoia is a psychopathological entity that survives the context in which it appears, and so in its essentials stays the same whatever its degree and whatever the disorder of which it is a part. That means that, as I see it, there are few essential differences between paranoia that is mild and paranoia that is severe, and that the paranoia of paranoid personality disorder closely resembles the paranoia of paranoid schizophrenia. Since I believe that paranoia breeds true, whatever its context, when I refer to paranoia I am in fact referring to a dynamic entity that I believe survives intact across all of the phenomenological boundaries of which it can become a component part, varying in some details but not substantively. Its core manifestations—the basic hypersensitivity and suspiciousness and the tendency to blame others for all one's flaws and the world for all one's troubles remain the identifiable irreducible soul of paranoia no matter what body that soul inhabits—whether the patient is complaining bitterly about how people take advantage of her or is hearing voices telling him that he is queer. Therefore, I disagree with clinicians who view the paranoia of everyday life as being somehow different from the paranoia that inhabits paranoid schizophrenia and delusional disorder—who, in other words, suggest that characterological suspiciousness is an entirely different phenomenon from delusions of persecution. Instead, I agree with clinicians who view one as either a more or less serious version of the other, and who, where others see a change, see only a transformation. I view serious persecutory delusions as lying on the right of a continuum from normal to abnormal, where lying somewhat to the left on the same continuum are such phenomena as the paranoia of everyday life that constitutes the highly suspicious nature, ideas of reference, illusions, overvalued ideas, shared myths, and persecutory histrionic imagery such as the belief that one is being followed and hears the footfalls to prove it (all terms will be defined and discussed later in the text). My clinical experience has convinced me that the overly suspicious lover who thinks, "You might be cheating on me" and is wrong about that has much in common with the patient who suspects that her surgeon has on the sly removed her esophagus just so that he could bill the operation to Medicare. Mine is a very American (as distinct from European) approach. It also fits my own tendency to be relativistic about many things, and about paranoia in particular.

My view of the inherent immutability of paranoia whatever the disorder of which it is a part leads me to a specific therapeutic philosophy. I look for and recommend sound, doable, helpful generic therapeutic techniques that are potentially useful for all individuals who are paranoid, ranging from those who suffer from the paranoia of everyday life to those who suffer from paranoid schizophrenia. Therefore in my book I often speak of the treatment of paranoia, not of the treatment of paranoid personality disorder, delusional disorder, or paranoid schizophrenia. One advantage of this, a thoroughly pragmatic view, is that it relieves us all of the need to be preoccupied with making precise distinctions between different subtypes of paranoid disorder that lie close to each other on a continuum—a difficult and somewhat agonizing process that reminds me of the futile exercise of distinguishing between a day that is partly cloudy and a day that is partly sunny. This, a process that occupies center stage in too much of what has already been written about paranoia, shifts the focus from treatment to classification and so away from what should be the main concern of all caretakers of paranoid individuals and of paranoid individuals themselves: identifying paranoia where it exists, understanding what it is all about, and finding methods that work for the vast majority of individuals who are paranoid, whether their paranoia is mild or severe, and whatever the specific guise their paranoia currently assumes.

PART I

Description

CHAPTER 1

Some Prominent Characteristics of Paranoid Individuals

A paranoid individual's characteristic problems with appearance, speech, thought, behavior, mood, insight, judgment, and intelligence when taken together trace a recognizable pattern called the mental status. Recognizing this characteristic pattern helps both clinicians and the general public spot the disorder, differentiate it from other disorders, and manage it correctively.

WHAT PARANOID INDIVIDUALS LOOK LIKE

Different paranoid individuals can look different depending on

- the exact nature of their comorbid personality structure (for example, obsessive paranoid individuals can look different from depressive paranoid individuals)
- the subtype of their paranoia (for example, those with prominent persecutory delusions often look different from those with prominent grandiose delusions)
- the degree of seriousness of their paranoia (the oddities in appearance characteristic of paranoid schizophrenia and delusional disorder tend to be softened in patients with the less-severe paranoid personality disorder)

Subtle Changes

In some paranoid individuals the signs of change in appearance that occur are subtle. They are often subtle because paranoid individuals choose to look as normal as possible because, as Theodore Millon (1981) puts it, they "refuse to submit to weakness [preferring instead to] struggle to 'pull themselves up by their own bootstraps'" (p. 398). Some such paranoid individuals merely look very *thin.* Their thinness may be due to anorexia that is the product of severe anxiety. Or it may be due to bizarre eating habits, as was the case for the patient who was skinny because "all I ever do is get on my stationary bike, eat cookies, and watch recorded reruns of old basketball games." Or it may be due to fad dieting based on false beliefs about eating and food originating in such delusions about eating and food as

- the food is poisoned
- my body is incapable of processing any sugar at all
- the food I eat won't go down because a surgeon on the sly removed my esophagus
- the only way to get rid of the mites crawling under my skin is to starve them out by eating nothing at all

Or they appear to be primarily *tense.* They pace about due to excessive sympathetic discharge, which may also drain the color from their face, making them look pasty. Or they seem to be stalking their prey in an angry, determined way, lips pursed tightly, or jaw jutted forward in hot pursuit of enemies or in defiance of all those who might get in their way.

Or they *mutter* to themselves, perhaps mulling aloud troublesome situations, reassuring themselves repeatedly that they are not in danger, or uttering magic phrases over and over again to ward off imagined evil. Or they are thinking out loud, perhaps contemplating what they might say to what has, according to Millon and Roger D. Davis (1996), been described as members of a fantasized "pseudo-community" (p. 691)—the adult equivalent of a cadre of imaginary playmates.

Or they appear to be excessively *reserved.* They appear to shrink into themselves, developing an air of remoteness suggestive of schizoid withdrawal, obsessional preoccupation, or histrionic indifference. Or they develop a faraway look, having turned inward as if they are thinking through their problem and working hard, and constantly, on ways to solve it.

Or they choose the *stance of simplicity* or calculatedly limit any changes in their appearance to *peripheral* ones so that we see nothing more than an inappropriate selection of accessory items like shoes, hats, rings, and umbrellas. For example, one patient wore a formal suit on all occasions, even to go supermarket shopping, because he feared that if he did not wear a suit others would derisively dub him antiestablishment. Or they limit the changes in their appearance to *cosmetic or otherwise superficial* ones. For one woman the only clue to the presence of a problem was a misapplication of cosmetics. This woman, feeling as if everyone were calling her an old hag, tried to look younger than her actual years by covering every liver spot on her hands and every mole on her face with makeup that, though artfully applied, only called attention to the underlying lesions. Her counterpart, a woman in her late fifties, tried to pass as a woman in her twenties by wearing too much bright lipstick, which she carried up over her lips, making her look a bit like a clown. She also wore her hair long and cascading, dyed it blonde, and demurely flicked it back into place whenever it moved just a bit off center. A man whose fear of a homosexual seduction made it difficult for him to change in the gym's locker room avoided putting the matter to a test by always working out in street clothes and, in the summertime, not in the standard sneakers, but in sandals.

In some paranoid individuals the changes in appearance resemble those found in individuals who are depressed. Paranoid individuals like individuals who are depressed feel pessimistic due to the belief that they will never have any sort of life. They then live out their pessimism in their appearance, as did the paranoid man who carried a black umbrella even on sunny days because he constantly feared that it would rain on him and spot his only good suit. He had other, better, suits but he never wore them because he felt that if the rain did not spot them then the careless people who smoked and carried sharp objects on crowded city streets would almost certainly brush against him ruinously.

Depressed paranoid individuals may use what they believe to be *positive* changes in their appearance to compensate for feeling defective. For example, a patient who was in fact unemployed always wore a dark gray suit and carried an attaché case so that others would think that he was on his way to the office, not a loser who could not find a job. Another patient dealt with his conviction that others were calling him old and ugly by overdressing to look alluring, managing instead to look not only unappealing but manic as well, as he wore a long fur coat with many outlandish rings on his fingers and two earrings matching the large medallion dangling on his chest from the heavy gold chain he had around his neck.

Gross Changes

Other paranoid individuals present with major deviations of appearance. Some display a marked bizarreness of appearance. Examples include the mountain man look and the militaristic look of the individual who wears camouflage both as a shield to keep others from seeing and attacking him and as a sword to send others the warpath message: "look out and buzz off." Others adopt a sinister, hostile, distancing, rebellious look to tell the world that they plan to overthrow a society that they hate and that they believe hates them. They get that look by piercing their tongues, tattooing their necks, arms, and legs, getting 1960s-style haircuts, and wearing long, scraggly beards—specifically meant to tell the detested square establishment that they are still back at the time of and grieving for the end of Woodstock. Some wear T-shirts with a message that broadcasts their paranoia. For example, a patient prone to attacks of road rage wore a T-shirt that said "Sticks and stones can break my bones, but no Chevy will ever pass me." Another paranoid individual took

the next step and wore a T-shirt that listed, in graphic detail, whom exactly he intended to slay.

Some paranoid individuals, including those who suffer from a paranoid personality disorder, display a degree of general deterioration of their appearance. They may seriously neglect their appearance because they are too preoccupied with or too caught up in the enfolding story of their worries, delusions, or hallucinations to maintain much interest in how they look. Often for that reason they become seedy and threadbare, like the man who wore a neatly pressed but frayed suit and the same clean but old washed-out shirt day after day. Or they look inappropriately retro, like the woman who as time went by came to look more and more dated because she never changed the style of her hairdo or clothes. Some, motivated to deliberately let their appearance go in order to become off-putting, might not shave in order to make themselves look unclean so that others will leave them alone. Others, motivated to avoid giving the impression that they have money because they fear that if others find out how much they have they will empty their bank accounts or kidnap them, dress in old, torn, second-hand or third-hand garments. Others actually age prematurely due to a combination of tension, neglect, deliberateness, and rebelliousness. I well remember a newspaper article that referred to one of my paranoid schizophrenic patients as an "old geezer." The patient was a mere 24 years old!

HOW PARANOID INDIVIDUALS SPEAK AND THINK

Paranoid individuals are often angry individuals who verbalize their rage by cursing a great deal. Often when they curse they favor words that refer to the excretory and sexual functions. As anyone who has said no to a paranoid panhandler demanding money can attest, they tend to get the angriest and curse the most when they feel crossed or rejected. To those of us who are analytically inclined, their curse words make a kind of dynamic sense. Thus they might tell someone to "kiss my ass" to humiliate them back, and in kind, for what they believe to be their having dishonored them by not granting them what they believe to have been a perfectly legitimate request.

Monomaniacal paranoid individuals, eager to make a single point, tend to speak passionately and precisely and to repeat what they just said, sometimes over and over again. In contrast, *withdrawn* paranoid individuals, eager to be evasive, shy away from specifics. Either they do not answer even reasonable questions at all, or they stall, or they answer them but only in a vague way—with circumlocutions, or by becoming deliberately tangential in order to reveal little or nothing at all. Often they speak in a way that seems, and may actually be, rehearsed—so that instead of talking spontaneously (thereby revealing too much) they cover their tracks by speaking in prepared statements and in a fashion that is so stilted and clipped that they seem to be reading from a script.

As highly suspicious individuals they often do not speak the truth, or at least the whole truth. For example, a woman known for a reticence bordering on paranoid secrecy, when asked "what property taxes do you pay?" as part of a general conversation about the rise of property taxes everywhere these days, believing that others were trying to find out just how much money she had, replied deceitfully, "I don't even know."

Many paranoid individuals, including those who suffer from a delusional disorder, think clearly but incorrectly. However, paranoid schizophrenics think both unclearly and incorrectly. They manifest a severe form of one or more of the following disorders of thinking: tangentiality, where they gradually lose sight of a point they intended to make as they move farther and farther away from it; circumstantiality, where they cover the same ground over and over again, orbiting around a point without actually ever making it; perseveration, where they make the same point over and over again; and loosening of associations, characterized by non sequiturs that sometimes disrupt ideation so much that what they say becomes close to or actually is an incomprehensible word salad.

Concrete thinking is a characteristic of the thinking not only of patients suffering from paranoid schizophrenia but also of less disturbed paranoid individuals such as those suffering from a paranoid personality disorder. People who think concretely do not capture the essence of a concept. They overlook nuance and miss true intent as they fail to read between the lines. They overlook the denotative (suggestive, or associative) significance of what others say or do and instead narrowly fix on only the more superficial connotative (exact) meaning, at least as they perceive it, in others' gestures, statements, or acts. As a result they take remarks meant figuratively too literally, or mild jokes or teasing too seriously. As an illustration, not meant to imply severe pathology, many of us have had the experience of calling up a company and, speaking to an associate, saying, "You didn't send me the item I ordered," only to be told, "*I* never spoke to you before." For such concrete-thinking individuals it is as if the "you" refers to "you personally," not, as obviously meant, "you collectively"—that is, to the company for which you work. A patient once kidded a New York woman for sending a recently purchased mink coat to a Connecticut address to save on the sales taxes, humorously comparing her to a famous hotelier who got nabbed sending empty boxes out of state. She felt he was accusing her of being a thief, and she never spoke to him again.

However, some paranoid individuals think not too concretely but too abstractly. They ponder every simple thought and communication from others, giving it a special complex meaning that it does not have, reading in import, creating mountains out of molehills.

Some brood in a detailed way about imponderables. Others just cannot stop thinking about gory details—like the patient who was a vegetarian because each time she smelled or saw meat, chicken, or fish she started thinking exactly about how the animals were killed. This spread to her being unable to build a dock in front of her house because she feared killing all the little creatures that lived under the river. She, like some such individuals, was taking some early steps along the road to becoming delusional, twisting what amounts to relatively benign or unimportant reality to become harsh serious delusional fear.

As will be discussed further in chapter 6, the thinking processes of many paranoid patients fall into a gray area of psychopathology—that is, somewhere on the continuum between normalcy and serious paranoia. In this gray area we find mild and transient delusions, what might be called nondelusional false ideas. Such delusions do not preoccupy extensively and are not particularly vivid. As delusional constructs they are only modestly distortive. They might take the form of a hunch not a conviction. Sometimes there is an ability to reality test the delusions, but that ability is temporarily suspended. Belonging to this gray area are delusions about food that fall somewhere between the belief that a particular food is poison, and the belief that a particular food is poisoned. For example, a mother had borderline food delusions that led her to impose a fad diet on her child. She fed her son exactly 14 peanuts a day because she believed that that, no more and no less, was just what the child's body needed to get all the protein he required as a growing lad. She also made him eat three melons a day because she believed that that would keep him from getting breast and testicular cysts. Also she would not let him drink diet soda because "diet soda makes you fat. The body isn't fooled. It thinks it has sugar in it and processes it the same way it processes glucose."

Or another individual with borderline delusions was almost but not quite convinced that, should she travel to Germany to actually meet a man with whom she had been corresponding over the Internet, she would be shackled, tortured, raped, and then strangled. She herself was then able to go on to correct her belief that something bad was about to happen in every encounter. As she noted, "the road to strangulation seems to be paved with remote possibilities, and an excessive fearfulness that some or another situation is off."

Also in the gray area are such semidelusional thoughts as ideas of reference, overvalued ideas, illusions, and the tendency to buy into the strange social myths of others or to create strange social myths of one's own. As we will see, many such phenomena are the product of a high level of suggestibility. Semidelusional phenomena are discussed further in chapters 2, 5, and 6.

Healthier paranoid individuals often clean up their delusional ideas once formed in order to make them appear to be less frightening to themselves and more acceptable to others. For example, many individuals arrange to appear grandiose (which seems healthier than appearing to feel persecuted) by transferring the unwelcome fear of being assaulted to become the desirable sensation of being the center of attention—even if that attention does involve being a target.

HOW PARANOID INDIVIDUALS BEHAVE

General Considerations

Behavior can be unremarkable even in patients who are seriously delusional. For example, behavior is unremarkable when delusions suggest that the person act normal to avoid detection, or to be on one's best behavior in order to accomplish a specific end—for example, to commit an act of terrorism without first being detected.

Some behavioral changes can occur. They can occur as a general by-product of having a chronic illness. However, when they occur, behavioral changes are mostly the product of, and therefore consistent or congruent with, specific delusional thinking. As examples of behavioral changes that are congruent with delusional thinking, an erotomanic paranoid individual may dress up for an imaginary beloved, while grandiose paranoid individuals may dress up for the audience they believe they have now, or anticipate that they will soon command.

Withdrawal

Some paranoid individuals, perhaps especially teenagers, withdraw to their rooms to play violent computer games or to send viruses out into cyberspace to infect (that is, punish and neutralize) the dangerous "them." If they relate to others at all, it is only to people who are similarly withdrawn, such as isolated computer hackers or members of militaristic, Nazi-style, or terrorist hate groups. These friends

- give them the feeling that they are not alone
- help them vent their anger
- validate their false beliefs as rational, intellectual, and desirable philosophical positions
- reduce their fear that they are in worldly danger by providing them with the safety of, and strength in, numbers
- offer them group support, which includes someone to complain or brag to about how bad they feel they are, and positive feedback that helps them view themselves as big somebodies
- help them clarify a previously diffuse identity, as epitomized by the Harley-Davidson T-shirt that reads, "You don't stand out if you take the bus"

However, the positive group effect often breaks down when external delusional enemies—the usual cadre of blacks, Jews, establishment, big government, and the like—become insufficient to satisfy the gang's thirst for adversaries. Now the gang, with nowhere else to turn, turns on its individual members, scapegoating and extruding some of them. Often the whole gang comes under a cloud, and people avoid them or attack them verbally or physically, to the point that each and every member of the gang becomes even more paranoid than before.

Anger

As mentioned throughout, paranoid individuals are angry people. Typically they use others as ready-made lightening rods for their own rage, then complain that, and act as if, other people are responsible for setting off their landmines.

Healthier paranoid individuals deal with their anger differently from those who are less healthy. Healthier paranoid individuals tend to simply wait their anger out until it subsides. Less healthy paranoid individuals tend to express their anger in a limited, controlled, but still counterproductive way. They may content themselves with making and repeating a single complaint (about noise) or criticism (of homosexuality), or they may express their anger passive-aggressively by making Freudian slips or by having self-destructive "accidents on purpose." We are all familiar with those individuals in the public eye who have succumbed to their hostile impulses and adversarial fantasies to the point that they have embarrassed themselves, and perhaps even ended their careers, by slipping and saying precisely what they thought about imagined enemies—finally coming out as the cruel, bigoted, or irrational individuals that they actually happen to be.

Those paranoid individuals whose adjustment is very precarious can display a loss of emotional stability should their anger, having successfully pressed for expression, shatter all controls and intrapsychic boundaries. In the more favorable cases the individual develops a violent personality where he or she becomes continuously embroiled in adversarial situations in which he or she is always the innocent victim and everyone else is a perpetrator, often as a member of a conspiracy. In the more unfavorable cases there is a full-blown rage attack and perhaps even violence.

After becoming angry, mildly paranoid individuals react by regretting having said too much. In contrast, seriously paranoid individuals do not regret having said too much. Instead they regret not having said nearly enough.

Dissociation facilitates the breakthrough of anger by creating an altered state in which self-awareness is so compromised that self-control becomes impossible to the point that irrationally angry thoughts and feelings emerge as if effortlessly. Patients in dissociation sometimes describe themselves as being unable to control their feelings because they are too remote from them to be able to have meaningful input into them. They say that it is as if they are viewing, in a state of disbelief, a car crash that they are not involved in, but are merely witnessing. Paranoid individuals also put others into a kind of dissociative state, a state of passive acceptance where victims, as if hypnotized, fail to challenge what are clearly false principles but instead accept them without questioning their legitimacy.

In my experience, in spite of all their rage, very few paranoid individuals think of themselves as unduly angry people. They feel that there is every reason to be angry and therefore no reason at all to suppress or control their anger. They reason that if they got angry it was because they were provoked, that is, others are to blame for how they feel and for what they said and did. It follows that when their angry positions are challenged or condemned they rarely apologize. If they do apologize they do so in a superficial way, just to deflect criticism, even though they have no intention of changing either their beliefs or their behavior. When pressured, they often offer admissions of guilt, but these stop short of real regrets and remorse. They admit not that they were wrong but that they could have handled matters better. So in similar future situations they behave in exactly the same way. A few acknowledge their anger fully and afterwards apologize, seemingly sincerely, but they do so perfunctorily just to keep a relationship going—so that they can have a victim waiting in the wings to strike out against once again.

THE MOOD OF PARANOID INDIVIDUALS

Often paranoia is associated with an ongoing bad mood. That can make it very difficult to distinguish paranoia from depression, creating both diagnostic and therapeutic problems for therapists treating psychologically and for psychiatrists and other physicians treating pharmacologically. However, though paranoid individuals have a disorder of mood, only depressed or bipolar (manic-depressive) patients have a true mood disorder. In a true depressive mood disorder the affect is sad, anguished, painful, and contrite, and the individual comes across as a tragic figure. In the pseudo-mood disorder associated with paranoia the affect tends to be more flat than depressed, that is, it consists of a diminished range of emotional response and expression. Flattening occurs for several reasons. First, the importance of negative emotions, like simmering resentment, has as its concomitant the relative unimportance of positive, upbeat emotions, such as joy. Second, a loss of affect occurs when affect is projected outward along with thought. For example, the paranoid patient feels that the other person is in a bad mood, when in fact it is he or she who is in the bad mood. Third, feelings may be blunted because of the general degenerative process that can accompany almost any chronic illness. However, affect does not appear to be flattened when there are persecutory delusions associated with a high level of fear, when there are grandiose delusions associated with euphoria, or when the hostility is intense enough to create what Arnold M. Cooper (1994) calls a piercing "cold paranoid fury" (p. 146).

THE INSIGHT OF PARANOID INDIVIDUALS

Some paranoid individuals have *little or no insight* into themselves. As such they have little or no ability to reality test their false beliefs. As a result they fully believe their distortions of reality. Any modest recognition that they are at all paranoid is swamped by their inability to realize that they are over-reacting and making much too much out of unimportant things, or out of nothing. They cannot dismiss their troublesome ideas from their minds, put their distortions into perspective, and distance themselves from their irra-tional fears. Instead they believe that their reality entirely justifies their in-terpretation of reality. Unable to identify which of their beliefs are irrational, they are unable to control them or any actions based on them. For example, a patient looking for love on the Internet only looked for love from foreign suitors because "as far as pen pals go, I'd no sooner convinced myself that I was most secure meeting a *foreign* one because it would be hard to plan to bring a gun or knife with him through the airport, when I thought of poison, or that he might just snap and push me down the stairs. So I concluded that, absolutely, Cupid has it in for me."

Serious lack of insight is often fixed. So often a lover in a jealous rage never doubts that it is justified to pursue and destroy a rival he or she imagines is seducing his or her mate; an erotomanic individual that his or her love is true, that he or she can be equally loved in turn, and that protestations to the contrary only prove the point because people in love are often slow to realize, and shy about confessing, it; a shooter that being dissed (invalidated) is as good a reason as any to pull the trigger; and a terrorist that it is right to kill innocent people simply because these people live in a country that the terrorist hates for what he or she perceives to be rational reasons—and that further-more since violence is justified, remorse is contraindicated, and being pun-ished inappropriate.

But even serious lack of insight can be transient and the negative actions that are a product of the transient lack of insight followed by regrets. Transient loss of insight often occurs during an acute paranoid episode. Thus the in-dividual with road rage but momentarily thinks it justified to go into a cold blind paranoid fury over having been slowed down by a driver in front making a legal turn, or a shopper with supermarket rage but momentarily feels it is justified to become hostile, agitated, and antagonistic because the person in front on the express line has more than the allotted items or takes time out to write a check.

Some paranoid individuals retain *a modest degree of insight* into themselves. As such, to at least some extent, they seem to know that they are troubled. Many of them take the next step and try to keep quiet about their paranoia, which they therefore only manifest in the subtlest of ways. For example, the only clue to the fact that the head of a department of psychiatry was hearing voices was his need to constantly change the room he gave his classes in—in the midst of a class that was already in session. However, some who know that they are troubled nevertheless still elect to pass their delusions on, but only after prefacing them with a caveat, such as "I have no proof of this but I sometimes think that . . ." or "Let me make it perfectly clear that my ideas are only one person's theory" or "It's *as if* people are persecuting me" or "I *worry* a lot about who is for and who is against me." In effect they are admitting "I guess I am a little paranoid and I shouldn't get so worried/depressed over such a minor matter."

But even those who retain the ability to recognize their paranoia often lose sight of its extent. They recognize that sometimes their thoughts and feelings are inappropriate, that they make too much of unimportant matters, and that they are occasionally hypersensitive, unnecessarily retaliative, and even unrealistic, but they do not recognize the degree to which they are troubled.

Some of these paranoid individuals are aware of the existence of past but not of present delusions. They know that they were delusional once, but they deny being delusional now. As a result, they look to the casual observer as if they are recovering when in fact they are still ill. Others of these paranoid individuals deny past delusions but admit to present delusions because these give them the most discomfort. As a result, they look to the casual observer as if they have an acute illness when in fact their illness is chronic.

Some paranoid individuals at least appear to have *excellent insight.* They know that they are paranoid and recognize the extent of their paranoia. They look for signs of paranoia in themselves and learn exactly when they get paranoid—for example, they learn that they get paranoid when they are being stressed, and what it is exactly that stresses them. As an illustration, many sexually jealous people know that they are being foolish and getting paranoid over nothing. However, so often the self-awareness does not last but tends instead to weaken as they begin to worry about what might happen if their delusional fears should come to pass—for example, they might be abandoned, harmed, or even killed. So their insight readily gives way, offering the individual no reliable help in controlling his or her thoughts or actions.

A patient stood waiting to get out of a crowded subway. The person in front did not move when the door opened and the patient was pushed into her from behind. In turn the person in front kicked back at the patient's shins. With the rush of anger, the patient's first thought was, "She did this because she hates me." This imputed attitude on her part enraged him more than any physical discomfort. He wanted to strike back, but he was afraid that if he touched her it would make matters worse. As he put it, "She might retaliate by calling the police and making trouble."

The incident was barely over before he began to wonder whether he might yet get into difficulty. He tried to reassure himself that the matter would pass, that he had not done anything wrong. Repeatedly he told himself not to get so excited and not to be so paranoid. "She doesn't know you exist, she would have done this to anyone who came along, not just you, and because she kicked you doesn't mean that she is going to report you for pushing her." He struggled thus for hours, brooding over whether his mistreatment was justified, whether there was something about him that led to his being mistreated, whether the mistreatment was or was not meant for him personally, whether he was the victim or the perpetrator, whether he should leave the city because of the danger of such encounters, whether he was yet going to get into trouble with the police, whether he might run into the woman together with her boyfriend who would beat him up, and so on.

Ultimately, he was able to put the episode into its proper perspective, dismiss it from his mind, and even chide himself for having become so emotionally involved. But the next time he got pushed and kicked, he responded in exactly the same way.

Possibly we should reclassify a *delusion* as an *obsession* based on the degree of insight present, as measured by the extent to which the ability to reality test is retained. Probably a fear, not a conviction, that a mate is cheating is an obsession about, not a delusion of, infidelity. A patient who is obsessed by someone he hopes is a true beloved but knows is just a fantasy lover is more hopelessly obsessively enamored than truly erotomanic. In contrast, a patient who is convinced that she has a chance with an in-fact disinterested, unavailable partner is less hopelessly enamored than delusionally smitten.

THE JUDGMENT OF PARANOID INDIVIDUALS

Nonparanoid patients more often contemplate than implement their negative impulses. For example, many obsessive-compulsives, instead of becoming violent, quake in the face of any possible violent behavior on their parts, while many depressives, instead of becoming violent over, just despair about a situation. In contrast, paranoid individuals often do act on their false beliefs because they are convinced that they are justified in doing so. They show frequent and sometimes serious lapses of self-control where they put others down, destroy property, happily defeat imagined rivals, or harm or maim presumed adversaries.

The depth and breadth of a delusional system is not always a reliable predictor of problems with judgment. The relationship between delusion and behavior is too complex to say with any degree of conviction that the more delusional a patient is the more affected his or her judgment will be. Some patients reality test even the most extensive delusional complexes and suppress any behavior they sense to be driven by delusion. Conversely, modest delusions may paradoxically go untested and lead to unproductive or dangerous behavior, including horrific crimes.

Of course, not all paranoid ideas when lived out produce self-destructive, antisocial, criminal, or violent activity that is the essence of bad judgment. While the positive aspects of paranoia, however significant, are rarely the basis for a compliment, it is nonetheless sometimes true that paranoid ideation can produce good behavior that at least on the surface looks as if it is the product of good judgment. Persecutory delusions might impel patients to do good deeds in order to be spared retribution at the hands of those they imagine to be against them, and grandiose delusions commonly lead to behavior that has clear, definite, and lasting social benefits. Paranoia itself is often associated with, and even productive of, such worthy, valuable, and self-protective personality traits as enhanced empathy, motivation to get to the top in order to defeat one's true adversaries, and a radar-like sensitivity to danger that warns that real enemies are approaching. It can also be associated with true and valuable talent such as the ability to be a good debater on talk shows or in the courtroom, or the ability to think and write like Franz Kafka.

The relationship between paranoia and judgmental defect is also discussed in chapter 8 on the relationship between psychiatry and the law.

THE MEMORY OF PARANOID INDIVIDUALS

Paranoid individuals often suffer from a memory that is too good (hypermnesis). They endow each little component of their self-created neoreality with a precision and luminosity otherwise unimaginable. They have a marvelous recall for adversarial situations and for every one of their feelings and instincts that they can connect with such situations. On the other hand, their bad memory (hypomnesia) is remarkably profound when it comes to remembering anything that interferes with their image of the world as populated by the weak and the wicked. Selectively remembering what is bad and forgetting, that is, repressing, what is good about a person or an event is in fact more central to the process of delusional formation than the textbooks usually suggest.

THE INTELLIGENCE OF PARANOID INDIVIDUALS

Intelligence can be impaired when paranoid individuals become too opinionated, too critical, too anxious, or too angry to accurately evaluate and assimilate a situation. That is why it is sometimes hard to distinguish between fanaticism and stupidity. However, intelligence can remain unimpaired when delusional thought and aroused emotions are successfully encapsulated.

Some paranoid individuals at least seem to possess above-average intelligence. The paranoid-style ability to uncover relationships between apparently unrelated issues—relationships that most of us miss—partly defines the concept of intelligence, which consists in part of the capacity for insightful supersleuthing that leads to recognizing overarching principles in the midst of what to others looks like chaos. The paranoid individual's special and often cunning ability to see into the heart of matters, put a finger on the basics, and then decide what exactly the next right move should be are all parameters of that elusive gift that we call being brilliant.

CHAPTER 2

Delusional Disorder

DELUSIONS

A delusional disorder is characterized by the presence of prominent, relatively fixed, and mostly nonbizarre delusions generally originating from within and usually unaccompanied by hallucinations. The *DSM-IV* (American Psychiatric Association, 1994) defines a delusion as a "false belief based on incorrect inferences about external reality" (p. 765). Andrew Sims (1988) defines a delusion as "a false unshakable idea or belief which is out of keeping with the patient's educational, cultural and social background . . . held with extraordinary conviction and subjective certainty . . . indistinguishable from a true belief" (p. 82). Alistair Munro (1999) defines delusions as persistent forceful ideas or beliefs that, however unlikely, exert "undue influence on [the patient's] life [altering it] to an inexplicable extent" (p. 35). He adds that these ideas are unquestioningly accepted, that is, they are minimally or not at all subject to correction by the patient himself or herself attempting to argue with them or by others trying to talk sense to the patient, so that any attempt to question the belief is met with "hostile secretiveness or suspicion" (p. 35). Delusions are typically allowed to "overwhelm . . . other elements of the psyche," (p. 35) creating "belief[s] and behavior that are uncharacteristic and alien" (p. 35). The result can be abnormal and sometimes violent behaviors, which are however "understandable in the light of the delusional beliefs" (p. 35).

The following two clinical vignettes illustrate what Munro likely means when he refers to the unquestioning acceptance of delusions. An erotomanic woman believed that Jerry Springer, the entertainer, was in love with her. She even advanced as proof a personal fan letter that she had received from him.

Her son-in-law countered that the letter was not personal, just one of perhaps thousands of copies Springer had merely signed in the original page. Her son-in-law's comment did not change her mind about the personal nature of the letter. Instead his comment changed her mind about the wisdom of talking to her son-in-law.

An often-told story in medical circles is that of a patient who had the somatic delusion that he had a snake in his abdomen. A technician did an X-ray to prove to him that there was no snake inside. Instead of agreeing that he was wrong about the snake, the patient insisted that the snake was radiolucent, and that anyway the X-ray was not his. He concluded that the technician and the doctors were all in it together, participating in a cover-up.

However, not all observers accept the just-mentioned premises that delusions

- Are all false beliefs based on incorrect inferences about *external* reality. For example, somatic delusions are false beliefs partly based on incorrect inferences about *internal* reality.

- Are all false ideas coming entirely from within. While some observers go so far as to suggest that that which comes from without is not a true delusion but is the product of histrionic suggestibility or is a shared cultural belief, other observers believe that truly delusional thinking can originate in and be an elaboration of external, stressful circumstances. Thus the term *Othello syndrome*, referring to delusions of jealousy, gets its name from the Shakespearean character whose delusions were not pure fantasy but were partly the product of false information planted in Othello's mind by Iago.

- That all delusions are fixed and therefore not subject to correction by argument. While some observers believe that that which can be challenged effectively is, as previously mentioned, not a true delusion but either an obsession—that is, a worry— or the product of histrionic suggestibility, other observers, myself included, believe that many delusional people have enough insight into their delusions to be able to correct them, if only temporarily and with great difficulty. Many interpersonal therapists and modern cognitive therapists have reported successfully and effectively challenging their patients' delusional beliefs. The (debatable) fixity of delusions and the futility of arguing with them may not even be a characteristic of the delusions themselves. Rather it may be a manifestation of the paranoid individual's character, specifically, a need to always be dominant and a stubbornness that makes the individual reluctant to give others the satisfaction of ever being right about anything. Some patients with a delusional disorder want to exasperate us. Like the patient who argued about the snake being in his abdomen, they want to give us a hard time. This they are able to do successfully because they are fast and clever individuals able to think on their feet, whose sophistic protestations come as naturally to them as obsessions come to an obsessive or as phobias come to a phobic. Besides, they have been practicing—honing and refining—their defensive thinking for a long time. Also, their goals—to defeat a rival or to proselytize in order to create additional paranoid people in their own image (that is, to create companions in paranoia)— are more sincerely held and of greater personal import than our goal of arguing them out of what we perceive to be their false beliefs for their, rather than solely for our, benefit.

Delusional beliefs are characteristically found not only in delusional disorder but also in schizophrenia and in paraphrenia. Paraphrenia is a disorder that lies on a continuum between paranoid schizophrenia and delusional disorder in terms of disorganization of thought, pervasiveness of delusions and hallucinations, and degree of disturbance of functionality. While not all observers agree, the presence of delusions is generally thought to be incompatible with the diagnosis of paranoid personality disorder.

Delusions are not confined to psychotic-spectrum disorders such as paranoid schizophrenia, paraphrenia, or delusional disorder. They are also found in depression, where they tend to be of a somatic nature—for example, the false belief that one's body stinks. Borderline delusional beliefs (what some observers call nondelusional false ideas) can be found in a number of disorders, including obsessive-compulsive disorder, for example, the false belief that dangerous germs lurk everywhere and if proper precautions are not taken are about to strike, and histrionic personality disorder where, as previously mentioned, they are often the product of extreme suggestibility.

Here are some important characteristics of the delusions found in delusional disorder:

- They tend to be very vivid.
- While they are often frightening they may also be pleasurable and even funny.
- They caricature people and cast them freely into roles.
- They can be single or multiple. While the delusions of patients with paranoid schizophrenia are often multiple and shifting, the delusions of patients with a delusional disorder are often single—that is, they constitute a monomania. However, multiple delusions can exist in a patient with a delusional disorder. For example, grandiose ideas of extreme youth and beauty often coexist with erotomanic fantasies of amorous pursuit by an in-reality disinterested stranger.
- They tend to be clearly organized. As such they tell a simple and comprehensible, though misguided, story that involves the individual and his or her relationship to the world—for example, "electromagnetic wires are poisoning me with harmful rays." However, sometimes the story that a so-called simple delusion tells is more complex and far-reaching than at first meets the eye. Often patients summarize their delusional ideas instead of reporting them in their entirety. As a result the simplicity can be deceiving—not entirely reflective of what the patient is actually thinking.
- They tend to be nonbizarre, unlike the bizarre delusions (defined below) found in patients with paranoid schizophrenia or paraphrenia. It is nonbizarre to imagine that an in-fact faithful partner is being unfaithful, that one is being watched by the FBI or otherwise targeted for surveillance, or that one has been, or is going to be, abducted and killed by kidnappers. Bizarre—strange and otherworldly—ideas about predatory aliens and the like are not typical of (but do not necessarily exclude the

diagnosis of) delusional disorder. However, because there is a great deal of latitude in determining what is and is not bizarre, the recent literature downplays the differential diagnostic significance of this criterion.

Here are some examples of nonbizarre delusions:

A patient dined regularly in a restaurant in Greenwich Village. His favorite waiter told him a good story, which he repeated to his therapist. Soon he became convinced that the therapist was the waiter's lover, that the therapist would repeat the story to his lover, the waiter, and that the waiter, recognizing its source, would learn that his customer, the patient, was a therapy case and would refuse to continue to serve him.

The patient, who was in love with Jerry Springer, the entertainer, and moreover was convinced that he loved her too, also thought that George Harrison of the Beatles was knifed in his home by an intruder because he was set up by his wife, who wanted him out of the picture because he was controlling her. Her evidence? "I can tell she did it because she has that squinty look in her slanty little eyes."

A patient accused her therapist of going around spreading the Chinese flu. She told her therapist that everyone agreed that the patient was right, and that meant that her therapist was in big trouble not only professionally but also personally.

Here is an example of a delusion that lies somewhere on a continuum between bizarre and nonbizarre:

An adolescent thinks, "I insulted one of the animals, and it told all the rest of the animals what I said, so that now no animals are speaking to me."

Here are some examples of essentially bizarre delusions:

A man speaks each night to angels whom he calls "evolutionary technicians." He feels that his life's purpose is to intercede with people having problems passing from this life to another. The heavenly angel-bodies help him explain what is happening to the bereaved relatives. "The angels help me help people. I communicate with the angels by their tapping me on the shoulder. When I want them to say yes they tap me on the right shoulder; and when I want them to say no they tap me on the left shoulder."

A man thinks, "I am having trouble with Neptune. Neptune controls watery business. Therefore I have to redo my bathroom due to Neptune causing it to malfunction."

A patient believes that a microchip has been inserted into his penis by the government in order to control, and mainly to interfere with, his sex life, and to check on him to see if he is queer.

All these delusions, nonbizarre and bizarre, tell an organized story, that is, one that we can follow. But some, the nonbizarre delusions, describe events that could conceivably happen and do occur, although not necessarily very often, or events that could conceivably happen but almost never, or never, do. Others, the bizarre delusions, describe events that simply do not occur in the real world and that most observers would dub impossible. The more unlikely and impossible the events described, the more bizarre the delusion.

The content of delusions in delusional disorder is often fixed, but it can change over time. The delusions themselves may be either constant or intermittent. They may be intermittent because they are selectively activated only in certain contexts, waxing and waning according to extraneous, often seemingly unimportant, matters, such as "who says what to me that day" or "what side of the bed I got up on that morning." This is not surprising, because delusions are partly the product of emotions, and emotions are partly the product of experience.

The delusions (or hallucinations) of delusional disorder may be, but are not necessarily, overtly persecutory. They may also be jealous, hypochondriacal (bodily, or somatic), erotomanic, grandiose, or litigious. Today we use the term *paranoia* in connection with all these delusions. Therefore, people may be said to be paranoiacs in the absence of overtly persecutory delusions. Thus a person with delusions of jealousy rather than delusions of persecution would still be classified as a paranoiac. While in the *DSM-III* (American Psychiatric Association, 1987) the stress in the definition of paranoid schizophrenia was on persecutory delusions or hallucinations, in the *DSM-IV* (American Psychiatric Association, 1994) the criterion for making the diagnosis of paranoid schizophrenia is not persecutory delusions but "delusions or auditory hallucinations . . . related to the content of the delusional theme" (p. 287).

In patients with a delusional disorder the delusions occur in an otherwise clear sensorium. There is little or no confusion or disorganization of thinking either in or out of the delusions. Negative symptoms that seriously impair functioning such as flattening of affect or withdrawal and mutism are mostly absent. If present, the possibility that the individual is suffering from schizophrenia or paraphrenia should be seriously entertained. Indeed, it might be said that patients with a delusional disorder encapsulate their delusions expressly so that they *can* continue to function without gross or global impairment. Such patients *intend* that their function be somewhat spared. This they can do because their strong ego has significant conflict-free areas that can be brought into play to challenge the disease process, keep it under control, and see to it that it does not excessively influence thinking and behavior. Paradoxically, it is often the paranoid ideation itself that motivates the patient with delusional disorder to continue to function well. Many of these patients wish to remain organized both so that they can better convince others that they are right, and so that they can more effectively vanquish those whom they presume to be their adversaries and enemies.

As previously noted, sometimes the delusional ideation itself and the behavioral changes that are the product of that ideation are positive, not negative/antisocial. Many worthy causes have been espoused and many worthy sociopolitical actions taken as products of thinking that is close to, or actually is, delusional. The usual cautions about determining what is and what is not reality in delusional patients also apply to positive delusions. For example, who is to say that some people have or have not actually been the recipients of, and are responding to, divine messages? Do we know for certain what the reality is for the nurse who bought a new home, then prayed for a sign from God that she had done the right thing and got one, she believed, in the form of a white dove that came and sat on her roof?

Frequently, however, the delusional beliefs of patients with a delusional disorder produce negative ideation and subsequent negative behavioral changes. For example, a patient who thinks that he is being followed might suspiciously look around to see if anyone is behind him. A woman who feels that her therapist is a Venutian sent down to spy on her might flee from the therapist's office in a panic or even try to assault him. A patient who believed that encoded messages were coming over the electrical and telephone wires tore the wiring out of the wall in an attempt to get the broadcasts to stop. On the psychiatry board examinations, my examination patient announced at the very beginning of our interview, referring to me and to my examiner, that "everyone in this hospital except the two of you is against me." I over-optimistically thought that we had established a good working relationship. Predictably, our rapport was shattered a few minutes into the interview when she announced, pointing first to my examiner and then to me, "On second thought, I am not so sure about you, or you." Then she ran out of the examination room (with me right behind her, trying to calm her down so that the interview could continue).

Often what functional impairment exists in delusional disorder is selective. Some paranoid individuals have problems at work but not at home. For others it is just the opposite. Often paranoid individuals arrange to have a positive relationship with one person who acts as companion, protector, and confidant and gives emotional support, while everyone else is regarded with distrust or hostility. But then sometimes that person is dropped to become a part of the paranoid "them," leaving the patient with no friends—unless, as often happens, the patient reconciles with former enemies and makes the former friend his or her new main adversarial outlet, the subject of his or her now evolving monomania. In the latter event, the new-found peace with the world is broadcast as incompatible with a paranoid outlook by a patient who presently intends to look generally healthy in order to better focus his or her hostilities onto the former friend, now recast as the enemy, the one who is the source of all of the patient's difficulties.

Some observers believe that there is an important clinical distinction to be made between primary and secondary delusions, particularly because this distinction has prognostic value, with secondary delusions more treatable than primary delusions.

Primary Delusions

Primary delusions, also called first rank or Schneiderian delusions, at least appear to be independent of life's events. They appear to be autochthonous, that is, they seem to just spring from the soil, coming at us as if out of nowhere after one day having just popped into the patient's mind without antecedent. As Sir Martin Roth (1989) says, "primary delusions [seem to] come . . . out of a clear sky without predisposing features in the personality that render the individual vulnerable to exaggerated suspiciousness and ideas of reference [and are not] understandable in the light of the premorbid personality and the situational stresses that precede illness" (p. 1634). Not surprisingly the patient suffering from <u>primary delusion</u>s, when challenged, often claims, referring to his or her delusional beliefs, "<u>I know it is so because I know it is so</u>."

I believe that it is productive to view the primary nature of delusions dynamically as at least partly the product of the defense of isolation, that same defense that helps create obsessions. Obsessions, like autochthonous primary delusions, pop into mind as if from nowhere and seem to be disconnected from mainstream thought and feeling. Speaking psychodynamically, the disconnected quality of obsessions is defensive because it separates or isolates the obsessional thought from mainstream thinking. That makes it look as if the thought is untethered to other elements both in the patient's psyche and in the patient's life. That helps reduce anxiety and guilt by turning a potentially emotionally laden construct into "just a stupid thought that I cannot get out of my mind." I have found the same to be true of primary delusions, and the techniques that psychodynamically oriented therapists use to restore the connections and reestablish the linkages between obsessions and mainstream thought, feeling, and life can at times accomplish the same thing with some primary delusions and lead to an equally beneficial therapeutic response.

Secondary Delusions

Secondary delusions have more or less obvious antecedents in the person's life, current circumstances, or personality. For example, a natively suspicious individual believed that the real estate agents in a developing area of town conspired to fill the storefronts with sham tenants to give him the illusion that the area was becoming gentrified, creating what was in fact a theater set just so that, as a prospective purchaser, he would think that the area was booming and so eagerly sign up for a condominium unit for sale in the neighborhood. Secondary delusions often arise from a traumatic incident, such as an actual rejection. As with delusions of jealousy, they may have some basis in fact. For example, a patient believed that his boss, his host at an office dinner party, was poisoning his food. This belief had its origin in actual evidence that the boss had his eyes on the patient's beautiful wife and was trying to make out, and off, with her.

Secondary delusions often seem to evolve from the core material of paranoid personality traits/paranoid personality disorder. They are elaborations of the substance of paranoid personality traits/paranoid personality disorder now presented differently and in association with new material. As David

Shapiro (1994) says, to fully understand paranoia we have to have a more complete understanding "of the nature and workings of paranoid character or personality" (p. 51) and of how "the severely rigid character's defensiveness is the pivot of the transformation of an internal tension into one that is experienced as external" (p. 54). As an example, a patient's unjustified suspicion that his wife was cheating on him became the nucleus of a developing delusional conviction that all the people on the city bus were calling him queer. In many cases delusions of persecution seem to be the evolutionary outcome of a failure of basic trust that itself is the product of generalized suspiciousness, hypersensitivity to criticism, and an excessive preoccupation with the possibility of rejection.

The following personality traits/traits characteristic of paranoid personality disorder commonly evolve into paranoid delusions:

- distrustfulness
- jealousy
- grandiosity (in the sense of being always correct about everything, perfectly in tune and at one with the right-thinking universe, and superior to ordinary mortals and, in some fantasies, to extraordinary mortals and even immortals)
- hypersensitivity and excessive vigilance, particularly with regard to the negative judgments of others
- overreactivity—a tendency to view and respond to others as if they are more critical, hostile, and malevolent than they actually are; for example, a tendency to view advice about possible consequences of one's actions as a criticism that one has done or is planning to do the very thing that one is being advised against
- sadomasochism—paranoid individuals masochistically torture themselves by transforming the world into a place full of adversaries, and they also sadistically torture others, making them suffer by accusing them unfairly of this and that, often doing so in order to antagonize them, and doing that in order to justify the bad feelings they already feel about them
- blaming tendencies—making others entirely responsible for everything that goes wrong in one's life, associated with the tendency toward knee-jerk self-absolution in order to relieve guilt and shame (just recently I waited on hold for many minutes for a salesman to pick up the phone; I then gave up, hung up, and called back later, at which time the salesman did not apologize for not answering sooner, but instead severely chastised me for not waiting longer)
- a proneness to be biased, judgmental, and rigid (Shapiro, 1994, pp. 54–55)
- a vagueness about distinguishing what is in the mind from what is in the world— what one is thinking about from what one has actually seen
- rationalizing tendencies that reflexively protect one's false notions

I believe that the evolutionary process in question consists in the main of intensification and embellishment of old material with new material derived from the externalization process, catalyzed by vicious cycling. In this vicious cycling, first destructive characterological trends such as stubbornness and argumentativeness lead to negative behaviors that antagonize others. Others in turn behave back antagonistically. That intensifies and fixes the underlying hostility and suspiciousness until delusional thinking begins. For example, a sadomasochistic patient claimed that all her problems were due to the sequelae of childhood abuse at the hands of a cruel mother and stepfather. She went on to complain that her husband demeaned, criticized, and devalued her the same way her parents did. She became quite angry when her husband claimed, with some justification, that it was not the patient who was being abused, it was she who, by constantly criticizing him, was being abusive. Instead of recognizing the partial validity of her husband's point, she blew up, then walked out on him because he is "always picking on me the same way my mother did." She then became extremely lonely and began to feel that "The world is a terrible place, one where everyone hates me" and developed generalized delusions of persecution.

An analogy with dreams to some extent illustrates the difference between primary and secondary delusions. Some dreams at least seem to make little or no sense. Therefore observers attempting to understand them have postulated that they are the product of the brain cleansing itself of detritus or have offered other similar organic or pseudo-neurological explanations. Other dreams are clearly Freudian in nature—they elaborate the day's residue, and in this and other ways obviously fit into an individual's life context. It is possible that both explanations are true for the same person having different types of dreams and for different people who dream differently. These two types of dream parallel the just-mentioned two types of delusion—primary delusions (that often have a high organic loading such as might occur in patients who as children suffered from fetal alcohol syndrome or in patients who seriously damaged their brains by substance abuse during adolescence or later), and secondary delusions that are almost certainly the product of emotions such as anxiety or anger and personality problems such as an undue suspiciousness or excessive fear of rejection, or are reactive to traumatic life events such as being fired from an important job.

Some observers, particularly Europeans, note a distinct difference in quality of thought and feeling as being characteristic of different kinds of mental disorder. For example, they might note that patients with primary delusions as compared to patients with secondary delusions have an otherworldly quality, reminding us as they do more of space aliens than of terrestrials. I myself have noted a distinctly creepy quality to delusional patients whose delusions appear to be mostly primary, a quality that indicates a possible genetic/organic basis for their mental disorder. This quality was particularly notable in a man who slashed a famous mural because he felt that it was saying bad things about him. A good deal of his creepy quality came from his appearance—one that could only be called monstrous, for his head was too large for his torso and seriously misshapen, and his body was physically deformed to the point of being grotesque. However, in general this different quality thesis has not been popular in the United States.

This said, many observers including Munro believe that there is almost never or in fact never a significant connection between paranoid traits/ paranoid personality disorder and delusional disorder. Such observers note that paranoid traits/paranoid personality disorder and delusional disorder are like two circles with only modest, if any, overlap, and certainly not as large an overlap as was once believed. They cite how the overlap is no more extensive than the limited overlap between histrionic personality disorder and conversion disorder, or schizoid personality disorder and schizophrenia. (As Henry Pinsker [personal communication, 1999] notes, the term *schizoid personality disorder* was coined because the individuals so diagnosed shared such characteristics with schizophrenics as the omnipotence of words, isolation, and autism. It was once thought that these were essential lesions and therefore that schizoid young people were at high risk for developing schizophrenia. Now we believe something different: that shy children grow up to become shy adults, not mental patients.)

At any rate, there is a great deal of latitude as to whether a given delusion is indeed primary in nature and so, as Sims (1988) quoting Jaspers says, "understandable" (p. 85), or secondary in nature. As Sims (1988) goes on to state, "several writers have claimed that all delusions are understandable if one knows enough about the patient" (p. 85). I believe that even primary delusions that seem to have few or no antecedents in the patient's personality, and no clear umbilical cord into the body of the patient's past or present life, can, after deep probing, often be understood in a personal context. Who can fail to at least dimly perceive the meaning of one patient's primary delusion that the government had inserted a microchip into his penis, the meaning of another patient's primary delusion that Hunter College, which was at the time an all-girl's school, was emitting rays and directing them into her vagina, or the meaning in a soon-to-be divorced woman of the belief that little moths that no one else but she could see were invading her loft, destroying her possessions, and getting under her skin making her body tingle all over?

TYPES OF DELUSIONAL THINKING/DELUSIONS

Persecutory Ideas/Delusions of Persecution

Patients with persecutory ideas/delusions of persecution falsely believe that they are or might become the object of a cabal or conspiracy. A patient was offered a blind date with a criminal lawyer but refused it because she feared his clients would come after her. (But then she accepted it because she realized that a good criminal lawyer could afford a body guard for his moll.) Another patient believed that her doctor, the hospital staff, and her neighbors were involved in a conspiracy to steal her money. She secreted her funds and falsely

claimed poverty. She would not sign anything, including her Medicare benefits form, lest someone obtain her signature and forge it on a bank withdrawal
slip.

Even delusions that are not overtly persecutory usually have a covert persecutory meaning. Patients with delusions of jealousy feel persecuted by their
rivals; patients with erotomanic delusions feel persecuted by love; patients
with litigious delusions feel persecuted by a legal system that treats them
unjustly; and patients with somatic delusions feel persecuted by their infes-
tations and by doctors who do not believe that they are physically ill, will not
treat them as they need and expect to be treated, or have actually made them
sick or deformed through carelessness or deliberate cruelty. In particular, individuals who suffer from grandiose delusions almost always feel persecuted
on some level. They feel persecuted by envious others. Additionally, grandiosity and persecution are opposite sides of the same coin, as illustrated by the
related and generally inseparable beliefs, "I am important enough to be singled out for persecution" and "I am singled out for persecution because I am
important enough."

The defense of projection is central to the formation of persecutory ideas/
delusions. Like such other defense mechanisms as repression and denial, projection is easier to describe ("I hate him" becomes "he hates me") than to
fathom (how, exactly, is "I hate him" transformed into "he hates me"?). This
is partly because projection, unlike more intellectual defenses such as rationalization and doing and undoing, is an emergency reflexive, biological response, making it in some ways as conceptually unfathomable as piloerection
(goose bumps).

Projection primarily involves reattributing to others tendencies originally
located, identified, and then condemned and disavowed in oneself. However,
as described in chapter 10, where I go into the mechanism of projection in
detail, reattribution is but one component of projection, for projection is a
complex defense mechanism made up of a number of other, equally primary,
defense mechanisms such as denial and identification.

Morbid Jealousy/Delusions of Jealousy

Some paranoid individuals are morbidly jealous people virtually convinced
that someone important to them might be cheating on them—either sexually
or by being personally disloyal. For example, a lover notices that his lover is
taking a blank Christmas card to work with him. He thinks, "He is sending
that card to someone he is having an affair with. I know this is so because he
didn't fill out the address at home, and that is because he doesn't want me to
know who his lover is, and where he lives." (In fact, the card is for a professional colleague whose home address the first man only had on his files at
work.) Morbidly jealous individuals are apt to go beyond condemning their
partners for being unfaithful to them to abusing them physically, or even

stalking and killing them and/or their imaginary lovers. (It is important to distinguish morbid jealousy in semidelusional or delusional individuals that leads to paranoid violence from jealousy that, while perhaps excessive, is to lesser or greater degree justified and leads to crimes of passion.)

Dynamically, morbid jealousy/delusions of jealousy is often the product of a patient's own guilty wishes to be the one participating in a sexual activity in which the partner is presumed to be involved, and for which the partner is being condemned. Such individuals want to cheat themselves, but they cannot own up to it, so they turn the problem from "I want to cheat on you" into "I condemn you for wanting to cheat, or fear that you are actually cheating, on me." In many cases the fantasized cheating on the partner's part can ultimately become a guilt-reducing excuse to cheat oneself, along the lines of the characteristically paranoid formulation, "I am cheating on you because you cheated on me"—the "you did it first" subvariant of paranoid "not me" thinking about relationships and about life itself.

you demand because you are divorcing me.

As Freud pointed out, sometimes forbidden homoerotic feelings are the primary focus and driving force behind morbid jealousy/delusions of jealousy. Some observers delight in shooting down this formulation, but in my opinion that is just another form of the somewhat paranoid activity of Freud-bashing. A closeted homosexual man who believed that his wife was cheating on him in fact had a secret guilty attraction to the man with whom his wife was presumably cheating. The patient then aligned himself with his guilty conscience and condemned his wife because she represented, and was presumably living out, the patient's own disavowed sexual desires. Now his paranoid cry become the equivalent of "I condemn you for doing what I condemn myself for having done in the past, and wanting to do in the future."

Since morbid jealousy/delusions of jealousy, like most or all symptoms, is overdetermined—that is, since one delusional attitude/delusion has many meanings—there are other components of delusions of jealousy besides the disavowal and projection of heterosexual or homosexual wishes. These delusions also take root in the disappointed narcissism of self-centered individuals who demand to be the only one in another's thoughts and actions. Under such circumstances imagined rejection is easily forthcoming, with the morbid jealousy/delusions of jealousy created from, that is fueled and fired by, the resulting disappointment and rage. These delusions also take root in low self-esteem, that is, in a poor self-image, whether or not that poor self-image is warranted. Individuals with low self-esteem and a poor self-image are especially prone to morbid jealousy/delusions of jealousy because they think, "I am not surprised that my lover would cheat on me. After all, how difficult can it be to find someone better than I am?"

Somatic (Hypochondriacal) Delusions

The patient with a somatic delusion believes that his or her body is being, or has become, damaged in a way that is

- possible and likely, but not true in a given case—for example, the false perception of mouth pain incorrectly attributed to bad teeth
- possible but unlikely—for example, the false belief that insects are crawling beneath one's skin or that coils of worms are living in one's abdomen
- completely impossible—for example, the false belief that one's esophagus is missing, and therefore one must not eat because if one does the food will fall directly into the thoracic cavity, or a pianist's belief that his left hand has turned to stone

Like many or most other delusions, somatic delusions, though not manifestly persecutory, have an implied persecutory element. This element, expressed in the bodily preoccupation itself, is often, as in the following case, a sexual persecutory fear translated into a bodily concern that hides a secret wish:

A patient felt that a bus driver attacked him after the patient had fallen asleep on the bus. As the patient put it, "he attacked my genitals with a pencil." The patient then developed delusional genital pain, his way of saying, "You hurt my genitals when you attacked them," as well as his way of expressing a more hopeful, "I still feel your pencil sticking into me."

Somatic delusions in patients who are predominantly depressed have a different quality and meaning from somatic delusions in patients who are predominantly paranoid. In the depressed patient we perceive a sense of hopelessness. We can translate the somatic delusion to mean, "All is lost because of what has happened to me." In the paranoid patient we perceive a lot of anger and can translate the somatic delusion to mean, "All is lost because of what you did to me."

Patients with somatic delusions tend to ultimately involve their physicians in their delusional constructs—requesting that the physician own up to the role that he or she supposedly played in neglecting a patient's illness, or in actually making the person sick, then demanding confession, atonement, and reparation. Some so-called cases of Munchausen's disorder involve more than mere illness-feigning. Rather they involve somatic delusions about being physically ill. These are not surprisingly associated with doctor shopping and requests for multiple hospitalizations that evolve into an angry delusional relationship with physicians and litigious delusions about the physician and/or the hospital.

Grandiose Ideas/Delusions

The patient with grandiose ideas/delusions believes that he or she is especially powerful, rich, or famous, or that he or she has become another person with some or all of these attributes—such as the Deity. Often specific grand identities are involved, which come and go in popularity throughout the years. Almost no one is Napoleon these days. Also in the infinite wisdom that many paranoid individuals retain, these days almost no one dares to be the Savior. At most they become one of His disciples, with a secret pretension (with oedipal overtones) to overthrowing the Father and moving up in the ranks.

In paranoid individuals, overtly persecutory ideas coexist alongside the grandiosity, contaminating the grandiosity with anger, suspiciousness, and adversarial fantasy, rendering it neither joyful nor infectious and so quite different in feel from true affective grandiosity. Bipolar patients with grandiose delusions are fundamentally high on themselves. If they express feelings of persecution at all, these at most represent a secondary concern that others will envy them and keep them from getting what they are entitled to, or take away what they already have. Paranoid patients who simultaneously feel both grandiose and persecuted seem instead to be less truly happy than defensively fantasizing their way out of fear. They are proclaiming their omnipotence in order to avoid the opposite, truer view of themselves as vulnerable and endangered. We can intuitively understand and follow their secondary and defensive shift from paranoid to grandiose. For example, it is not hard to fathom how some Don Juan personalities pride themselves on their heterosexual prowess to prove that the people whom they fear are taunting them for being homosexual are wrong, or how a person mollifies the idea that someone is persecuting him or her through the television set to become the secondary, protective, and defensive idea that "He can't get to me because of who and what I am." Such grandiose defenses can look counterphobic, or even hypomanic, but since they are counter to a paranoid attitude it is more dynamically correct to call them counterparanoid.

Unlike patients with persecutory ideas/delusions who are often aware that they are wrong to feel persecuted, patients with grandiose ideas/delusions often believe themselves to be special and rarely think that they are wrong about that. For them self-congratulations are in order—for their admirable moralistic stands, supposed ability to give excellent advice to everyone, altruistic motivation, and what they presume to be their actual good deeds, as in "I am God's messenger put on Earth to help the world gain peace," "I and only I can save the planet," or, another delusion found in a patient who believed himself to be a Christ disciple, "I have developed the secret of harnessing pyramid power to help mankind." They often go beyond claiming unusual or unique awareness and insight to begin proselytizing. As spokesmen of divine authority, they show an inordinate fondness for strenuous involvement in righteous, often openly religious, causes. Now they talk and act like the Savior they believe themselves to be, all the better to enlist others in their goal of creating a new world—of course, their way and in their own self-image. In the process they often assume a lofty air of charisma and speak in what they believe to be appropriately theatrical ringing, highfalutin tones.

So often the saintliness inherent in their proselytizing clearly represents an attempt to deny their own sinfulness. That is why their preoccupation with others' sinfulness focuses on the very sins that are close to the sins they identify in themselves. They take their own sins from within themselves and place them upon others' shoulders so that "You, not I, become the bad one." However, this defensive mechanism usually proves inadequate, and their presumed sins reemerge even stronger for the attempt to suppress them. So they have to try to suppress their own sinfulness even further, now by intensifying their suppression of other's presumed sinfulness—those presumed sins that, of course, resemble their own. Soon enough they feel that the sinners of this world need more than a good talking-to. They actually have to be taught a lesson. The lessons that grandiose paranoid individuals teach and the way they teach them are legion. In the worst possible scenario, their thoughts turn to violence, which not surprisingly consists of thoughts of killing bad others for their own good and for the greater glory of self, society, and God. Such individuals make us think that behind every saint is a sadist.

One of the sins their proselytizing attempts to deny is their intense anger at and hatred of others. Not surprisingly their anger and hatred still shine through in their words and deeds. Thus, they are not "put on Earth to save all you deserving people," but "to advise others that Christ is returning to warn sinners [not innocents!] that there will soon be an earthquake in New York."

Proselytizing is clearly related to and part of activism. The tenure of activists is often noted for certain real benefits such as making the trains run on time. However, to those who are not of equal mind the goodness paranoid activists see in themselves can look remarkably to others like badness, consisting when it does of totalitarian suppression, mayhem, destruction, and even murder. To many, burning SUVs because they damage the environment, blowing up buildings because they destroy the ecology, or destroying medical laboratories because they are used for legitimate animal experimentation are the actions of thugs. Not surprisingly, some grandiose activists seem to be hypocrites. It was hypocritical for an antiabortionist to demonstrate how sacred he held human life by killing an abortion doctor. A strict vegetarian did not eat, and demanded that others not eat, meat, meat products, or even eggs to protest the mishandling of chickens. She had no similar compunction however when it came to preserving her river view, although that entailed chopping down trees, oblivious to how she was doing that at nesting time when the nests were full of hatchlings.

Clearly, grandiose paranoid individuals are not nearly as withdrawn as other paranoid individuals. In fact they look quite related, if only in the sense of being very impassioned. The private, shy, internally oriented paranoid individual has now become an other-oriented, publicly demonstrative, vocal, and often quite convincing person—if only one who gets up on a soapbox to intimate, harangue, threaten, and warn.

In conclusion, in our society low self-esteem is often considered to be the problem, and making one's self-esteem higher the solution. That is not the case for the grandiose paranoid individual. For grandiose paranoid individuals the problem is one of self-esteem that is too high, to the point of megalo-mania, really megaloparanoia. Therefore the solution for them does not in-volve following the usual therapeutic exhortation to "improve your self-esteem." Such individuals do not need to elevate self-esteem that is too low. Instead they need to lower self-esteem that is too high.

Erotomanic Delusions

The literature is unclear as to whether the basic distortive belief held by an erotomanic individual is that one is loved by an in-fact disinterested stranger, or that one is productively in love with an in-fact unavailable person, or both. Some observers define erotomania as being in love with a stranger who is in reality disinterested and unavailable, associated with the grandiose notion that one has a chance with such a person, sometimes associated with a desire and a willingness to pursue one's love to the point of stalking the object of one's affections. Other observers define erotomania somewhat differently as the false belief that another person, someone who is in reality disinterested, is in love with the individual and may in fact be sexually approaching or even harassing him or her. Along these lines, Arnold Goldberg (1994) defines ero-tomania as a "systematized delusion of being convinced of the passionate love of another person" (p. 115). Both can, and often do, occur together: for ex-ample, "I am in love with Jerry Springer, and Jerry Springer is in love with me." In either case the love predictably goes bad, and the imaginary lover, seen as someone who ignores, disdains, and even hates the erotomanic indi-vidual, becomes an enemy and as such must be punished.

The patient who was in love with Jerry Springer was in her seventies. She savaged anybody who did not agree that she could pass for a woman in her early thirties. Her therapist thought her narcissistic, and her daughter called her excessively vain. One Thanksgiving she was asked to bring the desert for the family dinner—and in response brought a container of diet sherbet. The whole family, expecting a juicy pie, became upset about having only such a Spartan desert to eat, and the party broke up on a sour note.

At the time no one, therapist or family, thought to inquire why she brought sherbet rather than pie. Some months later the mother herself spoke about the incident, ex-plaining her thinking at the time. She had reasoned as follows: "sherbet has no fiber; fiber makes feces; alluring people do not make feces; I want to be alluring so that Jerry Springer will fall as much in love with me as I am in love with him. Therefore I only eat sherbet." When asked why she hid her intentions from all concerned, she replied, "I don't want anyone to know that I am after him romantically. They might criticize me, discourage me, take steps so that I do not marry him and leave him all my money, or get big ideas and try to get there first."

Eventually, after writing to Mr. Springer several times and receiving no personal reply, she became enraged at his lack of response and developed a strong hatred for him and for anything associated with him. She even began to fantasize punishing him for what she believed to be his rejection of her. The punishments that ran through her mind ranged from "I will never pay a cent to see anything he is in again" to "I hope he dies a horrible death as his comeuppance for ignoring me."

A friend wrote to me essentially as follows:

I need your opinion on something. Every morning for several years I take a walk at the beach early in the morning. There is a man that walks down there, a Vietnam vet, 64 years old. Once in a while I would chat with him. He was always very complimentary and I thought nothing of it. Now I believe he has become obsessed with me because I have been nice to him. He is single, always has been, claims he has an arsenal at home from the 'Nam days, and shakes when he talks about the war. A couple of times he tried to kiss me, supposedly as a friend, but the feeling I had was that he was a little too focused on me. So I said, John, I'm not interested, I'm happily married, and you even know my husband. I know you mean no harm, but people will talk, bla bla bla. He seemed okay for some time after that, and said "I don't mean any harm, but you don't know how much it means to me that a person like you talks to a nobody like me."

I have many friends down at the beach that I talk with, walk with, different ones all the time. The other day I ran into a good friend and colleague, Steve, a black lawyer that I worked with this past year. We walked a bit, and this guy John (the 'Nam guy) saw us and got visibly agitated. He knows Steve the lawyer for years, as John was his trash collector after John came back from Vietnam, so normally he would have said "hi" to both of us, but this time he acted like he was angry. Yesterday, I ran into two men that I know, and we were walking and talking, we see John, who also knows these men, and John turns his head in an obvious and infantile way, and walks in the other direction. The two men thought this was very strange, then figured out he was jealous because I wasn't talking only to John himself.

Today, he saw me walking alone and there was no turning his head. Instead he tried to put his arm around me. I pulled myself loose and he said, "Listen, I just want to tell you something because I love you as a friend, you know. People are talking saying you are a 'N . . . ' lover because they saw you walking with Steve the other day, then saw you get into his car (we went for coffee to get away from John!). I don't want to tell you what to do with your life, but you should be careful about what you do and whom you associate with. You know I have nothing against black people. I have a lot of black friends that I like better than whites . . . and I don't know if there is anything going on between you two or not, it's none of my business," etc. etc.

Yea, right. What an asshole. What I think is that no one said anything at all, in fact I think this is a ploy to have me talk and walk only with him. And God knows the rumors *he* is probably spreading.

I have tried varying the times that I walk, but he is always waiting for me in the lurch somewhere and pops out of nowhere. I am trying to remain cordial and polite, and calm, because I know he has weapons galore and he is isn't wrapped too tight.

I know you've worked with plenty of vets. How shall I handle this one? I have allergies and it is healthy down there. Also, there aren't many other places I feel safe walking, and besides I love the beach trail and don't feel I should have to stay away because of this nut.

I've tried everything I can think of for discouraging this guy nicely, without getting him to the breaking point, but my impulse is to tell him to go to hell, which I stop myself from doing. I have even brought Chet, my husband, with me on weekends. We hold hands, etc. John walks with us, he even went to coffee with us afterwards and when Chet got up to get napkins, he made a remark like "I hope your husband isn't jealous, hee hee hee" (as if he's just joking). I said there's nothing to be jealous about, but of course nothing I say seems to work. I've tried staying away from the beach for a couple of weeks, but then I went back, thinking: this is my favorite place to walk, why should I. . . . and of course there he was, saying "Laura, I missed you, you're my life, I was going to call you 'cause I got so worried something happened to you."

He bought a copy of the recording of a concerto I composed and remarked that when he heard it, he felt as if I was singing to him.

There are more details like this, but you get the picture. When I saw this coming (obviously way too late) I thought I had averted it pretty well. Then one day during Easter, there is an elderly toothless immigrant that I always kiss on both cheeks when I see him (it is customary in my culture). He's a lovely person and I said "Peter, Happy Easter." John pops up out of nowhere, and his face drops. He says "You won't kiss me, like I have leprosy, but you kiss him, thanks a lot." He said this right in front of Peter, making me sound like kiss-around-Kate or something. I was really humiliated.

Litigious Delusions

Litigious paranoid individuals feel as if they have been treated unjustly— for example, by the system—and therefore they feel that they deserve to be compensated. The emotional pain and suffering that they actually experience and complain about is, however, usually out of proportion to any actual harm done to them, and therefore the compensation that they often demand is too high considering only the nature of the injury itself. But of course that is because they seek not only monetary compensation but also personal redress, that is, vengeance, in the form of punitive damages. Being hurt and rejected figures heavily in the cause of their emotional state. That is one reason why the so-called misdeeds they uncover on the part of others are the actions of a formerly beloved person, such as a supposedly competent and trusted doctor, or a formerly adored spouse. Many doctors know that their best defense against an unjust malpractice suit is a good relationship with the patient, and that conversely anything that provides the patient with a negative grain of sand around which to grow a delusional pearl can set the stage for future personal and legal difficulty. Spouses involved in nasty divorce proceedings usually do not know: they can sometimes come out better if they treat their opponent as a litigious paranoid, that is, as someone who is suffering from a form of temporary, stress-related, paranoid, insanity, profitably handled using the generic techniques for handling paranoia described throughout this text.

Some litigious paranoid individuals who claim childhood abuse were actually and seriously abused when they were young. Others, however, are suffering from and acting on delusions of past abuse. Either they entirely imagine that they were abused, or they view abuse that actually occurred as more serious than it actually was. In either case they blame everything bad that happens to them for the rest of their lives on their early abuse and on others who, as they claim, abused them then and continue to abuse them now. This intensely adversarial view of the world even more strongly resembles a paranoid scenario when they turn "not me but my abuse" into a cause célèbre and then into a legal action.

Delusional subjugation to a false god, a phenomenon akin to the Stockholm syndrome, may be said to be the opposite of litigious paranoia. While litigious paranoiacs come to view someone they formerly perceived to be all good as now all bad, then retaliate, subjugated paranoid patients come to view someone they formerly perceived (and often rightly so) to be all bad, a true persecutor, as having become all good, even "my hero" or "my lover." While other paranoid individuals trust too little, these individuals trust too much, to the point that they wind up hurt or scammed. In some cases the idolatry is narcissistic in the extreme, and the true message is not "I admire you" but a grandiose "I want you, and everyone else too, to admire me, for my worshipfulness—for being a lover, not a hater—and for my extremely good taste." When the hero or heroine predictably falls short of unsustainable expectations and disappoints, the hatred that up to now has been suppressed by willing subjugation returns. Then there is a strong negative, and even a paranoid, "you let me down" reaction toward the formerly beloved. This process is seen in derivative form in the paranoia of everyday life of the opera lover whose hostility is unleashed when a formerly admired opera star disappoints in some, often trivial, way, for example, by missing a high note. Now with exposed feet of clay, the former hero becomes the hated incompetent—the stereotypical over-the-hill diva who beyond prime has lost her voice and therefore, having stolen my last dime for a ticket, deserves to be booed off the stage and permanently exiled.

Delusional Misidentification

Some patients with a delusional misidentification syndrome misidentify *other people*. They think, "You are not really you, you are actually someone else." A patient might experience delusions of a double (the Capgras syndrome), believing that his wife is not really his wife, but a replacement for his wife, who is elsewhere, perhaps married to someone else, or dead. Or a patient might experience delusions of familiarity and come to believe that he or she already knows people whom he or she is actually meeting for the first time. Some patients with delusions of reincarnation go so far as to state that they first met the other person in a previous life.

Other patients with a delusional misidentification syndrome misidentify not others but themselves. For example, patients with delusions of possession believe that "I am really me on the outside, but on the inside I am someone else, because an alien, or the devil, has taken over and is occupying my body, and now I am accursed and in need of exorcism." Or they think that "I am not really the peasant or the pauper I appear to be but am really the son or daughter of a famous man, even a Rockefeller or a king." Some cases of so-called multiple personality disorder (*DSM-IV* names it dissociative identity disorder) actually consist of multiple delusional paranoid personal misidentifications of this sort.

Culturally Determined Delusions

Culturally determined delusions lie on a continuum between social myth and personal distortion and therefore may not be true delusions. An example is the delusion that is central to the disorder called Koro. I have seen a number of somewhat different descriptions of this syndrome. In one the syndrome is said to consist of the rare and exotic delusion that one's penis is disappearing into one's abdomen and that to save one's life it is necessary to keep the organ from being swallowed up into the abdominal cavity, a feat that can only be accomplished if someone, perhaps a close relative, preferably one's mother, holds on to it for 24 hours with golden tweezers. In some cultures many people hear footsteps following them when nobody is there, believe that they are cursed or possessed by the devil and seek a religiously sanctioned exorcism, or have become convinced that they are being observed by an evil eye. Many observers call culturally determined delusions/hallucinations like this histrionic and call some of their episodic presentations *attaqués*. While these delusions differ from true paranoid delusions both dynamically and phenomenologically, similarities also exist, such as the readiness to believe something untrue accompanied by the suspension, however transient, of the ability to reality test. According to some observers these delusions (and the hallucinatory experiences/beliefs sometimes associated with them) occur more frequently in individuals with low IQs; those who lack extensive formal education; those who, having just immigrated, find themselves in a strange, disorienting place; or in the extremely, that is, overscrupulously, religious.

The following phenomena overlap with, but need to be differentiated from, delusions.

IDEAS OF REFERENCE

An idea of reference involves the false belief that others are thinking or talking about an individual, usually in a hostile way. Ideas of reference trace a continuum between rationality and irrationality. Those on the lower end of the continuum invoke but a small distortion of what is possible and likely. For example, a patient believes two people talking together are in fact bad-mouthing him. These two people may be, and are quite possibly, referring to him somewhat negatively, but if they are they are probably doing so only in passing, not because they know her well and are evaluating her personally. On the higher end of the continuum are those ideas of reference that come close to delusions, even hallucinations. That can happen when the patient goes beyond suspecting that others are talking about him or her in a general way and begins to think that he or she can actually hear them speaking and knows exactly the (usually bad) things that they are saying. Ideas of reference are also discussed in chapter 6.

OVERVALUED IDEAS

Overvalued ideas, further discussed in chapter 6 as phenomena belonging to the gray area, are preoccupying, often semipersecutory, beliefs, close to convictions, that lie on a lower end of the continuum between rationality and irrationality than do delusions. A close-to but not entirely rational overvalued idea occurred to the father of a Caucasian lesbian. His daughter had an Asian long-term partner. He was ashamed of his daughter's choice in lovers, first because the lover was a woman and second because the lover was an Asian. When his daughter decided to have a child through artificial insemination, her father, overcompensating, decided, over their continuing protests, that she be inseminated by an Asian. He reasoned, "Unless you do that, your lover will look like your nanny, and that will embarrass me forever."

Overvalued ideas, commonly found on the editorial page and in the letters to the editor column of the newspapers, may be as socially destructive as delusions, or even more so. An example of a potentially socially destructive overvalued idea is a bigot's preoccupying conviction that a certain group, often an ethnoreligious group such as the Zionists, is out to take over the world and must be stopped before it is too late. Another is the idea that all gypsies are constitutionally inferior. Overvalued ideas can be more dangerous than delusions. This is often the case because they seem very rational because they are well thought through by a person who, or a group that, has not clearly completely lost contact with reality and because they are expressed with conviction and passion, even more than the conviction and passion associated with those delusions that are paradoxically dispassionate constructs that come across as lacking in true emotional commitment. Overvalued ideas at times evolve into frank delusions, perhaps the way the overvalued idea that the Jews were responsible for everything bad in pre-Nazi Germany evolved into persecutory ideas about, and an actual persecution of, the Jewish people under Hitler.

HALLUCINATIONS

A hallucination is a false perception that can exist in all five senses, including taste (gustatory hallucination), smell (olfactory hallucination), and vision (visual hallucination). Many hallucinations are not emotionally caused but are the product of an organic disorder. Some have a dramatic quality that suggests that they are primarily histrionic. Like many delusions, true hallucinations tend to come from within more than from without. Also like delusions, they can either be subject to correction from within or from without, or be too fixed to so respond.

Some but not all observers believe that hallucinations are rare in delusional disorder and that their presence even invalidates the diagnosis. Others accept that some patients with a delusional disorder hallucinate. To make the diagnosis of delusional disorder they only require that the hallucinations be related to the content of the delusions, as was the case for the man whose hallucinations about being touched by angels were the product of his belief that he was in touch with them.

One cannot always readily distinguish a hallucination from a delusion. Many borderline phenomena exist that are difficult to classify. Especially difficult to classify are somatic delusions/hallucinations in which the patient both imagines and senses a bodily change—as occurs in patients who falsely believe that their insides are rotting out, or in patients who experience severe mouth pain in the absence of dental pathology. Also difficult to classify is the phenomenon of hearing one's thoughts, which may be more like an auditory obsession than an auditory hallucination.

Some patients who are hearing voices hear one voice only. Others hear many voices. Sometimes the patient always hears the same voice over and over again, and sometimes he or she hears one voice now and another voice at another time. Sometimes the voice/voices speak directly at or to the patient. At other times they speak with the patient, and at still other times they speak about the patient, commenting, favorably or unfavorably, on the patient's behavior or egging the patient on to do good or bad things. At times they speak only to each other and the so-called uninvolved patient merely overhears them talking. As with delusions, some hallucinations refer to what is possible and likely ("other people on the bus are bad-mouthing me"), some to what is possible but unlikely ("God is speaking to me"), and some to the clearly impossible, as was the case for a chess player who believed that he was able to get tips on how to move pieces directly from the pieces themselves, and as was the case for the previously mentioned head of the department of psychiatry who had the bathroom adjoining his office bricked up so that he would no longer have to listen to the voices coming out of the toilet.

Like delusions, hallucinations may or may not be meaningful in the context of the patient's life. As an example of a meaningful hallucination, a man communicates with his dead wife under a certain lamppost, and she gives him the numbers to play at the day's races. Another patient, upon being ushered into a closed ward, said, revealingly, that she did not want to go inside because she could smell all the lesbians waiting in there to pounce.

Some patients know that they are hallucinating. For example, some describe the experience as having nightmares while awake. Others are unable to distinguish their hallucinations from reality and respond and even talk back to their voices as if they are real. A problem in evaluating hallucinations is that those patients who recognize the pathological significance of their hallucinations tend to deny that they are hallucinating—something that they can do easily. Patients are especially prone to deny auditory hallucinations. Patients with other hallucinations such as hallucinations of taste and smell tend to confess that they are hallucinating. They admit to their hallucinations because they attribute them to a medical condition that they are not ashamed of having.

Individuals may or may not appear to be responding to their hallucinations. Some people ignore their hallucinations. Others, those with poor insight, poor judgment, and a lack of self-control, respond as if they are real. They talk back to them or follow their commands even when they command them to do horrific things, for example, to harm others first then kill themselves next. Responding to commands were one patient who was told to "gouge out your mother's eyes because the devil is in them" and a boy who brandished a knife after hearing voices telling him to kill his parents.

ILLUSIONS

Sensory illusions overlap phenomenologically with, but need to be differentiated from, hallucinations. Sensory illusions occur and can appear in all the senses. These closely resemble hallucinations but differ from them in the ordinariness of their content, understandable context, and lack of bizarreness. Examples, also mentioned above, include seeing shadows, hearing footsteps, or having religious sightings.

Intellectual illusions occur in a large proportion of the population. The belief that one has paranormal powers that can influence the outcome of a throw of the dice; the belief in such urban myths as the one that all New York apartments must be 80 percent carpeted; the serious belief in the principles of feng shui as occurred in a woman who virtually blocked off the only navigable entrance to her house because she was convinced that bad vibes were entering by that route; and the belief that playing a song backwards reveals a secret satanic message are just a few illustrations of widely accepted erroneous information that while illusory is often less than frankly delusional, differing from delusions because the ideas involved are not at all or only mildly persecutory, and tend to be susceptible to self-questioning and challenges from others and to correction by better information. However, there are some points of contact—like the overwhelming need to believe something, and the desire to accept rather than to question something suspected to be fundamentally untrue.

CHAPTER 3

Paranoid Personality Disorder

Paranoid personality disorder is perhaps the commonest form of paranoia the general public has to cope with. Paranoid personality disorder involves a fixed system of false notions about the world and the people in it. These may arise de novo or in the context of specific interpersonal events. They typically take the form of rigid ongoing interpersonal attitudes of a generally perverse and pessimistic nature, making patients with a paranoid personality disorder overly circumspect, evasive, highly suspicious, blaming individuals.

OVERLY CIRCUMSPECT, EVASIVE INDIVIDUALS

As overly circumspect, evasive individuals they do not readily show their hand because they feel that to do so would compromise their safety in what they believe to be a world full of wickedness and danger. If you ask them a simple question, they feel that you are trying to probe into their deepest secrets. So they do everything that they can to throw you off the scent. Saying "I do not know" is one of their favorite diversions. Alternatively, they might speak quietly and swallow their words, or speak in a careful, clipped, reserved, often repetitive pseudo-obsessional way, weighing everything that they say so as to be absolutely certain that they do not open up too widely and say the wrong thing, thereby embarrassing themselves or making themselves vulnerable to harm at the hands of known or unseen enemies.

HIGHLY SUSPICIOUS INDIVIDUALS

These are untrusting individuals who regularly feel that others are plotting against or are otherwise out to get them. A woman believes that her neighbor's "polar" tree (she really means poplar tree) was deliberately put there for two reasons: to grow tall and fall over onto her house, and to hide in its shadow the bad things that her neighbors are doing. A man sends the following e-mail to a friend, subtly accusing the recipient of doing things behind his back with the e-mail sender's estranged wife:

"OK I'm trying to find out the status of things without really knowing what happened. I was under the impression that you recently received a communication from my wife Marge. I don't know what it said, only that I was told that if I were to see you it wouldn't be with her. Although I may not always agree with my wife's reasoning, she is entitled to her point of view. Nevertheless, being left in the dark is not that cool. This is not a request for any personal exchanges between you and her. This e-mail is just between us so that I know what's going on. Anyway, do what you want to do. I am used to being mistreated."

BLAMING INDIVIDUALS

These individuals consider themselves completely blameless after blaming others for things that go wrong in their own lives. As a result, they develop an overly positive view of themselves based on the formulas "I am not responsible for anything; you are responsible for everything" and "All my troubles in life can be attributed to you." The resultant self-view, a self-view that Munro (1999) describes as full of hauteur and grandiosity (p. 35), is one of their most off-putting qualities. Victims do not usually like to be blamed for something that they did not do or to be told that they are responsible for everything that happens to someone else. In a typical sequence they first feel guilty though they are innocent and afterwards feel resentful about having been falsely accused. They next do a slow burn and then become overtly angry and may even drop the person permanently.

When a neighbor who lived across the street asked a patient to stop leaving the trash out where the animals could get at it, the patient replied not "I am sorry and I promise not to do that again," but "Miss, if that's all you have to worry about it would be a nice world, wouldn't it?" shifting the problem from leaving the garbage out and its being scattered all over the lawn to the neighbor's complaining too much, and the response from appropriate trash disposal to condemning and avenging herself against a carping neighbor. When the same neighbor complained that the patient's child was making too much noise, the patient shifted the problem of the child's making noise to how the neighbor's complaints devalued and permanently traumatized her son, and the response from asking her son to be quieter to vowing to retaliate. When a man complained to her that when she was parked next to him she hit his car door when she opened hers, she responded, "That's because you parked too close to me." When the management of a theater asked her to keep her cellular phone from ringing at a concert, she replied that the problem was their making big mountains out of molehills—their turning a situation that was un-important in the infinite scheme of things into one on a par with the twin problems of world hunger and disease—so that instead of apologizing and shutting off the phone, she told management to get their priorities straight and deal with what was really important in life. Instead of looking askance at herself for sending a bill off late, she felt only justified rage at the stupid post office for delivering the mail so slowly. When she forgot a date she felt only annoyance at others for their failure to confirm. Instead of blaming her own careless impulsivity for her decision to move into a neighborhood that she should have known was crowded and noisy, she blamed her real estate agent for hiding problems with the area, so that instead of feeling that she had made a mistake she felt only rage about how she was misled. Once she left an emergency message on a friend's answering machine without including her unlisted phone number in the message, so that the friend, who was away from home at the time without his list of phone numbers, had no way to return her call. When the friend explained why he did not call her back, instead of apologizing for her oversight she criticized him for leaving home without his address book.

When a patient confessed to his doctor that he picked up a disease known to be sexually transmitted through homosexual contact, the doctor asked not "How do you feel?" but "Why did you do that?" By asking that question the doctor was condemning the patient for sexual practices the doctor condemned in himself, to which he was attracted, and which, to his annoyance, constantly intruded into his fantasy life. Instead—though that would have been bad enough—of criticizing and condemning himself, the doctor criticized and condemned his patient—his way to turn being ashamed of himself for being amoral into being proud of himself for condemning immorality in others—the very same immorality he discovered, and tried to quash, in himself.

Like this doctor, most individuals with a paranoid personality disorder do not permit themselves to feel guilty for very long about their sexual feelings. Instead they turn their unacceptable sexual feelings around to become feelings of shock and outrage about what others might be doing with their bodies and/or how others might be attempting to seduce or recruit them. Getting up on their moral soapbox, they make others feel guilty as a substitute for feeling guilty themselves. They then tell others what to do as their way to control their own thoughts and behavior.

In such individuals the blaming process often involves blaming their past, and the people in it, for all their present failures. They point the finger at their poverty, childhood trauma, and sexual abuse as the sole causes of all their present problems, doing so even though the abuse was slight to nonexistent, and even though they themselves contributed mightily to being abused then, the same way they contribute to being abused now.

If they do accept any blame at all, they do so with sweeping self-extenuation. Thus an individual may acknowledge that his or her failure to take some action resulted in disaster, but will likely point to others as the cause of his or her failure to take the action—citing inadequate information in the form of poor briefing or training as the real culprits. Some are capable of a degree of self-evaluation and self-condemnation. But this attitude is superficial and generalized. It has no effect on their specific fantasies and no constructive influence on their subsequent behavior.

EXCESSIVE GUILT ASSOCIATED WITH A PARADOXICAL INABILITY/REFUSAL TO FEEL GUILTY PROTRACTEDLY

As the case vignette of the doctor illustrates, one reason individuals with a paranoid personality disorder find it difficult to accept blame is that they tend to become extremely, painfully, guilty, even or especially about small things. As Shapiro (1994) says, their "shame or weakness" (p. 54) exacerbates their problems. However, at the same time these individuals are unable or unwilling to feel guilty in a serious, meaningful, sustained, and productive way. So they employ several mechanisms for evading their guilt, chief of which involves turning a guilty self-accusation into a perceived unwarranted accusation or criticism from others, in effect blaming their bad behavior on some form of devil.

EXCESSIVE, INAPPROPRIATELY RIGID MORALITY

The severe guilt that they regularly experience often starts with an inappropriately rigid morality, which may take the form of religious scrupulosity or extreme prudishness. For example, an overly moralistic father of a two-month-old baby girl fired her male pediatrician and demanded that his daughter see a female pediatrician instead. He reasoned that it was a violation of his daughter's integrity to be naked in the presence of any male, even his daughter's doctor.

HYPERCRITICAL TENDENCIES

Blaming paranoid individuals are often fanatically critical people not easily distracted from their complaints about others. For example, a patient's mother asked her if the patient had ever told anyone that the patient's brother was gay and died of AIDS. The patient did not answer the question directly. Rather, she feinted and said that if someone asked her she would be honest and tell them the truth since she would not see any reason to lie. The mother interpreted her statement as a willingness to go against and embarrass the family and retaliated by not talking to her daughter for over a year.

Some of these highly critical individuals are content with making a single critical point—about noise or pollution, or about others' stupidity or homosexuality. They go on to make their negative point with clarity and precision, then, having said all that they have to say, repeat or perseverate without saying anything new. Others move from topic to related topic—as do hard-core bigots who readily shift from hating Jews to blacks to gays to doctors who perform abortions to foreigners. For such individuals their rage at the world is too infinite, and too insatiable, for them to adequately quell it by directing it to one target only.

These are also fussy perfectionists who complain a great deal about damage done to their property. However, their complaints emphasize not the spoilage *Couches* of their property but the symbolic damage done to their person. The property is regarded as an extension of the self, and the damage done to the property is seen as symbolic of others' wish to do damage to them—and ultimately to ruin their lives.

TENDENCY TO COLLECT INJUSTICES

They also collect injustices and traumata to give themselves reasons, or further reasons, to criticize and condemn others. As they perceive it, theirs now becomes not a case of misinterpretation of reality but a natural, expected response to the real, personal lack of consideration, antagonism, or malice implied in others' negligence. The injustices they collect tend to revolve around someone having hurt them physically, taken advantage of them sexually, or scammed or otherwise used them financially. With injustice-collectors you cannot win. If you say hello you are trying to seduce them, but if you do not say hello you are ignoring and rejecting them. For them, all advice, however well-intended, is an unwelcome sales pitch, and all offers of help not an admirable attempt to assist but an unwelcome attempt to control them or a selfish manipulation meant to enrich you at their expense.

Their tendency to collect traumata makes it difficult to determine if the past traumatic incidents they speak of actually occurred or if theirs are false memories that are the product of a retrospective distortion of the past arising out of a need to fantasize old and create new adversarial situations in order to give themselves an excuse to attack or to sue—guilt and consequence free. They differ in several important respects from truly traumatized victims with actual posttraumatic stress disorder (PTSD). In patients with posttraumatic stress disorder the traumatic content is relatively major compared with the minor contribution made by paranoid fantasies of having been mistreated, with the reverse holding true for patients with a paranoid personality disorder. Also, true victims of PTSD tend to dwell on the trauma more than on complaints about those who have traumatized them. In contrast, when a markedly paranoid element exists, the posttraumatic symptoms tend to resemble serious interpersonal complaints. For example, a Vietnam War veteran constantly complained that the noise from a shooting range he lived near reactivated old combat experiences. But for him the noise was less significant then his need to bombard and harangue others with the complaint, "Look at what the world did and is continuing to do to me." Also, individuals with a paranoid personality disorder tend to focus less on collecting monetary damages for harm done than on extracting a pound of emotional flesh from those believed to have harmed them. While patients with true PTSD are often looking for a paycheck, patients with a paranoid personality disorder are instead often looking for a payback.

TENDENCY TO FEUD

As part of their injustice and trauma collecting they continually embroil themselves in feuds. Their memories are especially long and their attitudes especially unforgiving when it comes to any issue that can conceivably give them the reason they need to feel injured. Unlike most people who soon lose interest in the battle, they have an ongoing mission. Therefore, they not only deliberately provoke feuds, they also purposely prolong them and refuse to back off, doing that so that they can

- wallow in their trauma
- convince themselves and others that they themselves are not just imagining that everyone is against them but that they are in fact on the side of the angels, that they themselves are pure and others are foul
- strengthen their case that their adversaries are not absent or nebulous but real
- have a self-vindicating pretext for putting the blame on the object of their aggression, so that they can view their own aggression not as first but as second strike—that is, not as generative of, but as reactive to, actual slights

Some have one feud only while others have many—with the neighbors, with the teenagers down the block, with organizations such as the department store that refused credit for an item returned, with delivery people who came late or scratched an appliance when they brought it, and with strangers such as the noisy crowd on the 7:42.

Sometimes the things they feud about involve problems they imagine entirely. As an example, a man felt that the people on his block were putting up their Christmas decorations to attack him personally for not being a Christian. In revenge he devised a lawn ornament meant to annoy, shock, and disgust them—an old toilet bowl inside of which he inserted a live potted pine tree that he arranged to have spring forth from the vessel. Then he covered the tree with tinsel and topped it off with a star.

At other times they feud about problems that are real but trivial and merely symbolic of what is really bothering them. A neighbor let a small patch of her lawn grow so that she could cultivate a few wildflowers. Her neighbor called the police, less because the woman next door did not mow all of her lawn and more because he was angry that she didn't think enough of him to respond positively when he asked her to clean up her property. Many feuding individuals, looking for reasons to feel provoked, jump at any chance they get to feel angered, letting almost any slight do the trick. Along these lines they do not differentiate between important and unimportant stressors so that an unreturned phone call becomes as serious a rejection as a broken engagement to get married. Should they fail to find actual events, situations, and relationships to fire them up, they find nonadversarial events to reframe into interpersonal aggravations, thus creating semidelusional scenarios that fuel their sadomasochistic need to become embroiled in some form of ongoing unpleasantness.

EXTREME PESSIMISM

Patients with a paranoid personality disorder are worrisome pessimists who every day see the possibility of injustices, scams, and physical assaults, regularly anticipate the worst, and find unfaithful spouses, potential kidnapers, and leering sexual predators everywhere they look. Theirs is a deep sense of foreboding associated with the belief that disaster is always on the horizon and that tomorrow will bring even worse news than yesterday, in the form of new revelations about more hostile, malignant enemies planning dangerous cabals and life-threatening conspiracies—further proof that "These days they're all out to get you."

They justify their pessimism by citing the things that actually go wrong in their lives, as if they do not go wrong in the lives of everybody. They then say, "I told you so," as if they were right all along. They want it to look as if they predicted a given negative outcome, which was then validated by circumstances. But their predictions in fact remain invalid because they view trivial events as important and unusual circumstances as completely validating their usual fears; because they make so many pessimistic predictions that some are bound to come true by chance alone; or because they make things go wrong, as planned, by antagonizing people with their anger and suspiciousness and by making themselves sufficiently unappealing so that people turn away, unable to tolerate their constant criticisms, demands for justice when no wrong has been done, and calls for vengeance when they have in fact experienced no harm.

ALOOFNESS AND WITHDRAWAL

Patients with paranoid personality disorder tend to be shy, cold, aloof loners. They withdraw from relationships because they believe that isolation protects them from others who might corner, attack, devour, and mutilate them, and, moving into their space, take over their lives, control them, and cause them to lose their individuality. They therefore often have a negative reaction to others who attempt to get too close to them, one that ranges from discomfort to counterattack. If they form relationships at all they tend to be loose, distant ones with others who themselves have problems with getting close—typically fanatics from fringe groups such as cults and militaristic, often Nazi-style organizations, that is, people who form bonds that are more ideational than interpersonal.

However, not all individuals with a paranoid personality disorder are cold and remote loners. Some actually dislike being alone because they fear that when they are by themselves they have no protection from dangerous outside forces. Those who are pathologically jealous are in some ways the opposite of loners: too intense and too involved for their own good and for the good of those they have incorporated into their delusional systems. Some swing between being related and unrelated and as a result appear to have a sort of split personality as they alternate between extreme dependency and a fear of being rejected on the one hand and extreme independence and a fear of being devoured on the other. Such individuals tend to be diagnosed not as paranoid but as having borderline personality disorder with paranoid features.

SADOMASOCHISTIC TENDENCIES

Some patients with a paranoid personality disorder are openly sadistic. That would include the straight man who told a gay neighbor who was in fact a good citizen to get out of here and go back to where he came from—and added that all of the neighbors on the block agree that that is a good idea. Sadistic paranoid individuals like him quest unremittingly for satisfaction in the ominous sense of triumph and vengeance. If they hack in cyberspace it is not (as they often claim in their rationalizations) to demonstrate that computers are vulnerable to being compromised as a basis for improving the system. Rather it is to destroy those whom they believe have it all and more than they do—particularly members of the hated establishment as symbolized by the big business interests of the very rich. Focused on turning the tables on their supposed persecutors they make the formulation "an eye for an eye" holy writ. While obsessionals justify the code of "an eye for an eye" as upholding the principle of desirable balance, entropy, and the notion that every reaction must be followed by an equal and opposite reaction, the "eye for an eye" of paranoid individuals expresses the notion that sin has its wages and that he who calls the tune must pay the piper. These people call not for balance but for atonement for sins and punishment for crimes. Unlike obsessionals who need symmetry and balance to *make* even, paranoid individuals need symmetry and balance to *get* even.

Other patients with paranoid personality disorders are less overtly than passive-aggressively sadistic. They hurt others not directly but indirectly. Instead of openly ridiculing, denouncing, and avenging themselves on others, they settle for becoming haughty, arrogant, and superior-acting, or even for passive malice—the enjoyment of others' bad luck, that is, schadenfreude. It is typical for them to simply refuse to grant a sensible request or to ask questions that hide accusations. When they ask a question such as "Are you upset with me?" they really mean "I am angry with you for mistreating me." Over-concern is another guise for their passive-aggression—their way to give others the impression that "I am humane and you are not," thereby invalidating others' positive self-view, making them look and feel bad while they make themselves look and feel good. Attempting to make someone who kept them waiting feel guilty about harming "a person as nice as I am," they assure him or her that they are not angry that they were kept waiting, only worried that something bad might have happened to the person they were waiting for. A bigot in favor of maintaining the criminalization of homosexuality notes that he does not want to see homosexuals in jail; he is merely seriously concerned about the effects they might have on future generations of children yet un-born. Overconcern can also take the form of the expression of good wishes to others meant to kill them with kindness. Thus a paranoid patient sends the following Christmas card (making sure that it will be opened and read before it gets thrown away by not including an alerting return address on the en-velope) containing a message entirely inappropriate for the spirit of the hol-iday season, geared to leaving the recipient wondering if the sender's motive was to reconcile or to attack all over again.

"I know that you are not speaking to me, but since that is the result of misunderstanding and miscommunication, it shouldn't negate the good will of the season. Take care."

In this Christmas card the primary motive was not to tell the victim that I want to wish you a happy holiday. The primary motive was to convey the message that, although you are not speaking to me and probably hate me, I love you anyway; therefore, I, not you, am a nice guy and you, not I, are the aggressor. The victim is also reminded that miscommunication doomed the relationship, by which the sender of the card meant, "I did not act badly; you misunderstood my intentions."

Other attacks on people in the guise of offering them good wishes are "some of my best friends are Jewish" and the knuckle-rapping paranoid homophobic "love the sinner, hate the sin."

Worry is another form of passive-aggressive attack. The man who con-demned a friend for seeing his wife behind his back, "leaving me in the dark as to just what is going on anyway," covered his antagonism with a falsely altruistic protest that he wasn't angry with his friend for betraying him. Rather he was just worried that by not being there and joining in the festivities he might have given his friend the wrong impression—that he was ignoring him.

Somatizing is a common way for passive-aggressive paranoid individuals to express their anger indirectly. As an example, frozen, rigid, empty bodily com-plaints such as a persistent global headache or severe crimp in the neck can be installed to convey the message "You give me a pain." A patient with, as she put it, "allergies to everything," who was in fact not physically but emo-tionally allergic to certain foods, repetitively told the hostess of a dinner party that she was attending that the hostess must not use the same spatula for the patient's food as she used for everyone else's. Unconsciously she intended to make the hostess miserable by constantly reminding her that even one mistake could "put me at risk of having a deadly anaphylactic shock."

Activist platforms are known for attacks on others using a positive self-statement, along the lines of "I would never kill an animal for its fur," leaving unsaid the real message in the communication: "Like you would."

Irritability and irascibility are other passive-aggressive ways paranoid individuals have of expressing their anger indirectly. In passive-aggressive paranoid individuals the irritability and irascibility tend to be lit from behind with the glow of suspicion, making their irritability and irascibility different from manic irritability and irascibility, which is lit from behind with the glow of euphoria. Also, while manics tend to snap, paranoid individuals tend to seethe. Often the paranoid individual displays a seemingly benign, apologetic, or conciliatory manner, but that is belied by a tight-lipped snarling facial expression and frown that seem to warn of unpleasantness to come. Even this façade can, however, wear away quickly as anger builds, takes over, and gets out of control. Now we may hear the characteristic hisses, curses, and broken sentences that finally end in severe outbursts accompanied by four-letter words. The resultant attacks on others on one level seem very personal, and they often are and should be taken that way. But on another level they are impersonal in the sense that the paranoid individual has merely used his or her victim as a docking station whose attachment points are a convenient place for the paranoid individual to park and unload his or her burdensome angry cargo.

In summary, as Cooper (1994) says, "the extent of paranoid suspicion and rage is often underestimated, commingled as it is with the patient's narcissistic fears of humiliation, and obsessional defenses designed to control and hide the extent of his malignant expectations. Warfare is usually carried on at the level of guerrilla resistance rather than nuclear explosions, although occasional cold paranoid fury may burst through" (pp. 145–146).

A number of observers, including Bone and Oldham (1994), have noted that individuals with paranoid personality disorders are, being sadomasochists, as masochistic as they are sadistic (p. 3). In their masochistic mode these paranoid individuals are embroiled in self-destructive interpersonal interactions whose main goal appears to be to almost deliberately antagonize people—part of their plan to arrange for others to hurt them and make them suffer, so that they can now say, "Look at what they are doing to me, just like I told you." A coffee shop owner, who will be mentioned throughout, repeatedly asked his friends to keep him from destroying his business, only to not listen to them and instead proceed to antagonize any of the patrons who gave him the slightest bit of (mostly imagined) difficulty. Once a poet was sitting quietly in the corner writing poems. Concerned that the table was being hijacked, he walked over to him and told him, "You cannot do that here." The table lay empty until closing time, absent the coffee refills that the poet was ordering and paying full price for.

GRANDIOSITY

Grandiosity in individuals with a paranoid personality disorder is at least partly an attempt to overcome a fear of being a big nobody. As such it has a palpable *reactive* quality to it. Individuals with a paranoid personality disorder deal with their fear that no one loves them by convincing themselves that everyone does. They deal with their fear of being demolished by convincing themselves that they are invincible. They deal with their fear of becoming big nonentities with smirking self-congratulations meant to cope with low self-esteem and to deny the effect of imagined put-downs. For example, one such individual dealt with the feeling that others were criticizing him for being uneducated by becoming a know-it-all who shamelessly debated with anyone, no matter how expert, on any topic whatsoever.

As noted throughout, some, plagued by the idea that they are sinners, deal with that self-perception by considering themselves saintly spokespersons of divine authority put here on Earth for the righteous cause of rescuing sinners from themselves, with the emphasis less on helping the sinner than on magically casting out their own sins by cleansing the very same sins in others. This righteousness even extends to the most antisocial of their actions, lending these an air of guiltlessness that in turn allows them to view their even truly horrific behavior in an entirely favorable light. They become like a pilot who crashes his plane to kill himself and those aboard for a higher cause: so that all can join a beneficent God in a better world.

There is a palpable *narcissistic* component to their grandiosity. This takes the form of extreme self-interest. As far as they are concerned their persecution, their status in life, their court case, their body symptom, and their unrequited love affair come first, and if others have problems or needs of their own they can either get behind them in line or go away. Also inherent in their narcissism is a reluctance to see the other person's side of things. Though they care about "my persecution," they care not at all about how you might feel when I attack you for persecuting me. Feelings of narcissistic entitlement lead them to believe that they are owed, making them very sensitive to deprivation of all sorts. For example, jealous delusions often translate to "You are stealing someone I need and want (that is, not someone I love) away from me." Not surprisingly there is an infantile element to their complaints about others, making these complaints rather like childish temper tantrums taking place in an adult. For example, a woman demanded that her husband pay for her trip to France. She was going there to cheat on him with a man she had met over the Internet. She reasoned, "Husbands are supposed to provide their wives with a car; I don't have a car; therefore he owes me a certain amount of money for transportation." When he refused to pay the tariff she felt a combination of despair and anger at him and raged at him for depriving her of what she believed she was rightfully owed.

Should their defensive grandiosity fail them, their feelings of superiority readily transform into feelings of inferiority. They do not, however, merely feel as if they do not have what it takes. Instead they feel singled-out and persecuted by envious and jealous competitors who presumably hate them for having it all. As Shapiro (1994) puts it, they become bitter people who harbor "the hatred that a prideful inferior or subordinate harbors towards his [envied and] grudgingly admired betters" (p. 54).

PERSONALIZATION TENDENCIES

Patients with paranoid personality disorders tend to personalize the actions of others to the point that they come to believe that others play a central role in their lives, even when those others' thoughts and actions in fact have little or nothing to do with them. They believe that they are the sole or principal target of actions just because those actions affect them. Just as they relate impersonal events to themselves, they impute personal motives—usually hostile, and where there are no reasonable grounds—to others. Thus the neighbors would be quieter if they didn't hate the individual so much. In their view there is no such thing as an accident. Instead all adverse developments possibly caused or influenced by nonhuman or human agency, however random, are personally meaningful. What to a normal observer would be an error they construe as intentional. They feel that the police simply by virtue of being imperfect have it in for them. Loss of a job is attributed to enemies in high places. Neighborhood noise is attributed to a gang with a grudge. The failure to receive a check is attributed to thieving neighbors. In this tendency we find echoes of the atavistic need to animate or personify causative forces and transform them into persecuting demons.

THE TENDENCY TO THINK ILLOGICALLY

These individuals distort logic in order to defend their favored philosophical or pseudophilosophical positions and in order to justify their negative reactions to other people and to external events. A favored form of illogic involves comparing apples with oranges, as in the pornographer's defense that "Yes, but violence is worse, and the real sin." They often use the logic disorder of von Domarus to justify their persecutory beliefs (The classic example of which is, "I am a virgin; the Virgin Mary is a virgin; therefore, I am the Virgin Mary). For example, one patient thought, "I am a foreigner, everyone hates foreigners, therefore all people hate me." Their polemics depend on their using selective abstraction to omit facts that go contrary to, and might disprove, their often angry assertions. From paranoid homophobes we learn how to selectively quote from the Bible. For example, to back up their hatred of homosexuals they quote that part of Genesis that refers to homosexuality as an abomination but fail to mention that they do not necessarily subscribe to that part of the Bible that prohibits wearing garments made up of two kinds of material and sowing one's field with two kinds of seed (Leviticus, 19). They use part-to-whole errors to maintain their focus on the dark side of things. They make a lot negative out of things that are mostly positive by acknowledging only the base motives in complex behaviors, like rejection in an unavoidable cancellation of a date. For example, a patient's dinner engagement was canceled because the man of the couple suddenly discovered that he had to have a brain tumor removed. The patient saw that as a personal rejection and linked it to the hosts' similar rejecting behavior 10 years previously when they had to cancel another date for other, almost as good, reasons. He felt singled out because "they don't treat their other friends that way." Then he insisted that his conclusions arose from his assessment of reality, even though his assessment of reality was derived from his conclusions. Next, as is so often the case, his neo-reality became the basis of a pathological response. He refused to make any more dates with the couple to spare his own sensibilities, and even contemplated inviting the couple over for dinner then canceling out at the last minute to get his revenge.

Not surprisingly, individuals with paranoid personality disorders rationalize the logical errors they make after they make them. While depressed people are eager to confess their distortions so that they can look like sinners, these individuals are eager to hide them so that they can look like saints. For example, they try hard to give the impression that their conclusions about other people were arrived at not impulsively, but reluctantly, with regrets, because they simply could no longer ignore the evidence.

Their use, really misuse, of logic, is often impressive and convincing. They are not necessarily smarter than other people. Rather they are more highly motivated to prove that they are right—more so than other people are motivated to prove them wrong. They want to prove themselves right so that they can convince people that they have the word, and so that they can defend themselves against those who would call them misguided. Also their illogic, being a product of their illness, comes as second nature to them, much as rituals come as second nature to obsessive-compulsives or as a fear of heights comes as second nature to phobics.

Individuals with paranoid personality disorders often seek or demand consensual validation for their illogical thinking. They ask others to agree with them, hoping that the others will validate their invalid premises. Often they seek this agreement for practical as well as for emotional reasons. They might want others to join them in an antimanagement or antiestablishment coalition not only so that they can win an emotional personal feud or get others to admire and love them, but also so that they can defeat a feared or hated rival, or so that they can enlist allies to help them sway an intended audience.

Their search for validation puts the persons called on in a difficult position, because to agree is impossible, while to disagree makes you an enemy, a co-conspirator. While other, nonparanoid people refused validation sulk, drop the person, and look for someone else, these individuals, when others refuse to take their side or, worse, side with their adversaries, do not sulk, but attack, doing so with a vengeance because they have taken the disagreement both personally and to heart, as if others are not disagreeing with their ideas, but invalidating their person.

However, all assertions cannot be ignored and invalidated just because they come from a paranoid person. The assertions of individuals who are paranoid need to be taken seriously for two reasons. First, their assertions can only be discounted if they are known to be a product of illogical or delusional thoughts. But people who are paranoid in some respects are completely free of paranoia in others. Therefore not everything that they say or do comes from their delusional system. Besides, as noted throughout, it is often difficult to determine what is delusional and what is reality. Second, paranoid hyper-vigilance with its constant scanning can make these individuals quite insightful, and therefore right at least some of the time and brilliant in at least certain respects.

THE TENDENCY TO GET DEPRESSED

Individuals with paranoid personality disorders often appear to be clinically depressed for the following reasons. First, some deliberately revise their case presentations so that they can come across not as paranoid but as depressed. They want to avoid being thought of as paranoid, and to do so they change "I fear that people hate me" to "I fear that no one likes me." As Ansar M. Haroun (1999) says, "it is 'okay' to be depressed" (p. 335), but being paranoid means being angry, which is not okay (p. 335).

Second, individuals with paranoid personality disorders are often truly moody people whose sadness and withdrawal are real. But in paranoid individuals the sadness and withdrawal occur in the context of, and are a product of, an adversarial relationship less, as with depressives, with themselves, and more with others. Unlike depressives, who feel that all is lost because they made so many mistakes in life, paranoid individuals feel that all is lost because others have made so many mistakes with them. Another differential point is that while the affect in depression is anguished, sad, pained, and contrite, in paranoid individuals the affect is flattened or, when the hostility is intense, piercing. Also, while depressives look like tragic figures who suffer a great deal, individuals with paranoid personality disorders look like antagonists always ready to strike out at others and to make them suffer. In addition, while depressives suffer mainly from despair, paranoids suffer mainly from fear.

Sometimes there is true depressive mood originating in true depressive thought, but it does not prevail. Rather it is an evolutionary peak of the paranoid process, the ultimate product of rational negative thoughts about their plight and fate in life, often appearing when their paranoia is subsiding to the point that now they can just begin to see how badly off they are in life realistically, due to the cumulative ravages of their chronic illness.

Like depressives, patients with paranoid personality disorders, as previously noted, are pessimistic. But unlike depressives whose pessimism is often the function of low self-esteem (leading them to believe that they are too unworthy to have any good come into their lives), the pessimism of paranoid individuals is mostly due to what they believe to be experientially justified low expectations. They feel that they can never, no matter what they do, overcome life's serious adversities, as in "How can I get anywhere in life when everyone is against me?"

Patients with paranoid personality disorders, like depressives, can have a true sense of unwarranted low self-esteem. But with these individuals the unwarranted low self-esteem is less the product of a sense of guilt, as it is in depressives, than a response to the negative things they believe that their persecutors are saying about them, and the bad names they are presumably calling them. Sometimes their low self-esteem is little more than a cover for passive-aggressive retaliatory fault-finding, as when a lover says, "Life has nothing to offer me" and "I am no good and worthless," but really means, "because of what you do to me."

Those who appear to be grieving are often less preoccupied by the loss itself than they are with the negative effect that the loss has by implication brought down on them. Students who shoot up the school after a breakup may say that they did so because they were in a state of grief over having been rejected, but they may not be so much feeling grief as feeling humiliated. Now they shoot to kill both to affirm their wholeness and to revive their sense of power and control, as well as to simultaneously punish the ones they believe to have been responsible for their fate. The cry of a depressed griever is "I cannot live without you," while the cry of a paranoid griever is "I'll get back at you for what you did to me by leaving."

A DESIRE TO LOOK INTACT

Inherent in paranoid personality disorder is a desire to be able to continue to function effectively. This function is of course impaired, but the deficit may not apply equally to all parameters. It often leaves the capacity to work intact, while interfering with the capacity to love. It is quite common for individuals to accept being paranoid with their husbands or wives but to be "paranoid about being paranoid" with their boss or with strangers.

CALCULATING BEHAVIORS

As discussed throughout this text, feelings of persecution are not incompatible with a certain amount of calculation. The close relationship between delusional thinking and argumentativeness (being delusional, after all, involves arguing with reality) means that these individuals are natural debaters adept at conning others into believing that they are right and that others are wrong, often manipulatively and in large part so that they can adjust the matter along desired lines—by getting those they believe to be the culprits to make amends, to change their interfering ways, to confess their sins, or to award them compensatory damages for (often imagined) harm done. Many such individuals arrange to look normal when they want to and abnormal when that serves their purpose. They arrange to look normal when they want to leave the hospital and abnormal when, without a place to stay for the night, they want to be readmitted. In prison they do good deeds less because they are truly altruistic and more as part of their long-term plan to get out early. The most psychopathic among them simply lie if they think that that will produce an intended effect. Not surprisingly, those who lie defend their lies afterward, in true paranoid fashion, along such not-me lines as "The problem is not my lying, but your refusing to believe me."

CHAPTER 4

The Adverse Ways Paranoid Individuals Affect Others

On the positive side, paranoid individuals are often bright, interesting, effective, successful people who contribute a great deal to society. But on the negative side, they are mostly a troublesome group to deal with who pay a high price in the currency of their relationships for the intrapsychic advantages they get from their disorder. Most of us find that however much we would like to relate to them and offer them understanding, empathy, and constructive criticism, they tend to strain our patience and our sense of compassion. Indeed, sooner or later most of us give up trying to relate to, and think only of protecting ourselves from, them or, in less favorable circumstances, of retaliating for what they have done to us. We respond that way even though we recognize that they are not bad but sick. It is, after all, only human nature to dislike

People who see negative motives in our positive intentions, misinterpreting our offers of advice as control, our attempts to help them as taking over, and our statements of love as smothering them or having designs on them sexually.

People who are impossible to please, who exasperate us by putting us in a damned if we do and damned if we don't position, so that if we do not set limits on them they feel that we are uncaring, but if we do set limits on them and attempt to warn them to not do something self-destructive they take that as a statement that we have no faith in them, and criticize us for believing that they would do such stupid things.

People who are so hypersensitive that they take everything we say and do incorrectly and to heart, so that we always have to be 105 percent careful about saying and doing the wrong thing, constantly having to watch our step and walk on eggshells with them.

People who are so narcissistic that they condemn us for not meeting their very personal needs or being in tune with their very special agendas. An individual who read one of my books wrote to me that he was disappointed that I did not discuss a topic relevant to him. I wrote back that that particular topic was out of the area of my expertise. He then covered me with invective, saying that it was hard to comprehend how I could be so out of touch, that my response marginalized him, and that therefore he could not longer consider me his mentor because anything I had to say had no real applicability to him.

People who provoke us to anger just so that they can justify their own outrage with us as second not first strike, that is, as reaction not action.

People who criticize and blame us when we are innocent just so that they can view themselves as blameless.

People who cleanse themselves of the evil they see within themselves by transferring that evil onto us, condemning our sins to prove to themselves that they are not sinners, criticizing us for having their own disavowed characteristics, such as acquisitiveness, laziness, or femininity just so they can stop thinking of themselves as being bad or evil in that way. As an example, a grandiose boss took an inordinate amount of sick leave. When she did come to work she rarely put in a full day, and instead of just doing her work used the hours she did put in to deal with her guilt about being dishonest about time by railing against the erratic attendance records of those who worked for her, and complaining that she was the only one doing anything at all around the office. As Cooper (1994) notes, like any paranoid individual she was "defy[ing] rules to the brink" (p. 145) while proclaiming her innocence by blaming and criticizing others for not following the same rules—the typical hypocritical "do as I say, not as I do."

People who in their moralistic, bigoted way attempt to reform us, demanding that we be healed along their predetermined lines, which consist of black-and-white distinctions made in areas of gray, clear precepts of right and wrong and evil and good that we must share with them, whatever our personal beliefs happen to be, or else.

People who manipulate us so that they can obtain some unfair advantage for themselves, such as being let off easy after committing a crime on the grounds of being adjudged insane.

People who are passive-aggressive, who, as Cooper says, frustrate us by teasing us in a hostile way (p. 143). Especially frustrating is that the usual way we have for managing passive-aggressive individuals—recognizing the subtle blaming shift that is taking place, then putting the blame back on them, where it belongs—does not work very well with paranoid passive-aggressive individuals, who do not break down in the face of such obstacles but instead react by feeling guiltier than before, which inspires them not to apologize or to offer to change but to extract even harsher penalties from us, usually in the form of verbal malice—humiliating, criticizing, and destroying our positive sense of self as our punishment for having seen through and taken countermeasures against them. Equally frustrating is that our efforts to cope can be not only ineffective but dangerous should we undermine their defenses to the point that we cause them to break down completely and become highly agitated, openly angry, or even violent.

what is a clear example of this?

People who are difficult to get along with because they start and become embroiled in petty squabbles, then keep them going because they have long memories and quest unremittingly for vengeance, so that they do not accept apologies or back off but continuously pursue their mission to get their eye for an eye.

People who propose radical solutions for what are in fact trivial if not entirely imaginary problems. For example, a social worker dealt with his belief that he was too subordinate for his taste in two ways. First, he paralyzed all team meetings almost completely by not letting the team move forward unless and until a complete agenda for the meeting to come was outlined, then followed as if it were etched in stone. He then permitted no deviation from the agenda and, if by accident there should be one, insisted that the team go back and redo the initial agenda, revising it to include the new material. Second, he constantly squawked that everyone at work was taking advantage of his good nature by dumping on him and in response demanded complex procedural tracts that outlined the duties of all concerned just so that he could have an even playing field, that is, one where he did not have to do any more work than the next guy.

People who are unpleasantly cold, angry, and aloof, who wrap themselves up in themselves not so much because they want to be alone, but because they want to steer clear of others they are convinced are plotting against them.

People who, conversely, are *too* intrusive because as a product of their psychopathology they relate even more intensely than most people, although in an unhealthy way. This group includes grandiose paranoid individuals who demand an appreciative audience, and pathologically jealous paranoid individuals who demand an acceptable explanation.

Those of us with a tendency to be paranoid ourselves do especially poorly with other paranoid individuals. As Cooper (1994) puts it in another context, such individuals readily bring "out prominent paranoid defenses that [are] otherwise well contained" (p. 144). It follows that individuals who are themselves paranoid must be especially careful about relating to other paranoid individuals. They have to be very careful to choose partners who do not provoke them by being passive-aggressive, first making them angry with their suspicions then denying that that is what they did. They should avoid extremely jealous individuals who accuse them of cheating just so that they can cheat themselves. They should avoid people who make harsh often retaliative jokes at their expense, like the woman who responded to her new partner's saying, "We have been together for three weeks now," with, "Yes, but it feels like three years." They should also avoid insensitive people, like the woman who brought an old lover back into a new relationship, then responded when her new lover said that she felt hurt by telling her that she was falsely accusing her of being unkind due to her own being much too sensitive.

Of course, sometimes others with a tendency to be paranoid themselves merely imagine themselves to be provoked. They become pseudo, or so-called, victims who claim hostility where there is none, accuse others of hidden motivations they do not have, and develop an adversarial relationship with others based on presumed antagonisms that do not actually exist. The following is a letter from one such possibly paranoid pseudovictim:

Pondering the holidays, I realize that something I'm anxious about is mail. More specifically, I'm afraid that a gift that is sent could be an emotional booby trap. For instance, one member of the household (not the victim in this distinct case) receives a gift from the PA [passive-aggressive]. Notably the gift (which is obviously exposed to all in the household when opened on a holiday) is something that would remind another member of the household of some personal disappointment.

To illustrate with a hypothetical instance, assume a collection of five Christmas gifts sent to a wife by her sister includes among other things two tickets to an unremarkable musical titled "Crackerjack." The sender had a history of Passive Aggressive attacks on the wife's husband and everyone knows the husband has always loved to eat popcorn. If the husband had recently been diagnosed with severe diverticulitis (the dietary consequences of which were known and understood by the Passive Aggressive) would you consider this a Passive Aggressive attack by the gift sender on the husband?

This is what I'm wondering about characterizing as an emotional booby trap. I've seen reference to bringing up personal family stress/hurts in greeting cards, but this seems more subtle (and probably therefore more potent).

CHAPTER 5

Covert (Hidden) and Missed Paranoia

In this chapter I discuss covert or hidden paranoia, that is, mild to severe paranoia that is not immediately obvious even to, and so may be missed by, the careful observer. In the next chapter I discuss the related issue of paranoid phenomena that fall in the gray area, that is, that lie somewhere on a continuum between the mild paranoia of everyday life and the more severe clinical paranoia. Because of the overlap this chapter should be read in conjunction with the next chapter, which covers some of the same ground but in a different context.

As a general rule, where there is a strong indication of persecutory and grandiose ideation there is usually a sound basis for making the diagnosis of paranoia. But not all paranoid individuals are Nazi sympathizers, terrorists, religious fanatics, or deluded misfits. There are less obvious candidates where, as the *DSM-IV* (American Psychiatric Association, 1994) suggests, "delusional conviction [has to be] inferred from an individual's behavior" (p. 765). Here the hard indications of paranoia are seemingly slight or absent, and the only available diagnostic material consists of peripheral elements associated with paranoia such as malignant narcissism, cunning manipulativeness, or a tendency to be too highly critical of others. In such cases we should suspect paranoia and dig deeper to rule it in or out, using psychological detective work to trace its visible footprint back to its original and true source.

Covert paranoia is to be found in a variety of everyday situations and in people in all walks of life, where it typically presents as phenomena we call by other names. For example, many people we call argumentative and many people whom we say have an axe to grind are covertly paranoid individuals. Our suspicions should also be aroused by people in road rage; politicians who, overlooking the considerable differences, make exact comparisons between homosexuality, incest, bigamy, and bestiality; wife-beaters who like to claim "she provoked me" to explain and excuse their ferocious behavior; pseudo- and quack scientists such as those who seriously embrace the questionable energy concepts of feng shui as protective against malignant vibes, who claim that calcium cures cancer, or who state unequivocally that we are all cloned from aliens; and community activists who go beyond rational helpful complaints about social injustice and inequality and reasonable recommendations for its alleviation to become fringe fanatical, blaming extremists, totally and irrationally preoccupied with the evil certain men do. Even what appear to be mild personality quirks may owe their existence to hidden paranoia. For example, some individuals who on the surface appear to be just plain stubborn may in fact be displaying fixed delusions impervious to argument, and some individuals who on the surface appear to be merely withdrawn and remote may really be isolates due to a need to protect themselves from the imagined evil-doers all around them. Some people who superficially appear to be merely self-centered may in fact be personalizing random events referentially, or who appear to be merely highly rivalrous may in fact be competing not to prove what they can do but to "get them before they get me." People who upon first glance appear to be merely know-it-alls with little time for or interest in others' point of view may in fact believe themselves to be the Deity, or at least one of the disciples, not placed on Earth to listen to, but to be heard by, others. Even complaining neighbors who appear to be just average city folk justifiably annoyed by those living next to or above them may in fact be not merely hypercritical, irrational, angry individuals but paranoid people convinced that a neighbor is deliberately harassing them by sending smells under their door or by beaming noises at and into their bedroom.

Many of these paranoid individuals do not reveal their highly charged persecutory fantasies/impressions/thoughts/delusions because they are aware of their diagnostic significance and, unless they are schizophrenic, are generally intellectually intact enough to be capable of effectively dissimulating. Such individuals often whitewash their delusions as obsessions. Thus a patient who was convinced that gay men were putting the AIDS virus on exposed metal spurs on the supermarket carts so that he would prick his finger and get infected, in the telling changed this conviction to a worry that the carts were full of bad germs and that he might pick up a bug that was fatal. Many patients whitewash a delusional erotomanic preoccupation with a lover who has no interest in them at all by referring to it as an "obsession with love." Of course, paranoid individuals often hide their delusions under the cloak of reality, the familiar "I am not paranoid, I have real enemies." Adding to the diagnostic confusion is that many so-called paranoid people are often partly right, making it difficult to know where reality ends and delusion begins. Indeed, in many cases both reality and nonreality combine in a given paranoid idea. Because there is almost always a core of reality in paranoid ideation, most paranoid individuals can with minimal effort present themselves as suffering not with a problem of injustice-collecting but from the effects of real injustices.

Those paranoid individuals who reveal their delusions at all sometimes only reveal them in fragments. This makes each of their revelations appear neutral enough so that the true distortive nature of the underlying belief is disguised from others and sometimes even from themselves. Yet what they say is not so far removed from its origins that it does not express the distortive idea at all. Thus, with a persecutory fantasy the presented fragments (no one of which is itself paranoid) might be "You don't like me," "To all indications, I occupy a central position in your mind," and/or "I cannot stop thinking about you." To get the whole picture, for example, to be sure that the patient feels persecuted not just unloved or overworried, the diagnostician must hazard an empathic guess from one or two of the pieces, and sometimes be resigned to the fact that the whole picture can only be put together over time.

An elderly couple went to restaurants not to enjoy themselves but to find fault. Whether or not it was true, they would send every dish back to the kitchen saying that something was wrong with it. They invariably quoted an authority who, according to them, said that it was proper to send things back if something were amiss. Then they would give the waitress an excessively small tip, quoting another authority who, according to them, had clearly stated that a large tip was the reward for good service and should be reduced or withheld if the service was not acceptable. Finally, they would wrap the bread and take it home not because they wanted it but as restitution for the wrongs that they believed they had suffered, for which they desired to make the perpetrators pay.

These people, while they looked merely overcritical or picky, were in fact beyond that. They were hypercritical, petty individuals who felt persecuted, but expressed their persecutory feelings only indirectly and in a partial way. The mien of smug self-righteousness, excessive fault-finding, and hair-trigger response to every trivial or imagined slight both clothed and exposed the body of a typically paranoid attitude—the belief that the world is a dangerous and hostile place, a belief they revealed to others by merely citing small examples of the world's dangerousness and hostility. (Also revealed here is how typical it is for a manipulative "statue"—manipulative in the sense that a situation is deliberately created to validate a prior intention of giving a small tip—to have a paranoid "pedestal.")

There are several reasons why paranoid individuals keep their paranoia hidden. First, paranoid individuals are by nature shy, secretive, even shifty people who desire to exercise tight control over what they reveal—that is, they are too paranoid to admit that they are paranoid. As Cooper (1994) says, "secret-keeping is a routine aspect of paranoid behavior" (p. 143).

Second, many paranoiacs consciously intend to look normal. Some want to look healthy—in other words, to "malinger health"—in order to avoid being referred to a psychiatrist and perhaps forced to take medication, or in order to secure timely release from a mental hospital. Others want to look healthy so that they can continue to relate to and interact with people in order to keep alive the opportunity to prove a point of contention, or to maintain a needed adversarial relationship. In others it is their natural healing tendencies that lead them to recognize and struggle with, ignore, or not admit to, their delusions. As a result, healthier paranoid individuals often have their delusions under control to the point that they mention them only when something the interviewer says, asks, or does acts as a trigger. A patient, convinced that he was the object of a conspiracy by a large bank, only mentioned the problem when the interviewer set him off by opening up a discussion of his retirement finances. For months an internist treated the patient with the delusional belief that "I have no esophagus" for "esophageal spasm" because she complained to him that she had difficulty in swallowing without telling him the real reason why she believed that she couldn't swallow. I only found out about her delusional belief when I asked her specifically, "And why do you feel that your food will not go down?" A patient was referred to the Boston Psychoanalytic Institute for deep analysis after having been given the relatively benign, non-psychotic diagnosis of histrionic personality disorder. However, when the analyst pulled out his notepad at the start of the interview, she was stressed to the breaking point. Now she could no longer hide her delusions, so that what came tumbling out was, "I have to stop seeing you because you are taking notes about what I say. That proves what I already suspected—that you are a Martian put on earth to spy on and control me."

Often the reason paranoia remains hidden resides not in the paranoid patient or process itself but in the clinician, where it can arise out of personal attitudes about mental illness in general and about paranoia in particular. Now hidden paranoia becomes missed paranoia. Unfortunately, explanations are not difficult to come by for the collective tendency to overlook mental illness in general and paranoia in particular.

Those who are hostile to the mentally ill may deny that mental illness exists so that they can punish, not make excuses for, people who are emotionally disturbed—along the lines of "you brought this on yourself."

Those who feel more positively inclined to the mentally ill may still deny that mental illness exists, but they do so because they believe that calling individuals mentally ill is pejorative, and that the rules for classifying mental illness resemble the rules for identifying witches. Or they may admit that mental illness exists but refuse to call someone that they like personally a paranoid. A woman refused to think of a boyfriend with flat affect, catatonic stupor, and bizarre persecutory delusions as paranoid. Instead she insisted that he was suffering from a bipolar disorder and was currently depressed. Indeed she bragged about his being bipolar as if it were a badge of honor, one that said, "You belong to an admired, if unusual, group." Like her, many therapists stretch a point to make an affective diagnosis, so as to avoid making a paranoid diagnosis. Though recently it has lost some of its steam, a few decades ago there was a movement/trend afoot to reclassify almost all schizophrenia as affective disorder, and along with that a movement to reclassify much paranoia as depression. To do that it was merely necessary to misinterpret feeling persecuted as feeling unloved, and conceptualize severe withdrawal as prolonged guilty retreat from life. On the positive side, therapeutic miracles have occurred when so-called schizophrenic patients have been properly reclassified as having an affective disorder and treated with antidepressants or antimanic agents, and as a bonus these medications are much better tolerated than the phenothiazines. But on the negative side, as I emphasize throughout, and especially in chapter 15 on pharmacotherapy, a number of paranoid people have killed themselves and others after having been incorrectly diagnosed as depressed and either given activating antidepressants alone without a covering phenothiazine or treated, inadequately, solely with mood-stabilizing medication or with mood-stabilizing medication along with an antidepressant.

Alternatively, some mental health workers who feel favorably inclined to the mentally ill stretch a point so that they may view paranoid individuals not as psychotic but as neurotic. They might recast a withdrawn paranoid individual as a shy social phobic or as having an avoidant personality disorder. For example, in spite of evidence to the contrary, a psychiatrist refused to diagnose a woman's chronically withdrawn and mute brother as catatonic. Instead, going beyond stretching a point, he forced his illness into the procrustean bed of a neurosis: social phobia with hysterical mutism in a person with a chronic oppositional defiant disorder of childhood lasting into adulthood.

Many therapists and laypersons alike hesitate to call others paranoid because seeing themselves in and identifying with paranoid individuals, they become reluctant to brand behavior that resembles their own as disturbed. If mental illness of any sort, and paranoid mental illness in particular, rules others' lives, perhaps it rules one's own too, so perhaps one's own anger, hypersensitivity, suspiciousness, narrow thinking, grandiosity, and manipulativeness are seriously abnormal. Also if mental illness can rule, it means that we, just like those mentally ill people, have an unconscious, suggesting that not all of our will is free. The specter of others at the mercy of their angry and sexual passions does not sit well with those of us who like to feel we are, unlike the animals, always completely in control of ourselves.

Too many of us miss the pathological nature of paranoia because we secretly condone and admire people who are paranoid. We condone and admire the behavior of those politicians who campaign negatively, stirring up common hatreds to entice the masses over onto their side, and we excuse politicians who look for scapegoats, such as the last person in office, to blame for their failures. We secretly approve of people who dislike and condemn sexuality as we support those who view homosexuality as evil, and we buy into the assertions of those who incorrectly view a proper sexual approach between consenting adults as sexual harassment. It makes us feel good and chaste, even in line for beatification, as we congratulate ourselves for being among the few people left in the world not constantly on the make or otherwise out to gratify our base instincts.

Besides, who among us is willing to readily relinquish our paranoid tendencies to elevate part to become whole truths, using selective focus to prove our own favored, not entirely logical, points; willing to eschew the option to claim provocation as justification for doing wrong; or willing to forgo an opportunity to shift responsibility onto others using comforting blaming defenses to reduce our own anxiety and improve our self-image by making others feel guilty for our own questionable past, present, and future actions? Who when caught with his hand in the cookie jar has not thought to come to his or her self-defense by asking, "Why did you leave it out where I could find it"? What impotent man does not blame his wife's frigidity for his inability to perform, and what sexually dissatisfied woman does not at least think that it is her husband's anatomy that is her destiny?

In short, the paranoid person, acting for us, doing our bidding, is our alter ego, our hero or heroine realizing our secret desires—if only we could bring ourselves to admit, express, and act on them.

Social factors also determine the collective tendency to overlook manifestations of paranoia. The media encourage us to normalize paranoia by boiling complex social interactions down to struggles between all good and all evil, and by telling every story as if it has only one side to it. Many of us buy into popular social myths about mental illness in general and about paranoia in particular to the point that our judgment becomes clouded. Many of us believe the myth that thinking clearly and planning rationally is incompatible with being mentally ill. Thus, Christopher Lehmann-Haupt (1999), favorably reviewing Richard Rhodes's book *Why They Kill* in the *New York Times*, quotes Richard Rhodes as suggesting that violent criminals are sane because "they invariably made plans to commit violence, decided consciously to act and felt wholly responsible for what they have done." (As mentioned throughout, many paranoid individuals, and particularly those paranoid individuals with a delusional disorder, only reason badly up to the point where they form an initial irrational core generative premise. After that they go on to reason in an intact way, often impeccably, as they proceed to turn their initial, and often subtly, warped hypotheses into entirely plausible theory leading to manifestly logical decision making.) We also buy into the myth that for a patient to be mentally ill he or she must be dirty and disheveled, hear voices and be seriously disorganized, and necessarily have a chronic unremitting disorder that follows a downhill course. Behind the general public's collective tendency to overlook the possibility that a nice teenage neighbor can look normal one day, then go overnight from "good morning, ma'am" to murdering one of the neighbor's children and back again to "good morning, ma'am," is our tendency to forget that the severest manifestations of paranoia can be episodic and cyclical, that is, acute not chronic, with the violent psychotic break lasting for only a short time before the patient goes into what can at least appear to be a state of full remission, becoming once again that nice person whom we certainly think we know well enough to safely assert that he or she cannot possibly have done such a terrible thing.

Finally, too often our diagnostic judgment is compromised by practical, often financial, considerations. There are many practical/financial reasons for overlooking paranoia. Advocates for gun control claim that guns, not people, kill people, in order to avoid the simple and, for their purposes, telling observation that, since both apply, gun control, however admirable a goal, is inadequate unless the problem of gun misusage is also addressed. Advocates for the homeless avoid stigmatizing their subjects by calling them homeless to avoid calling them mentally ill, or paranoid, in effect understandably but somewhat questionably diagnosing an illness according to its consequences, doing so because they correctly perceive that, even when applicable, calling the homeless mentally ill reduces their status in the eyes of a public that has very little sympathy for people with emotional disorders and will thus be dissuaded, really, further dissuaded, from supporting and contributing to their cause. Advocates for the mentally ill find that diagnosing paranoia goes contrary to one or more of their charitable (humanitarian and financial) purposes. These advocates correctly recognize that labeling someone paranoid makes the person a frightening figure, while labeling someone bipolar or depressed makes the person appear to be more appealing by making him or her seem less troubled, more like the rest of us. In my view, a better solution involves not reclassifying paranoia as something else, but educating the general public to the fact that paranoia is not a judgment call, because, no matter how many evil thoughts paranoid individuals have and express, paranoia itself is not a form of evil, but is rather just one way for persons with an emotional problem to express, cope with, and master their anxiety and guilt.

Some practitioners, consciously or unconsciously, avoid giving their patients a paranoid diagnosis to avoid getting a certain reputation in the community that might lead new patients to shun them. I have sometimes heard, "Don't go to that doctor. He will slap a psychotic diagnosis on you, and you will suffer from that for the rest of your life." Some practitioners avoid the diagnosis of paranoia because they want to please, in order to get a free lunch from, the drug detail persons who tout antidepressants or mood-stabilizing agents because these happen to be their best sellers. A goodly proportion of the advertisements I get in the mail for refresher courses are about depression and bipolar disorder. I do not recall seeing even one about paranoia. Perhaps when a specific medication for paranoia becomes available, the diagnosis will be made more often. At the time of this writing Munro's (1999) advocacy of low-dose pimazole for patients suffering from delusional disorder has not, to the best of my knowledge, achieved widespread acceptance.

Finally, and most unfortunately, some people who write about, and even some people who treat, mental illness, make diagnostic errors due to their being more like amateurs than professionals. In fact, some of those who speak with the most authority about mental illness have never in their entire lives either seen or actually treated a patient—having never, like W. S. Gilbert's captain of the Queen's Navy, actually gone to sea. Therefore, I conclude this chapter with a cautionary quotation taken from the *DSM-IV* (American Psychiatric Association, 1994): "The diagnostic categories, criteria, and textual descriptions [in this book] are meant to be employed by individuals with appropriate clinical training and experience in diagnosis. It is important that *DSM-IV* not be applied mechanically by untrained individuals" (p. xxiii).

CHAPTER 6

The Gray Area and the Paranoia of Everyday Life

Roth (1989) speaks of how "the paranoid disorders are relatively common forms of illness, particularly when account is taken of the grey area that separates them from the major psychoses and personality disorders" (p. 1609). In this gray area lie phenomena on the boundary between normalcy and disorder, and thus between rational idea and delusion. These are the phenomena we are often referring to when we say that someone has "a touch of paranoia." Individuals with that touch of paranoia inhabit all walks of life and are to be found in all professions. They are usually identifiable by subtle rather than by overt psychological cues. What behavioral and ideational changes are present are usually merely hints of the existence of their paranoia—more suggestive than telling, and more alerting than pathognomonic. Such people are often described in the media. Because media presentations are famously distorted, I believe that it is inaccurate to analyze a person from the picture he or she presents to us via the newspapers or television. However, media presentations do offer useful clinical examples of all sorts of paranoid phenomena that, when disassociated from the big names they are attached to, can serve as valuable clinical vignettes—illustrative behaviors that teach us something even though the behaviors in question have little or nothing to do with the person charged. Indeed, to an extent they become valid *because* they have little or nothing to do with the person charged but instead mainly represent the paranoid fantasies of the individual doing the charging—exactly one of the things we are looking for.

Here is a sampling of people in the gray area, some of whom were mentioned in chapter 4:

People who are difficult because they are *contentious, angry, and argumentative,* such as people who with very little provocation blow up at friends because they see them instead as enemies. A gay man simply mentioned in passing to a lesbian friend that he did not get along with each and every gay man he met, only to have her shoot back, "Like all lesbians don't get along with you?" Many of these people have an unconscious bias to anything that confirms a preexisting hostile fantasy about others, so they see only the negative implications in others' basically positive words and deeds, and react like the mother in the joke who gave her son two ties as a gift, then when she saw him wearing one of them groused that he was a thankless person for not wearing the other. Or they respond like the woman who complained that others who were merely trying to get close were in fact attempting to control her. For example, she dropped a friend who merely wished her new relationship well in the belief that he was trying to tell her what to do with, and how to run, her life.

People who are difficult because they are *haughty and critical.* A woman entered the coffee shop referred to earlier and asked for a pastrami sandwich, only to have the owner shoot back, "This, as should be obvious, is a café, not a delicatessen." These are the people who often develop and hold grudges over very little. Also they readily smear other peoples' reputations, like the woman who when asked about her builder said that he always lies about when he is going to finish a job, just because once he was delayed a day and a half completing a small repair on her house.

People who *distort logic* for their own hostile purposes, such as muckraking newspaper reporters who realize their own agendas by leaving out the qualifiers when they are reporting the news. Just as a paranoid individual changes "some people are against me" to "everyone is against me," a newspaper reporter changed my assertion that "*some* gay men have emotional problems" to "gay men have emotional problems," I guessed just so that he could set me up to look bad, and himself to look good—as the hero who exposed and crushed the enemy homophobe establishment psychiatrist. Belonging here too was the critic who, generally advocating a counter-cultural approach to life, misinterpreted my suggestion that committed relationships were a good thing to have as a manifesto that was dangerous because it completely devalued people who preferred to remain single and polygamous. Politically correct to excess, these individuals imagine themselves to be keepers of a cause, in a mighty struggle with those who have fallen from grace. Sometimes behind their avowed motive to rescue the world is the real motive to aggrandize themselves by comparing themselves favorably in purity to what they aver to be the foulness of others.

People who *personalize,* seeing the evil conspiracies we all know to be occasionally afoot as directed to them as individuals. A fringe reviewer of one of my books proclaimed, without hard evidence to back it up, that an inordinate number of my cases of avoidant personality disorder were gay men. My guess is that he found himself in my book, felt that I was criticizing him personally, and got back at me by broadly implying that I was a homophobe criticizing gay men by pathologizing them.

People who are deliberately *trying to be evil* because they actually like themselves that way, such as the man at the gym who wore a T-shirt that said, "F—— you, you f——ing f——."

Hypocritical people who do things they should not do and continue to do them, then make themselves feel less guilty about what they have done by criticizing others for doing the very same things.

People who are *unable to trust* others, such as the boss who when out of the office calls 10 times a day to check up on her workers because she suspects that, being idiots, they are screwing everything up in her absence.

As Henry Pinsker notes (personal communication, 2003) people who are constantly *alert for unsuspected dangers* such as those said, without firm evidence, to be presented by transmission lines that emit dangerous magnetism, and those that come from genetically altered squash (and who simultaneously believe that the FDA has been in cahoots with the forces of big agriculture to convince the world that genetically altered foods are safe, despite an almost total lack of evidence of FDA complicity in the matter). Included here are people who believe that legitimate scientists are enemies trying to put something over on them, like the newspaper reporter Michael Liberatore (2003), who, apparently imagining that all medical scientists are both straight and resolutely homophobic, wrote, I "demand that HIV/AIDS be thoroughly investigated. . . . If the world's medical leaders can isolate a virus in the current Asian respiratory flu in two weeks, why can't science find conclusive evidence regarding the HIV 'virus' in over twenty years? There are two reasons: First, HIV/AIDS effects [sic] fags and drug addicts. Plain and simple. The Asian flu attacks businessmen traveling to the Far East. Second, there is clearly something WRONG with the HIV virus model. It's time to demand that science stop giving lip-service to Dr. Robert Gallo's 'discovery' in the mid-1980s and find what REALLY causes AIDS. A virus? A bacteria? A parasite? A combination of all three? We need answers, and we can't let this drag on any longer" (pp. 10, 28).

Junk scientists and quacks, particularly those who tout mysterious-ray theories such as the belief that arthritis can be cured by electrons emanating from a metal bracelet, or who, like Wilhelm Reich, envision the possibility that bodily evil can be neutralized by a box of his own design that concentrates healing energy from the atmosphere.

Fringe activists and fringe crusaders, who become like paranoid individuals to the extent that their passionate involvements arise not out of a need to express and fulfill themselves and share valuable information and insights that only they have, but out of a need to prove that "I am right, and you are wrong" and "I am sound, and you are compromised."

Terrorists, who are like paranoid individuals in their tendency to justify their first as second strike and their actions as reactions. They also resemble paranoid individuals in their tendency when brought up short to deny that they are bad and instead to portray themselves as good—for example, as world saviors, using the typically paranoid self-justification of "it depends on how you look at it," that is, "I am a defender and a crusader, not a terrorist, and the definition of a terrorist depends on whose side you are on and whose ox is being gored," which, predictably, is never yours, but theirs.

Literary critics, who act like paranoid individuals when they personalize others' writings, musical compositions, or the like, and respond as if something in those is a planned attack upon the critic, then, after becoming defensive, go on the offense.

A patient, a literary critic, found someone just like herself described in a book she was reviewing on relationships. She next became convinced that the author was criticizing her and her lifestyle personally. Having made her choice in life to be a loner, she did not like it when the author strongly recommended that we should all try to develop and maintain close relationships. So she set about making snide comments to defang the author. For example, she commented that more fun than reading the author's book would be ordering in Chinese food and staying home watching old reruns on television. The critic Bernard Holland's (2003) perceptive article on critics of his criticism illustrates, perhaps unwittingly, how his critics in their use of illogic in some ways come to resemble paranoid individuals. Like paranoid individuals, Holland's countercritics take a small matter and make it the whole thing, as when they call a spelling error a sign of illiteracy. Also like paranoid individuals they confound his mild questioning or criticism with an attack, so that Holland's phrase "cast some doubts on" becomes "a berating." Also like paranoid individuals they misconstrue comments of his that are not entirely positive as racial slurs that they attribute to covert bigotry on his part (p. 35).

Bigots, who share with paranoid individuals the tendency to distort focus by stereotyping and oversimplifying along adversarial lines, as did the reviewer of Raeleen Mautner's (2002) book *Living la Dolce Vita,* who in his critical comments reevaluated "all" Italian people as follows:

> Italians . . . use [clichés] to present the "bella figura" that masks the essential dysfunction of the entire culture. My experience growing up among Italian émigrés and natives is that they are suspicious, thin-skinned, and cold and they get away with it by spouting self-serving nonsense about family and friends. Italians despise the concept of therapy [even though] the whole country needs it.

Defense and prosecuting attorneys, whose struggles in the courtroom in some ways resemble the personal struggles between paranoid individuals and their adversaries, right down to the self-serving distortive thinking whose purpose it is to expose, shame, ridicule, and blame others in order to become less blameworthy oneself, to gain a particular advantage, and to achieve consensual validation for one's beliefs, here by a jury of peers that they employ as a substitute for the everyday backers most paranoid individuals need and actively seek.

Dictators, like Stalin and Hitler. Men like them are not the only *political leaders* who are possibly paranoid. Politicians of everyday life come to resemble paranoid individuals when in a process that closely overlaps with the selective abstraction and narrow self-serving ideational focus characteristic of paranoid thinking they focus strictly on others' negative points in order to create negative advertisements that are the product of the omission of crucial positive mitigating facts, the goal of which is the deliberate distortion of reality along desired lines.

Litigants, who acted consensually, then felt guilty and reduced their guilt and shame by blaming others entirely for their own actions.

Posttraumatic stress disorder patients, who blame their fate entirely on their upbringing and society, their parents, or the area in which they live, to deal with their shame about being either partially or entirely responsible for their antisocial behavior or poor showing in life.

However, not all the people we read about, or know personally, who at first appear to be are actually paranoid. The media describe many people who distort and misperceive in an apparently paranoid way who should not be catalogued by psychiatrists. The homily "you are not paranoid; people are actually persecuting you" applies to those individuals who look paranoid but are not because theirs is a rational explanation for what at first appear to be purely imaginary persecutory ideas. Also not strictly speaking paranoid are consciously manipulative people who seize upon paranoid mechanisms to distort and misperceive reality entirely, or almost entirely, for personal gain. Among these are *addicts* like the patient of mine who demanded that I write a prescription for large amounts of Valium so that he could sell the pills on the streets, then, when I refused, in paranoid fashion said that I turned him down because I was prejudiced against him. I would also include here house hunters who pick one or two negative qualities of a property and focus on those just so that they can get the price down, saying that it is good business, but overlooking how it is also "good paranoia." Naturally this category would include the politicians mentioned throughout who deliberately and calculatedly create adversaries strictly to woo voters, controlling the masses by conjuring up a common enemy. Even mass murderers like Mao or Stalin or Hitler or Hussein may not have been paranoid individuals in the sense that they were having and responding to persecutory and/or grandiose ideas, delusions, and/or hallucinations. They may have been that, or they may have simply been using paranoid mechanisms for manipulative purposes in a way that was more evil than sick. Finally this category would include any criminal who when apprehended blames his or her murderous rampages entirely on his or her upbringing to get the sympathy vote and to get off easy.

As suggested throughout, even the most innocent-looking behaviors can in actuality be seriously paranoid. The mother who brought the diet sherbet as desert for Thanksgiving dinner felt that she did not look a day over 30 though she was in fact in her early seventies. Her annoyance at those who refused to answer in the affirmative when she asked them if she still looked youthful covered a serious persecutory conviction—that they actually wanted her to get old and feeble so that they could steal her money, and to die so that they could inherit her house.

Individuals in the gray area may be said to suffer from what Millon (1981) calls a "personality pattern" (p. 10) or from what others have called a shadow syndrome. They are what I call seminormal individuals—that is, they suffer from pathology that is borderline in nature, degree, and extent. As Pinsker suggests in a personal communication (1999), while these people can be understood by using paranoia as a model, they are not automatically to be placed in the psychopathology group without considering other, mitigating factors.

However, just because they do not qualify for paranoid diagnoses does not mean that their behavior is completely normal. By analogy, depression is a widespread problem, but there is a distinction between the depression of everyday life and depressive illness. To make this distinction, mental health professionals call the more serious condition clinical depression. I propose an equivalent term, clinical paranoia. Whether modestly troubled individuals are suffering from a pronounced distortion of normal paranoid tendencies or a mild form of pathological paranoia is not certain, and therefore we do not know whether to say that they lie on the outer reaches of the normal continuum or suffer from a mild mental disorder. We do not know for certain how to answer the following question: since delusional people think that others are out to harm them, is everyone who is excessively and inappropriately concerned about being harmed (which is almost everyone) suffering from a touch of the same thing?

Seminormal individuals tend to be overreliant on defense mechanisms that deflect anxiety, but they are less single-minded in their use of these mechanisms than patients with a "symptom disorder" (again, Millon's, 1981, category, p. 10). They may make modest use of several such mechanisms, although in exceptional cases they may use one favored mechanism extensively but discontinuously. They are plagued by, and plague others with, suspicious ideas typical of apprehensive scanners, or with overvalued ideas, which as defined in chapter 2 and below resemble, but fall short of actually being, delusions. If they have true delusional ideas they are transient, and both are subject to a degree of reality testing by the patients themselves and admit of a certain degree of argument and correction by others. Often the delusional ideas are at least partly the product of environmental cues, particularly those arising out of situations that are inherently persecutory, such as actually being pursued by a jealous lover or being controlled and cowed by a sadistic authority figure such as one's boss or mother.

Or, their delusional ideas are *shared*. An example of a shared delusion is the formerly widespread belief that a moon and stars logo is satanic, or that the violinist and composer Paganini was somehow in cahoots with witches or was himself actually the devil. Another is the belief in an unlikely conspiracy theory to explain any one of a number of historical, recent, or current events, for example, a presidential assassination by one individual attributed without firm evidence to the work of a cabal, or a spell of bad weather attributed not to nature but to recent acts of terrorism. Shared delusions seriously challenge our ideas about what we should define as delusional. As Henry Pinsker noted in a personal communication (2003) if we accept that some delusional thinking involves personal acceptance and elaboration of external impressions, then culturally shared false beliefs begin to look more delusional after all. But if true delusions are to be defined as odd, autistic false beliefs that develop internally, these are myths, not delusions. People with shared delusions may not be in fact truly delusional. Rather they may simply be victims of mass hysteria, people whose main problem is suggestibility. Dynamically speaking, suggestible individuals show an intense need to belong as manifest by their adopting the beliefs of others, true or false, and embracing them fully, in effect subjugating themselves to a leader—often himself or herself a truly paranoid individual with a delusional theory that happens to resonate with the general public. In such cases these individuals' possible diagnosis is not delusional disorder but histrionic personality disorder. Scientists may be able to explain dynamically such individuals' willingness to follow that route, but they cannot diagnose these individuals as paranoid if all they have done is joined the crowd.

Indeed, individuals with shared delusional beliefs may not be suffering from any form of psychopatholgy whatsoever. The widespread belief that the government is concealing information about various wrongdoers may be no more an indicator of individual psychopathology than the belief that a beneficent God is running things. Also, how abnormal is it to believe and be reluctant to question something titillating—such as witchcraft—however untrue or preposterous the belief may be, when the goal is mainly to derive pleasure from being scared, and to get the good feeling we all get from having, and sharing, a common enemy—pleasures indulged in alike by the general public that believes in scary ghosts and the paranoid individual who believes in nonexistent persecution? Besides, it is intellectually troubling that the numbers belie our usual definition of psychopathology. If 80 percent of the population believes in something that is untrue, perhaps the other 20 percent of the population, the nonbelievers, are the crazy ones.

Still, shared delusions are not entirely benign. They run deep, and while many people when pressured laughingly brush them off, they continue to believe them, even if they do not admit it. The individual with a delusional disorder who believes in nonexistent persecution by rays and the general public that readily accedes to something similar at the hands of overhead wires or cell phones may have more in common than is generally recognized. The need to believe something untrue or preposterous and the reluctance to question it may in fact be pathological traits shared by paranoid individuals and the general public alike.

Seriously complicating matters is the difficulty of defining *shared* and *delusion*. Are commonly held delusions actually shared? If many New Yorkers believe that there are alligators in the sewers that will come up from the toilet and bite off their genitals and that belief persists without documented case histories, or if almost everyone in New York thinks that there is a law that they have to have 80 percent carpeting though there is no such law, did all of these people catch these delusions from one another, or did those who hold the belief all arrive at the same conclusion independently, via the same, possibly normative and possibly pathological, psychological mechanism(s)?

A healthy sign, although not necessarily proof that one is not delusional, is a suspicion that one's delusional thinking is incorrect as revealed by a willingness to ask people in a position to know if one is paranoid, or even crazy. Just recently a friend asked me if her boyfriend, the one who speaks each night to the angels who are evolutionary technicians, was treatable. She thought that he was treatable since even she could disabuse him of his beliefs, however temporarily and however great the effort required, because he himself wanted to know if he was paranoid or crazy, and because he both asked her the question repeatedly and cared about her answer deeply.

People with *overvalued ideas* (previously discussed in chapter 2) sometimes fall into the gray area. Sims (1988) defines an overvalued idea as "an acceptable, comprehensible idea pursued by the patient beyond the bounds of reason . . . usually [associated with strong affect and] abnormal personality" (p. 92). The *DSM-IV* (American Psychiatric Association, 1994) notes that "it is often difficult to distinguish between a delusion and an overvalued idea (in which case the individual has an unreasonable belief or idea but does not hold it as firmly as is the case with a delusion)" (p. 765). An overvalued idea is a single, often simple, idea that resembles a delusion in some ways and an obsession in others. It is dominant, preoccupying, and passionate, and often drives a specific political, religious, ethical, or scientific activity, typically explained and justified in pseudorational, particularly moral, or pseudomoral terms.

Some of the main characteristics of overvalued ideas are their inner certainty, the certainty that characterizes how they are presented to others, and the extent to which they become generalized, that is, applicable across all cases, however much each case is different. Though overvalued ideas share with delusions a degree of unshakability, they are generally more modestly distortive. They may, however, interfere significantly with living a normal life as much as, or more than, do delusions. Examples of overvalued ideas are readily found in the letters to the editor column and in newspaper editorials. Activists such as those who believe that *all* animal experimentation is unjustified or who condemn *all* patriotic support of one's country in time of war as a totalitarian suppression of free speech and dissent may be expressing overvalued ideas. Sometimes relatively ordinary people have them too, like those New York tenants who believe that *all* landlords are crooks who should be vilified and punished for making too much money and for taking advantage of the poor, and those patients who believe that *all* doctors overlook the physical cause of what are in fact emotional symptoms, or, conversely, are *all* out to perform unnecessary operative procedures on them just for the money.

Crackpot ideas are close to overvalued ideas, differing from them if at all in being even more irrational. Examples are the belief in pyramid power, the belief that eating a grapefruit will make you lose weight based on the idea that fats burn in the fires of grapefruit juice, and, once again, the energy theories of feng shui, which remind me of the quack orgone energy theories of Wilhelm Reich. Many crackpot ideas have a slight measure of truth buried in them. Some substances do increase metabolism, but thyroid hormone is likely to do that job better than grapefruit juice, and certain furniture arrangements are unwelcoming and thus do emit "bad vibes," but only figuratively, not literally. Sometimes it is hard to tell whether an idea is crackpot. What constitutes a quack medical theory depends on a number of factors, chiefly the extent and validity of our present knowledge. At one time it was thought that tonsils and adenoids poisoned the rest of the body and so had to come out; that ECT destroyed the core pathology of schizophrenia and so was the perfect treatment; and that stomach ulcers were caused entirely by the emotions of dependent people whose stomachs twisted and griped when they felt angry about being unloved and abandoned. If at the time of such theory-making we did not know the reality, is it fair to say that there was a delusional-like deviation from it? Of course, crackpot ideas can be advanced for a specific purpose, in particular to make money, as I believe was the case for the spinal manipulator who, crazy like a fox, advertised that he used an advanced chiropractic technique to help most people with multiple sclerosis and Parkinson's disease.

Superstitions are not far removed from overvalued and crackpot ideas, but unlike them they tend to be associated with a degree of insight. Those who hold superstitious ideas on one level really believe, and often act, on them, but on another level they know the truth. Down deep people know that black cats are not unlucky and that it is unlikely that a disaster will occur if one crosses your path; that positive thinking is simply not going to influence the luck of the draw; and that saying gesundheit when someone sneezes is probably not going to prevent the person from either getting or spreading the plague.

Ideas of reference, also discussed in chapter 2, often lie on the low end of the continuum between rationality and irrationality. For example, the belief that disinterested strangers are talking about an individual is either no distortion at all or only a small distortion of what is likely and possible. Some referential ideas are, however, frankly delusional. A paranoid schizophrenic looking out the window of his house saw two bicycle riders stop and talk to each other. Feeling that they were talking about him, he got into his car, pursued them, and would have assaulted, beaten, or killed them if he had been able to catch up with them.

There is no acid test to distinguish between normal and pathological individuals. However, the answers to the following questions can help point one in the right direction:

How consistent are the deviant elements? Is the patient delusional or semidelusional continuously and about the same thing all the time, or do his or her delusions or semidelusions come and go depending on his or her emotional state, especially the degree to which he or she feels, or is actually being, stressed by external circumstances?

How pervasive are the paranoid elements? Are they fully encapsulated, or do they spread and intrude themselves to affect the personality, compromising the patient's ability to function at work and in his or her relationships?

How flexible are the paranoid elements? Does the patient pass the test of vulnerability, that is, can he or she be successfully disabused of his or her false beliefs? Is he or she sufficiently reasonable to reconsider the false beliefs either under his or her own steam or when given new information? A patient looking out of the window of their shared home saw his lover, who had just pulled up, dallying at the car and "doing something" inside. He had the angry fearful thought, "He is covering up the evidence of a prior sexual exploit in the back seat so that I don't find out." Then he thought, "That's ridiculous," and calmed down immediately. A good marker for a paranoid individual's ability to be flexible about and reconsider his or her false beliefs is his or her prefacing them in the telling with a caveat. For example, he or she might say the equivalent of "I admit that I have no proof of this and wish to make it clear that my ideas are only hypothetical."

How close is the false idea to the textbook picture of a delusion? Most patients with a delusional disorder develop one (or more) of the standard delusions, of which there are relatively few. The likelihood that a construct is truly delusional increases to the extent that the delusional idea resembles one of the classics, such as the familiar ones populated by blacks, gays, Jews, Zionists, the government (especially the FBI and CIA), dangerous rays, fantasies of insertions of thoughts into one's head or microchips under the skin, and influencing machines of both the figurative and the literal variety.

How positive is the behavior that is the product of paranoia? People who use the paranoid knife not to kill but to cure are more technically than spiritually paranoid. Some individuals' so-called paranoid ideas and behaviors represent sensible precautionary or otherwise helpful behaviors. For instance, Proust's famous lining the room with cork may indicate that Proust was paranoid about rays coming at him through the masonry. Or, it may simply mean that he lived in a neighborhood that was so noisy that he could not help but be distracted from work that needed his full attention, and as a result was forced into that extreme remedy. Certainly if one were ever a defendant in court one would want an attorney who is aggressive, who is always nitpicking and anticipating attack, who is always wary, and whose motive is the semiparanoid "protecting others from danger"—that is, someone who uses paranoid ideation adaptively for its considerable personal and social value. Paranoia can even be creative. It is creative when it is the driving force that enables the individual to forge previously unrecognized connections or to create new ones between disparate facts or ideas, leading to the recognition of overarching principles that others miss, in effect putting old wine into new bottles, creating the equivalent of an unanticipated, inspired masterpiece.

CHAPTER 7

Interpersonal-Social Aspects of Paranoia/Paranoid Violence

INTERPERSONAL-SOCIAL ASPECTS OF PARANOIA

A general public that understands the social manifestations and effects of paranoia through and through will be in the best possible position to create, if not a utopia, then at least a less paranoid society, whose members

- defend reality against perception, avoiding self-deception and seeking absolute truth, not proof of prior contention
- accept responsibility for their own actions instead of blaming everyone else for their individual shortcomings and mistakes
- do not regularly send the message "until proven otherwise, look out for your neighbor because he is out to get you" but instead, when appropriate, send the message "love and trust thy neighbor first, and until you have a real reason not to"

Many paranoid individuals are among the people whom Millon and Davis (1996) refer to as fanatic, and who they imply are responsible for many of today's social problems. Millon and Davis divide fanatic individuals into two categories: the eccentric and the combative (p. 693), with each category characterized by a special set of less than positive and often openly negative social behaviors that are the product of overvalued ideas bordering on delusions pushed beyond the bounds of reason: vocally, vociferously, and sometimes dangerously.

Eccentric paranoid individuals, as Millon and Davis (1996) suggest, are often rebelling against traditional parental authority (p. 717) by becoming nonconformists. They are countercultural people who live on the fringe. They frequently have their own version of science and become persuasive quacks—rainmakers, music men, and gurus who shamelessly foist their questionable theories on the general public, possibly doing considerable damage to their followers' pocketbooks, health, and even lives. I recall a nurse who died of cancer because she never got the right treatment in the first place, having put all her hope and spent her last penny on a substance called laetril, a supposed cancer-fighting agent made from apricot pits, discovered by and advocated for by a prominent and perhaps overly grandiose university professor and physician of the day. The final chapters of Wilhelm Reich's 1949 book *Character Analysis* reveal the mental deterioration of the author as he went from brilliant creative psychoanalyst to paranoid physician touting a nonsensical orgone theory and pushing for a worthless treatment that involved placing all or part of oneself in a specially designed box that supposedly collected and concentrated healing energy from the atmosphere—Reich's version of the influencing machine. Not surprisingly, no one benefited, some neglected treatable conditions, and Reich himself ran afoul of the law.

Combative paranoid individuals, as Millon and Davis (1996) suggest, have a "a chip-on-the-shoulder attitude, bristling with anger and reacting before hostility and duplicity actually occur . . ." (pp. 718–719). These are highly critical people who condemn others as defective to defend themselves against a perception of being flawed, using projection defenses against troublesome unacceptable fantasies about themselves, "denying their own faults and weaknesses [and] maintain[ing their] self-esteem [by] attributing their shortcomings to others [and] repudiat[ing] their own failures [by] ascrib[ing] them to someone else" (Millon and Davis, 1996, p. 701). For example, I suspect that one anti-SUV fanatic contemplated destroying the polluting vehicles as a way to convince himself of a personal integrity that he doubted by acting in a manner that he felt to be pure as compared to others he condemned for spewing impurities into the atmosphere.

Inherent in the combatives' criticisms of others is an overestimation of the true worth of their own ideas and themselves. Not surprisingly they deride others just because others disagree with them. They have no compunction whatsoever about telling those who see things in a different way how they ought to think and what they ought to do. They readily, as Millon and Davis (1996) suggest, "impose their self-created standards on others" (p. 719) while humiliating and depreciating "anyone whose merits they question and whose attitudes and demeanor evoke their ire and contempt" (p. 701). These individuals grow even more grandiose and persecutory when they achieve positions of influence and power both because the adulation of the masses feeds their self-importance and because the approbation of their critics elicits their defenses.

Often, combative paranoid individuals go beyond merely complaining about their adversaries to actually taking them on. To do that they might become computer hackers—graffiti artists on the face of cyberspace—or litigious paranoid individuals who with very little reason and with even less prompting sue for the justice and compensation to which they feel completely entitled. Some victimize others with false accusations, as Millon and Davis (1996) note, "demand[ing] 'protection' and . . . accus[ing] innocent victims of committing indignities, of making lewd suggestions, or of molesting them" (p. 709). Others falsely accuse their victims of child abuse, expressing what Millon and Davis (1996) call "past beliefs of danger [that] have not always proven true" (p. 725). Some become semiviolent criminals who do serious damage to their victims' sensibility and property by painting swastikas on the walls of synagogues or burning crosses in backyards. Still others become truly violent individuals who shoot up the school to get back at the other kids whom they believe have humiliated them, or who after being fired return to the workplace to shoot up the boss and/or coworkers they believe have treated them unfairly.

VIOLENCE

Of course, not all violence is the product of combative paranoia. Sol Levine (1999) offers a comprehensive list of "the many *DSM-IV* disorders that [in addition to paranoia] predispose to overt manifestations of aggressive and even violent behavior, even at a very young age" (p. 344). These are "impulsive disorders, substance abuse disorders, hypomanic behavior . . . thought disorders, psychoses, psychopathy, and other psychiatric conditions" (p. 344). I have seen violence in

- *borderline* patients angry about being rejected *or* about being accepted
- *antisocial* patients angry about not getting their way or about not getting something for nothing
- patients with an impulse disorder, unable to muster even a little self-control about most things, and especially about their hostility
- *manics* whose euphoria is in fact a display of irritability, causing them to snap and strike out
- patients with an *organic disorder* whose dyscontrol is primarily the product of physical or structural brain damage

Also, not all violence originates in mental illness. Two examples are violence incited by leaders who undermine traditional authority and encourage insubordination using their own paranoia to supply others who are not mentally ill with both the reason for and the logic of the violence, and the socially sanctioned violence of wartime.

Additionally, there are no good statistics that tell us with any degree of certainty if any important association exists between paranoia and violence. Many paranoid people are hypersensitive, easily aggravated individuals prone to rage reactions, but only a few actually become violent. The evidence for the relationship between paranoia and violence rests to a great extent on the clinical similarity between the two conditions. Thus, paraphrasing the *DSM-IV* (American Psychiatric Association, 1994), both paranoid and violent persons tend to be distrustful, suspicious, pessimistic individuals ready to feel injured and slighted, who expect the worst from others and are by nature combative people who additionally experience brief psychotic episodes lasting minutes to hours as a response to stress (pp. 634–638).

Therefore, I believe that most of our fears of paranoid individuals (and of the mentally ill in general) are to an extent unwarranted. We must not allow our irrational fears that paranoid individuals will actually become violent lead us to mistreat all those who carry a paranoid diagnosis by placing more and more restrictions on them. That is because, while there is a proven association between paranoia and the *potential* for becoming violent, it is, I think, relatively uncommon for paranoid individuals to *actually* act out their violent fantasies. Indeed, at least theoretically, one's paranoia can protect one from actually becoming violent—paranoia does, after all, keep some people safely withdrawn and even indoors all their lives. Willpower, a meaningful force in many paranoid individuals, often provides them with a measure of self-control. Besides, many paranoid individuals, by nature highly self-protective people, know the wisdom of not acting up in a self-destructive fashion, and by nature ambitious people know that if they do not act up they are likely to avoid antagonizing those in a position to do them good, give them something of value, and protect them. They know that by not acting violent they improve their chances of getting others to side with them and increase the likelihood of remaining in contact with their adversaries so that they can win out over them or successfully challenge the injustices they presume have taken place at their hands. Finally, violent tendencies often diminish with age, even in patients who are paranoid. They recede due to the same chemical (hormonal) changes and the same wisdom of the years that develop in everyone else.

But, this said, understanding violence through and through does require putting clinical information about paranoia to work. For, to a great extent paranoia *is* at the root of much violent behavior, as a number of recent well-publicized incidents of random, unexpected, and seemingly unexplainable violence in individuals who might have been paranoid—in the schools, in the workplace, in the neighborhood, and on the subway platforms—seem to suggest. Those who like Rhodes (1999) completely overlook or deny the clinical relationship between covert and overt paranoia and violence miss an opportunity to psychotherapeutically manage violent behaviors ranging from road rage to terrorism. Focusing exclusively on the causative role that society and the media play in creating and promoting violence, or viewing the problem of violence strictly in terms of easy access to firearms, overlooks how psychological tools can be used to predict so-called random, and prevent so-called inevitable, violence. Merely censoring video games or taking guns away may help some, but not nearly enough. In order to adequately manage danger-ousness, we have to understand it through and thorough, and that can mean understanding and managing the paranoid rationale both for buying the guns (itself a sometime quintessential paranoid act) and for using them.

I envision two scenarios of violence:

Violent acts as the work of paranoid individuals whose mental illness has gone unrec-ognized because it was mild, at least up to the point where the individual snapped, with the violence the product of paranoid rage occurring in individuals with sim-mering paranoid personality disorders who decompensate into brief but severe acute paranoid psychotic episodes—that is, "previolent" individuals whose careful identification and proper management could possibly prevent violent acts.

Violent acts as the work of paranoid individuals whose illness was severe and recog-nized but went untreated or was mistreated for all the reasons and in all the ways I outline in this text. In such cases we might say that what killed people was not just guns, and not just people, but guns in the hands of the wrong people, who were the wrong people because they were paranoid, were misdiagnosed, and as a result were receiving less than optimal therapy.

The Scientific Literature on Violence

Much of the scientific literature does recognize the widespread role that emotional problems in general, and paranoia in particular, play in causing an individual to become violent. For example, Jan Fawcett (1999) emphasizes the paranoid-like belief of violent individuals that the "ends justify the means" (p. 333), with an "adversary simply an opponent to be defeated, at any cost" (p. 333); the paranoid-like "fight-flight reaction to perceived danger" (p. 333); the paranoid-like "self-justification" (p 333) involved in violence; and how a "touch of paranoia" (p. 333) contributes to violence the element of "I better get them before they get me" (p. 333). Haroun (1999) mentions that many terrorists are (like paranoid individuals) frighteningly rational to the point that they are able to offer sophisticated justification for their revenge fantasies (p. 336). Levine (1999) emphasizes the roles played by: the paranoid-like "ex-pression of . . . anger at traditional authority" (p. 344); "smug self-satisfaction" (p. 345); self-aggrandizement making oneself "notorious or glamorous" (p. 345); the feeling of being special (p. 345); and "passionate zealotry, intol-erance, and occasionally, danger to others" (p. 345) along with the motive of "physical intimidation" (p. 347). Haroun and Allen C. Snyder (1999) note that a focus on faulty premises can suggest "delusions of persecution" (p. 361). Salman Akhtar (1999) includes in his multifactorial dynamic analysis of ter-rorism "the narrowed cognition characteristic of paranoid mentality" (pp. 351–352) and mentions the relevance of the Kleinian paranoid position (explained in chapter 18) to the making of grudges, refusal to compromise, omnipotence, and refusal to settle for less than the ideal as all being characteristic of the violent individual (p. 353). He also notes how violent individuals, just like paranoid individuals, "mistrust . . . others, loath . . . passivity and dread . . . the recurrence of a violation of their psychophysical boundaries" (p. 351). Theirs is also an "intense anxiety over future loss . . . driven by the semiconscious inner knowledge that passivity ensures victimization" (p. 351), so that "to eliminate this fear such individuals kill off their view of themselves as [passive] victims . . . by turn[ing] passivity into activity, masochism into sadism, and victimhood into victimizing others. Hatred and violent tendencies toward others thus develop. Devaluing others buttresses fragile self-esteem. The resulting 'malignant narcissism' renders mute the voice of reason and morality. Sociopathic behavior and outright cruelty are thus justified. The narrow cognition characteristic of paranoid mentality, along with a thin patina of political rationalization, gives a gloss of logic to the entire psychic organization" (p. 352). The violent person, in effect projecting, "attacks . . . those parts of his own personality that seem aligned [with others]" (p. 353). He or she is a "sociopolitical Ahab: grievously injured, possessed by the lust of revenge, unmindful of reality, boundless in his demonic hope, ruthless and cruel toward others, and, ultimately, not even good for his own self" (p. 354).

This said, some of the scientific literature fails to recognize the causal role emotional disorder in general and paranoia in particular play in violence. A psychiatrist discussing the case of an adolescent boy who was singing the praises of Adolph Hitler, passing out Nazi literature in the school, and stealing on the Internet—charging computers to stolen credit card numbers and having the computers delivered to the houses of friends—and, on a less lofty level, going around calling the neighbors names like dickhead concluded, "This boy is watching the wrong television shows, and has gotten in with a bad bunch," and recommended suspension from school for the rest of the semester. He did not recommend the professional care that I thought was indicated for someone who was possibly mentally ill: psychotherapy certainly, medication possibly, and hospitalization perhaps.

The Lay Literature

In contrast to the scientific literature, the literature meant for the general public, especially some of the popular literature on criminology, too often contents itself with a superficial view of what is a much deeper problem, recommending incomplete and even trivial solutions for solving the problem of social violence, such as school prayer, reducing movie and television violence or the violence in computer games, fighting poverty, dispersing gangs, changing the way we live, instituting gun control, and the like.

When the literature for the general public does recognize the part mental illness plays in generating violence, it generally gives recognition only to the most serious forms of mental illness. Those who recognize that murder can be a product of emotional disorder, and that some violent individuals have a history of mental illness, generally equate mental illness with having hallu-cinations or delusions, and fail to note the role played by other, milder, forms of mental illness, particularly paranoid personality disorder which is, in my opinion, a major determinant of violent behavior.

Sometimes the literature recognizes the presence of a mental illness but credits the wrong mental illness. A boy shoots six students at his high school. The media explain his actions as due to his being *depressed* because he just broke up with his girlfriend. Yet in this case he seems to have shot others because he viewed them in a distorted negative, adversarial light, which sug-gests that his violence may have been due less to depression than to paranoia.

Clinical Observations

It makes sense to recognize that some paranoid individuals have at least the potential for becoming violent. In part this is so because what falls on deaf ears with other people with these individuals turns into a slight, and then into an argument, which can then easily turn into a fight.

Many paranoid individuals are landmines ready to explode, often about almost anything. Some are set off by an important stressful professional or interpersonal problem such as the loss of a job or of a loved-one—especially when they believe the loss to imply, signify, or actually contain an element of rejection. Others handle the big things better than the little things. They find themselves most troubled by unimportant matters such as a cancellation of a dinner date. For them, more important than the actual stress they are under is their tendency to reframe neutral or minimally stressful events to become serious adversarial, sometimes delusional-adversarial, scenarios. They are of-ten simultaneously impulsive and immature individuals who find it very dif-ficult to control themselves, especially their tendency to flare up in angry outbursts before first thoroughly checking the facts. They are also unforgiving individuals with an ongoing simmering need for revenge that can even carry across the generations. True to form is their tendency to be reluctant to take the blame for any violence that they go on to express—the same way they are reluctant to take the blame for anything else that they say or do. Instead they seriously believe, and often claim, that others provoked them to act in a violent fashion.

The progression to violence seems especially likely to occur in individuals with a history of past abuse. For example, because of their past exposure to combat, many of the veterans I evaluated in a veteran's clinic were much more likely than other patients to respond with violence to being treated badly. On the job they were less accommodating and less tolerant of mistreatment than their superiors recognized or, recognizing, chose to admit. Many of them developed violent fantasies toward their superiors. Some of them came very close to acting these out, that is, to "going postal."

Some violent paranoid individuals are an exception to the rule that having a mental illness is nothing to be ashamed of. At some point what is illness merges with what is unacceptable, abhorrent, and evil. There is no shame in wrongly feeling like a big nobody when one is in fact successful. In contrast, in my opinion, there is true shame in feeling like a big somebody because one has just pulled the arms off a teenager in a torture chamber. Some violent paranoid individuals I have treated are simply not nice people. They have dark, terrible, primitive thoughts, masturbate to erotic fantasies involving deformed dwarfs, and do horrific things that their mental illness helps explain but does not, in my opinion, fully justify or excuse.

It is of interest that violence is as much the cause of paranoia as the other way around. As noted throughout, paranoia is a way to defend against one's violent tendencies. In a sense we can interpret actual violent behavior to mean that the paranoia has not been adequate to handle the violence. Therefore, some violent paranoid individuals are, paradoxically, not nearly paranoid enough.

Managing Violence in Paranoid Individuals

Special care must be taken not to provoke a potentially violent paranoid individual's paranoia. Potentially violent paranoid people, tigers out of a cage, cannot be poked. Avoiding provoking them means first identifying their paranoia, then recognizing exactly what sets it off. The following section describes some things that are likely to provoke paranoid individuals and that therefore present a special risk to patients who are both paranoid and potentially violent. Specific remedies are implied. This section is profitably read in connection with chapters 18 and 19 on handling any individual who might be paranoid, potentially violent or not.

As noted throughout, paranoid individuals often find *passive-aggressive* individuals particularly provocative and upsetting. Passive-aggressive individuals provoke paranoid individuals by making them the butt of their covert hostility, then denying that that is what they did, confusing them and leading them to wonder if they are losing their minds completely. For example, when driving a car a passive-aggressive man sped, cut people off, and pushed people off the road just to be bad and to make them mad. At home he provoked his wife in similar fashion. Even though he knew that because they had plenty of money her pleas that he use the cell phone to make long-distance phone calls partly originated in her delusions of poverty, he still refused to comply with her wishes, and instead insisted on using the land line just because he wanted to, leading her to complain that he was deliberately and unnecessarily running up high telephone bills just to drive her crazy.

Rejecting people also seriously challenge and upset individuals who are paranoid. Some seemingly independent paranoid individuals are cold and aloof not because that is the way they are, but as a defense. Their coldness and aloofness is their way to distance themselves from others to avoid the threats associated with a closeness that they actually desire but also fear. Otherwise, why would some paranoid individuals with delusions of jealousy become so furiously angry with possible interlopers? One reason that such individuals cannot tolerate closeness is that they fear being first used and then cast aside. As a consequence they do especially poorly with people who first lead them on, then threaten to or actually do abandon them. These individuals much prefer, and do much better with, partners who either make it clear right from the start that they do not want to get close, or who make it clear that they do want to get close and can be counted on to hold that thought over the long haul.

Men who become violent to wives they think are cheating on them often do so not only because they feel that the cheating casts a negative light on their masculinity, threatens their sense of dominance and power, and signifies that they are not in control, but also because they feel left out. As such any domestic violence on their parts can represent vengeful retaliation meant to hurt someone who presumably abandoned them. Knowing that dynamic can be the basis for some surprisingly simple remedies even in a number of every-day situations. For example, if you live in an apartment building and are having a party, you can usually avoid having the neighbors complain about the noise simply by recognizing that, when they say they are disturbed by the din that they in fact are complaining, or are also complaining, that they are being left out of the festivities. Clearly the remedy is not to act angry, but to instead invite them over to join in the fun.

Paranoid individuals feel threatened by *people they think are on to them*. They particularly hate being stared at because they believe that you can see right through them. Therefore it is unwise and even dangerous to make prolonged eye contact with a driver (or anyone else) who is at all paranoid or, if you are a gay man or lesbian, to look long and hard at someone who is probably both rough and straight, no matter how much you might fancy that person.

Highly critical people challenge, provoke, and upset paranoid individuals by undermining their belief in themselves. They challenge their defensive superiority by reminding them that they are not the hot stuff that they imagine themselves to be. A favorite snide comment that highly critical people like to make to paranoid individuals is of the "why should the CIA be interested in you, you big nobody?" variety. In effect that says to the paranoid person, "You don't count quite as much as you think"—not something he or she wants to hear, or will always calmly tolerate.

Paranoid individuals hate *people who put them down*. Though some readers will find the concept of castration anxiety quaint, I believe that male paranoid individuals classically flare when their masculinity is called into question by people they imagine to be (and often are in fact) ballbusters. For example, in my experience, road rage is a typical phallocentric need for dominance and power expressed by symbolically reaffirming that "I am number one" and "I stand out, at least behind the wheel." Horn-honkers are not really in the rush they appear to be in. Rather they are people who do not take kindly to being put in a position of being number two, even if it is only by someone in front of them in line. They hate it when others occupy the place that they want to and think that they have a right to be in, and that they want the others out of. Refusing to yield makes them feel that they are being thrust aside, and that makes them feel as if they are being declawed and defanged. That helps explain why acting submissive and giving them what they want tends to calm them down; it returns them to the powerful position they like, and feel rightfully entitled, to occupy. This sort of soothing behavior can save one's life.

A man's car died on a Memorial Day weekend. This was a symbolic castration so, though the car was safely ensconced in the parking lot of his place of work, he insisted at that very moment on calling a tow truck and bringing the car over to the repair shop. When the family made fun of him for being impatient, he felt even less intact and as if he were losing control, provoking a violent outburst against them. In like manner, I often get the impression that a student who shoots up the school after breaking up with a girlfriend does so in a homosexual panic, the breakup having called his masculinity into question. He then shoots from the hip as a way to prove his masculinity to himself and to those whom he believes doubt it.

Paranoid people hate people who *dishonor* them. Honor is an especially sacred cow for paranoid individuals. I often get the impression that students who shoot up the school do so to get back at people for dissing, that is, for humiliating and defiling, them. Therefore teachers and principals must identify those at risk for feeling grievously humiliated and respond accordingly. Gay men should be equally aware of this dynamic. Homophobic young men who beat up or kill gay men who try to pick them up and have sex with them are typically doing that in order to handle forbidden homosexual impulses brought to light by the homosexual pass in order to establish, beyond a shadow of a doubt, that they are free of dishonorable homosexual desire. Judging others the way they judge themselves, they destroy others of like mind in order to convince themselves and the world that "I am not for, but against, that kind of thing."

Paranoid people often feel discomfited by people exercising traditional *authority*. Some paranoid individuals tend to have this difficulty because in their backgrounds are, as Millon and Davis (1996) put it, a failure to learn "impulse controls" (p. 717) due to having "gain[ed] their outlook in life wandering 'on the street' in concert with equally destitute and disillusioned peers [with] few congenial and socially successful models for them to emulate [so that they come to view] the traditional values and standards of society . . . as alien, if not downright hypocritical and hostile. [As a result] aggressive toughness seems mandatory for survival, and [they] learn quickly to adopt a dog-eat-dog attitude and to counter hostility with the same" (pp. 718–719). It is not surprising, therefore, that such paranoid people have special problems at school with teachers and with the principal, and outside of school with the police—

relationships that require more cooperation and submissiveness than they find comfortable. A policeman in a small town stopped a man simply because he was walking the streets at 3:00 A.M., going to an all-night supermarket to pick up some milk. Some would say, "This policeman is protecting the town," but this man, speaking from his paranoia, thought instead, "He is trying to take my freedom away from me by violating my civil rights by falsely accusing me of being a criminal."

As a general rule, being adolescent goes hand in hand with being paranoid. The watchword for many adolescents seems to be "the more that you suspect authority, the less authority can hurt you." Adolescents are also at that stage of life where it seems only right to make inherently insignificant matters into issues of serious importance both in the here and now and in the infinite scheme of things. Therefore, all of us have to be on special guard to avoid making adolescents paranoid, or more paranoid, by being critical, humiliating, overcontrolling, and unsupportive of and to them. One student had an acute paranoid break and became somewhat violent because, as he reported it, he hated all his teachers: a math teacher who played favorites so that no matter what he did she told him that a rival she favored did it better; a Latin teacher who instead of taking him aside humiliated him in front of the whole class for using a cheat sheet to translate the works of Julius Caesar; an English teacher who made fun of him publicly for mouth breathing and for saying *towel paper* instead of *paper towels;* a geography teacher who laughed at him when he pointed a compass to the north on a map and asked why the compass didn't point north, not realizing that for the compass to point north the page had to point north too; and a guidance counselor who condemned his healthy independence as rebelliousness and his originality as insubordination. However cynical most adolescents may be about authority, they take what authority says to and about them to heart. They would not be so rebellious, or become so violent, if they did not care so deeply.

In conclusion, I believe that, outside of legitimate violence during wartime, much violence is purely paranoid and almost all violence has a paranoid tinge. Do students ever shoot up a school where they do not feel somehow put down by someone there? Do drivers ever argue with someone they do not believe is taking unfair advantage of them? Do husbands ever abuse wives they do not unreasonably fear are taking advantage of, rejecting, or cheating on them? Do postal workers ever shoot up a place where they do not feel unwelcome, unloved, and treated wrongly? Do straight men ever kill gays whom they do not imagine are threatening their masculinity? Do serial killers ever rape, torture, and kill people they do not inappropriately view as their adversaries or enemies? That doesn't mean that paranoid individuals are more prone to violence than most other people. It does, however, mean that potentially or actually violent people should always be viewed as if they may be paranoid.

Therefore, I believe that some violence can be prevented if we take steps to identify its paranoid basis and make a special attempt to avoid deaffirming, criticizing, or otherwise upsetting potentially violent paranoid individuals. The spouse in an abusive marriage who does not correct for his or her mate's paranoia is part of the problem, as is the teacher who fails to tailor his or her behavior to adolescent sensitivities, or the boss in the post office hierarchy who abuses his Vietnam veteran workers in a way that reminds them of combat, by his actions thereby becoming the real reason why these workers go (really are pushed) postal.

I recommend that all caretakers, potential or actual, take seriously their responsibility to develop insights into all things paranoid, and to turn their newly developing understanding of abnormal psychology into a commonsense approach to handling one of its most serious manifestations. As psychotherapists we should understand the necessity of not aggravating paranoia by humiliating, rejecting, criticizing, persecuting, or abusing paranoid patients to the point that they decompensate in a paranoid huff and take their anger out on the world. As pharmacotherapists who elect to use medicine for people who might be paranoid, we should give medicine for paranoia, not medicine for depression, social phobia, attention deficit hyperactivity disorder, post-traumatic stress disorder, or obsessive-compulsive disorder. As parents we should be supportive of children who are difficult because they are paranoid, yet at the same time set proper limits on them, and especially on their hostile behaviors. As teachers we should avoid making fun of sensitive adolescent men who throw the ball like a girl or sensitive adolescent girls who are overweight or have acne or hair on their faces, and we should step in to keep bullies from doing the same thing. The general public, newly allied with professionals, should consider the possibility that anyone whose hero is Adolph Hitler is more than a little perverse, that anyone who is seriously antigovernment is more than a little rebellious, and that people who come to work in army fatigues may be making a threat rather than a fashion statement.

This is not a suggestion to blame the individual who is paranoid or his or her victim for anything. Rather it is a call to study the contribution all concerned make to the violence that is a product of individual paranoia in order to profitably take corrective measures to reduce the incidence and prevalence of violence and its negative interpersonal and social effects.

CHAPTER 8

Forensic Issues

This chapter makes no pretense at offering a complete discussion of the relationship between paranoia and the law. I am neither a forensic psychiatrist nor an expert on forensic issues, and since I am a physician mine is more a medical than a legal point of view. Also, my goal is a limited one: to introduce readers to some general principles that might prove useful for understanding the many and unfortunate cases they read and hear about or have personal knowledge of in which so-called criminal behavior seems to be the product of paranoia, raising the possibilities that the diagnosis of paranoia

- justifies an insanity defense
- is a possible reason to judge an accused incompetent to stand trial
- means that the patient meets the criteria for involuntary commitment
- is a reason to justify forcing a patient to take medication against his or her will, having concluded that the medication is deemed medically necessary to treat his or her mental condition

I will consider three viewpoints about these matters: the psychiatric viewpoint, the legal viewpoint, and the viewpoint of the general public.

THE PSYCHIATRIC VIEWPOINT

The Insanity Defense (Not Guilty by Reason of Insanity, or NGRI)

Because paranoia can affect insight, judgment, and behavior, it can be a determinant of antisocial or criminal behavior, raising the possibility that a so-called criminal can and should be adjudged not guilty of having committed a crime by reason of insanity, or NGRI.

There are a number of rules, varying from state to state, for determining whether a patient's mental illness/paranoia is reason enough for him or her to be adjudged not guilty by reason of insanity. These rules refer directly or indirectly to, and attempt to make specific determinations about, the effect a mental illness such as paranoia has on the mental status parameters of insight, judgment, and behavior. Here are some of the rules that might apply, adapted from Ralph Slovenko's (1985) article on forensic psychiatry:

At the time of the alleged crime, due to his or her paranoia, the person because of "a defect of reason, from disease of the mind [did not] know the nature and quality of the act he was doing; or if he did know it, then he did not know that he was doing what was wrong" (p. 1966). This is the M'n-aghten standard.

At the time of the alleged crime, due to his or her paranoia, the person "lacked substantial capacity either to appreciate the criminality of his conduct or to conform his conduct to the requirement of the law" (p. 1967). "The terms 'mental disease or defect' [may not be defined] by repeated criminal or otherwise antisocial conduct" (p. 1967).

At the time of the alleged crime, the person, due to his or her paranoia, was "as a result of mental disease or defect . . . unable to appreciate the wrongfulness of his conduct" (p. 1968).

At the time of the alleged crime, due to his or her paranoia, the person was "not criminally responsible [because] his unlawful act was the product of mental disease or mental defect" (p. 1967). This is the Durham, or product, rule.

At the time of the alleged crime, due to his or her paranoia, the person was under the spell of an irresistible impulse.

As Robert M. Wettstein (1988) summarizes things, "current social policy in criminal law is based on the belief that an individual cannot be held culpable for committing a crime if he lacks the mens rea or criminal intent for that act" (p. 1063), and "the mental culpability elements of an offense include, among others, purpose (or intention), deliberation, knowledge, recklessness, or negligence" (p. 1063).

In short, our concern is with individuals who at the time of the alleged crime suffered from a paranoid mental condition to the extent that in fact no crime, in the strictest sense of the term, was committed.

As I see it, these tests seem easy to understand, but that is very deceptive. First, problems of definition prevail. What, for example, is a *defect of reason* or *an irresistible impulse*, and what exactly do we mean by *appreciate* or *disease*?

Second, in some paranoid individuals there is a direct relationship between the paranoia and the crime committed. But in other paranoid individuals this is not the case, for not all crimes committed by persons who are paranoid are committed as a direct result of their paranoia. Because paranoia tends to be delimited, especially in patients with paranoid personality disorders or delusional disorders, that is, because it tends to affect a part but not all of the mental apparatus, it may not participate in, and thus may not help explain and account for, a specific criminal act. Alternatively, in some cases paranoia does have an effect on insight, judgment, and behavior, but the effect is only partial, not complete, and therefore the patient retains a capacity, however diminished, to reality test his or her delusions or to correct his or her faulty thinking.

Third, paranoia may be not an enabling or an aggravating but rather a *restraining* factor. For example, paranoia can render people so fearful of being caught that they do not dare to do anything unlawful, or it can keep them safely at home for a good portion of their lives.

Therefore, the question to be answered is not the general one—is paranoia an adequate reason for the insanity defense?—(it often is, at least theoretically), but the more precise one—can we, following the above rules and others, determine whether an individual's paranoia is in some way specifically and meaningfully connected to a given criminal act, making the act not a criminal one but the symptomatic action of someone who is mentally deranged? This is very difficult, if not impossible, to determine exactly in a specific instance. The complex intellectual, as well as emotional and procedural, issues surrounding the application of these rules make for an unfortunate truth—that the harder we try to formulate and apply the rules, the more we move the whole discussion into such murk that experts and members of the jury alike often complain that they would prefer to be elsewhere.

This said, I believe that many psychiatrists and most lawyers underestimate the hold that paranoia has on those who are suffering from it, to the point that they minimize the extent to which paranoia affects insight, judgment, and behavior, and that they therefore downplay the extent to which criminal-like behavior can be the product of paranoid ideation. Some paranoid individuals are let off too easy. But there are others who are much more psychotic than they actually appear to be, and these individuals are sometimes denied, merely on theoretical and procedural grounds, the NGRI defense to which they are in fact entitled.

Part of the problem is that too often the courts forget that the ability to reason clearly is compatible with the diagnosis of paranoia. It is so easy to forget that an individual who reasons perfectly clearly and retains the ability to plan and calculate may still be paranoid and therefore may possibly be insane, and insane enough for the defense of not guilty by reason of insanity to apply. It is easy to forget that it is in the nature of paranoia that thinking is clear, and that the ability to plan and calculate is retained, although both are misguided. Indeed, paranoid individuals often plan and calculate all too well. Their logic is too airtight for its and their own good. The problem is not illogic, but instead logic that proceeds smoothly, but from an incorrect premise. Many terrorists are coolly rational and offer sophisticated persuasive rationalizations and justifications for their actions, only their entire argument turns on a false hypothesis—the belief, based entirely on fabricated evidence, that a specific targeted group is evil.

In conclusion, there is really no fully reliable, practical way to determine whether an individual's so-called antisocial/criminal behavior proceeded from his or her paranoia to the extent that he or she should be not punished for a crime but treated for a mental illness. This is unfortunate, because I as a psychiatrist believe that many more individuals than generally recognized should be judged NGRI, having committed their crimes as a result of a mental illness, paranoia, that has seriously affected, however subtly, their insight, judgment, and behavior.

Competency to Stand Trial

Some paranoid individuals are clearly *incompetent to stand trial.* Medically speaking, a paranoid individual might be incompetent to stand trial if he or she feels that his or her attorney is an agent of the devil put on Earth to oversee the patient's downfall. Paranoid schizophrenics are the most obviously impaired individuals and so the most likely to be adjudged incompetent to stand trial. However, in my medical opinion, even the moderate emotional upheavals and cognitive distortions characteristic of mild paranoia can potentially affect insight, judgment, and behavior enough to render a person effectively incompetent to stand trial. I believed that this was the case for a patient who was not overtly delusional, but was so pathologically suspicious of her own (entirely competent) attorney that she fired him for conspiring against her, and so grandiose that she decided to act as her own counsel because she felt that she alone was prepared to do that job well. I believe that this was also the case for a man I know who told me that he was starting a new relationship and he wanted me to help him avoid f——ing it up. I agreed to do what I could. At the first sign that he was indeed risking his relationship over some minor annoyance, I reminded him not to do anything to screw it up. To that he replied that he could handle his own relationships and please would I butt out of his business. When this man subsequently committed a crime, I felt he was not entirely competent to work with his lawyer, just as he was not entirely competent to work with me.

Legally, both these individuals would certainly be adjudged competent to stand trial. First, as the trial attorney Stephan H. Peskin (personal communication, 2003) notes, the rule is that there is no such thing as legally *diminished* competency, for that would be the equivalent of being a little bit pregnant. Second, the legal standard for incompetency is so high—too high to apply to the less severely ill paranoid patients—that those whose competency to stand trial is, medically speaking, merely diminished will still be adjudged legally competent. As one lawyer said, the only people he knows of that were adjudged incompetent to stand trial were those who were truly mystified by the difference between the judge and a lemon. Again, quoting

Peskin (personal communication, 2003), "the rules for determining competency involve, at least in the State of New York, a fairly minimal standard: Do you know the charges, and do you know the role that you play in your defense, the prosecutor's role, the defense attorney's role, and the Judge's role? That's all there is!"

Meeting the Criteria for Involuntary Hospitalization

It is notable that an individual adjudged not free of legal responsibility by reason of insanity and judged competent to stand trial may still meet a state's criteria for involuntary hospitalization. As a practical matter, highly delusional individuals often escape being committed because they think clearly and precisely, while disorganized schizophrenics are more likely to be committed because they look crazy. As Pinsker relates in a personal communication (2003), in a study done by a lawyer involved with providing mental hygiene legal services to psychiatric inpatients, a comparison between the assessment of experienced psychiatrists and the outcome of commitment hearings revealed that disorganized schizophrenics were likely to be committed because they looked insane, while patients with delusional disorders were likely to win their commitment hearings because they tried hard to look normal because they wanted to convince us that, as they were themselves convinced, they were not crazy and so should not be hospitalized against their will, and they succeeded at looking normal because they reasoned well, albeit from a false initial premise.

Medicating a Patient against His or Her Will

A particularly controversial area, one where medicine and the law frequently clash, involves the issue of forcing a paranoid patient to take medication against his or her will. Most doctors feel comfortable asking themselves, "Does this delusional paranoid patient need to be given medication against his or her will for the benefit of his or her health?" However, the answer to that question varies from doctor to doctor. In response, some doctors, depending on their personal and professional orientation, answer, "We will not force medication because all patients are entitled to, and have a civil right to, make a decision about whether they need or want medication," and "moreover, individuals have a civil right to keep their illness if they so desire." Other doctors answer, "We will force medication because this patient is delusional about taking the medication and will not take it even though he or she needs it, and we have to override his or her so-called personal preference and his or her civil rights for his or her own ultimate good. Some individuals are by virtue of their emotional disorders just not capable of having enough free will left after their illnesses destroys it or exercising what free will they have to make appropriate decisions for themselves, and therefore it is in their best interests to have a professional take over and decide what should be done for them, and then make sure that they actually do it."

Procedurally, according to Wettstein (1988), there are "three basic models of the disposition of patients who refuse psychotropic medication" (p. 1073). One simply involves the decision "to override the patient's refusal, and devise the treatment plan for the use of medication" (p. 1073). Another involves getting a "second opinion" (p. 1074). A third involves administration taking over and appealing to the courts "to declare the patient incompetent to . . . refuse medication" (p. 1074). (Wettstein does not mention a fourth possibility, letting the patient go unmedicated.)

In contrast, few doctors feel comfortable asking, "Does this delusional paranoid patient need to be given medication against his or her will to make him or her competent to stand trial or be executed?" and answering in the affirmative. Also, few feel comfortable asking and deciding in the affirmative that medication should be withheld so that the patient looks crazy enough at trial to be adjudged not guilty by reason of insanity or incompetent to stand trial.

I personally can see both sides of these controversies. It reminds me of a debate I had recently about e-therapy. Some lined up to approve of it in spite of its disadvantages because without it some people would get no therapy at all. Others lined up to disapprove of it as invalid and unethical because the patient is not there to be examined directly, eyeball to eyeball, and so is not there to provide nonverbal cues and to correct misconceptions. To me, it is not a matter of which is the one right thing. Rather it is a matter of picking one's poison, or antidote—that is, there is no really good choice that fits all cases at all times. In part this is because knowing as little as we often do about any one paranoid individual it is difficult or impossible to make the single right choice that fits a given case perfectly. Also inherent in the problem is that no matter which side you are on there are advantages to be obtained, as well as a price to pay, for not being on the other.

My personal stand on the matter is rooted in medical tradition. I do not feel that diapering or restraining a patient with Alzheimer's disease is interfering with his or her civil rights. Rather I feel that it is taking over, but only to treat the manifestations of an illness. Along the same lines I believe that giving some paranoid patients medication without their full, voluntary consent is humane and therapeutic, and has social value too. I therefore believe that unilateral intervention is sometimes indicated, even though it does deprive the patient of a degree of autonomy.

I am certainly against dealing with mental illness too permissively when that is just a way to trivialize it, ignoring how it can devastate the mind as severely as a physical disease such as senile dementia can devastate the brain, leaving the patient just as helpless and in need of humane unilateral intervention as is the patient with Alzheimer's disease. As a paradigm, I do not believe that people are, as some would have it, entitled to commit suicide if they so choose. Certainly some believe that there is something to be said for that argument, and to an extent how we argue that point reflects the individual's current predicament. For example, our response might be one thing if a patient is existentially depressed, but quite another thing if a patient is actually dying, and a third if a patient is both. But as a general principle, I believe that it is far better to intervene and keep the patient's body together than to steer clear and do only what is good for the patient's soul. In the full recognition that many scholars, philosophers, and religious leaders disagree with me, I believe that it is sadistic to let a person die just for purely theoretical reasons. So I might certainly consider medicating a patient against his or her will when I believe that not forcibly medicating the patient can mean letting him or her stay indefinitely in confinement and suffering without adequate treatment. I do not favor protecting civil rights at the expense of enhancing real personal liberty when that depends to any extent on a person's medical well-being.

However, this said, I recognize that it is a matter of judgment as to what constitutes severe paranoia and therefore when and with whom we should intervene unilaterally. I also take pains to remind myself that just because a patient is paranoid does not mean that his or her insight and judgment about taking medication is affected to the point that he or she is completely wrong about the disadvantages of taking medication. Therefore, I make a case-by-case determination that takes many, often elusive factors into account. As a result, my decisions in these matters are almost always based much more on art than on science.

In conclusion, the complexity, variability, and unpredictability of paranoid illness often makes it difficult to impossible to determine with any degree of certainty in a given case the presence, scope, and effect of the disorder. First, it is often hard enough to make the diagnosis. Some paranoid individuals confess their paranoia, that is, they speak honestly and tell us all about themselves, making paranoia the obvious culprit. In contrast, others are so secretive about their paranoia that they hide it from most or all observers, making it difficult or impossible to spot. Second, not all paranoid illnesses are alike in degree of severity and subsequent impairment. Not only are there shades of paranoia, but the same shade has different effects upon different individuals with different emotional makeups, different realities, and different goals in life. Some paranoid individuals encapsulate their illness so that it does not affect important aspects of their judgment, while others choose not to or cannot do so, with the result that it takes over and more or less completely guides their thoughts and actions.

Additionally, we have to take into account that, to put it mildly, not all psychiatrists agree about everything. About the issues I just discussed, many disagree with one another on either theoretical or practical grounds, or both. Since there is usually more than one right way to do things, the choice of one method over the other is often an arbitrary and extremely personal one. Of course, practical matters often rule too. Different forensic psychiatrists have different agendas for different reasons, not the least of which is their willingness to let their loyalty to those who hire them to testify in an adversarial proceeding affect their objectivity.

As a result of all these considerations (and there are others), it is very difficult to determine precisely and scientifically in a given instance if and to what extent criminal behavior is the outcome of paranoia so that the individual can fairly and reasonably be adjudged sane or insane, have his or her competency to stand trial reasonably questioned, avoid being committed involuntarily, or be given the option to refuse medication. There are few clear precepts to follow, and the application of even those is made difficult because of an understandable tendency on the part of all concerned—paranoid patient, physician, and attorney—to bend the rules in order to attain specific, often very personal, and sometimes quite self-serving, objectives.

Linda Greenhouse's *New York Times* article (Tuesday, March 4), "Forcing Psychiatric Drugs on Defendants Is Weighed" (2003), quotes Supreme Court Justice Scalia's pithy description of the complex issues involved: "We can't try [someone] because his mind is not working properly, but you say he is entitled to [that is, his mind is working properly enough for him or her to be able to decide to] refuse the drugs that would make his mind work properly. It's just a crazy situation, what can we do about it?" (p. A 18).

THE LEGAL VIEWPOINT

Psychiatrists and attorneys do not think exactly alike, partly because they tend to have different personalities, and partly because they are in different professions with different orientations, philosophies, needs, and requirements. As an example, while I as a psychiatrist, like most psychiatrists, consider a patient's past history to be entirely relevant to his or her present and future behavior, an individual's past history is generally speaking not to be considered in court when attempting to determine whether he or she is not guilty by reason of insanity (NGRI). As Pinsker notes (personal communication, 1999) legally the verdict NGRI is applicable to a single criminal act, and that must be adjudged independently. Therefore, when the insanity defense is attempted, it is not relevant to demonstrate (as prosecutors may attempt to do) that the accused acted reasonably before the crime when he or she purchased the gun, or after the crime when he or she attempted to avoid detection, or when he or she looked normal to passers-by. The focus must be on the moment when the defendant snapped. Also, while most psychiatrists and psychologists, when making a diagnosis, include statements from outside observers in their diagnostic assessment, attorneys often consider these to be hearsay and therefore impermissible as evidence for prosecuting or for mounting a defense.

Too, psychiatrists and psychologists tend to admit of shades of gray, where courts see mostly black or white. Courts more than psychiatrists and psychologists tend to sort people and issues into either-or categories. As previously mentioned, while a psychiatrist recognizes that in some cases competency to stand trial is merely diminished, in court you are either competent or incompetent.

Many psychiatrists, emulating Freud, create a general theory from a specific case, along the lines of that which is applicable to one is by extension applicable to many. Attorneys often make their determinations based on reasoning that goes in the opposite direction: that which has been determined to be applicable to many (precedent) is therefore by extension applicable to one.

Psychiatry and the law mix well when all concerned seek truth without regard for the utilitarian value of what they find. However, when the goal is not determining transcendental truth but proving a point, it is the persuasiveness of the advocate, not the accuracy of the science, that often determines, if not the truth, then at least the reality.

THE VIEWPOINT OF THE GENERAL PUBLIC

So often the general public's impression of the legal issues associated with mental illness in general and with paranoia in particular comes primarily from news accounts of trials in which two experts present opposing views. As Pinsker notes (personal communication, 1999) the public does not know that some controversies are not 50–50, that is, that each contrary point does not deserve equal weight. The public is also exposed to a large body of fringe critics who only seem believable as they assail generally accepted information persuasively but incorrectly. For example, one often reads of ECT as a "controversial treatment" instead of as a mainstream treatment that is highly offensive to some.

Most of the public has no trouble intellectually with the idea that seriously mentally ill individuals, including those who are paranoid, are not fully responsible for any horrific acts that they may commit. But they do have a great deal of difficulty with that concept emotionally, and for that reason they have a great deal of difficulty applying it. Coupled with the ideational murk referred to above, the gut response of the general public presents a serious barrier to lawyers attempting the insanity defense, increasing the likelihood that it will fail. For one thing, the general public is almost as paranoid about paranoid individuals as paranoid individuals are about the general public. The relationship that the general public has with paranoid individuals is an ambivalent one. On the one hand, the public tends to be cowed into believing the silliest or craziest of paranoid notions, as illustrated once again by the feng shui or evil vibes phenomenon. On the other hand, the general public tends to mistrust all paranoid individuals completely, knowing that many paranoid people, especially those who are on trial for having committed crimes, filter and distort what they say with one eye open to achieving a specific effect. The general public certainly suspects that some paranoid individuals want to get off easy after committing crimes, and so are not beyond claiming that crimes come from their paranoia, when what really comes from their paranoia are the (often effective) self-justifications of crimes already committed. The general public senses when logic is after the fact, that is, when the reasoning goes not, as it should, forward to organize seemingly disparate facts into a meaningful whole, but backward to prove a desired, already predetermined, unreasonable, and irrational contention. The general public knows when a paranoid individual is selectively abstracting facts to prove a misguided preconception, or otherwise using pseudologic in the service of self-justification. And the general public wants the truth, not partisan proof—a fair assessment of reality, not just another example of what it already suspects—that for some paranoid individuals stealth is their watchword and winning over an adversary their all.

Even those members of the general public who intellectually accept the notion that emotional disorder can excuse an individual from being responsible for his or her crime can secretly believe that many emotionally troubled persons brought a present, valid, emotional disorder on themselves by their irresponsible past behavior. Therefore, as they see it, at least some people with valid emotional disorders are ultimately at least partly responsible for having become emotionally disturbed. It is hard to convince some members of the general public that mentally ill persons are entirely passive victims of mental disorders the same way that feverish people are mainly passive victims of their flu. The general public subscribes more to the obesity or drug-addition paradigm of illness with its considerable component of "you bring these things on yourself" than it does to the Alzheimer's paradigm of illness—the paradigm of the endogenously deteriorating brain. Many members of the general public believe that somewhere along the line people who are presently ill at one time in their lives made a personal, free-will choice to go that route. Therefore, they claim that an individual should be held at least partially responsible for his or her present mental illness if the person unwisely and even deliberately took action in the past that somehow led to the present debacle. So, the general public wants to know "in what way is a person who got paranoid after snorting cocaine and refusing to enroll in a drug detoxification program entirely free from responsibility for his or her present delusional disorder?"

Besides, many members of the general public sincerely believe that even seriously mentally ill people should be able to control themselves. To many it doesn't matter that mental illness explains bad behavior; it still does not excuse it. Therefore, while few admit it, almost everyone believes, at least on some level, that mentally ill patients deserve to be punished. Emotional positions like this, somewhat paranoid in themselves, have a great deal of hold on all our thinking, and therefore a great deal of influence upon the outcome of any attempted insanity defense. The general public seems to understand, but not to really believe, that when an ill individual does something criminal due to his or her mental illness, in fact no crime has actually been committed.

That the emotional needs and wishes of the community often depart from purely medicolegal considerations is exemplified by Pinsker's (personal communication, 2003) experience in the case of a lawyer who killed his wife and children. As Pinsker put it, "I said that because he was judged NGRI he had not been convicted of any crime and so should be allowed to continue to practice law. The Bar Association said, 'we don't want murderers practicing law.' I was right from the legal perspective. They were right from society's perspective."

Of course, adding to the problem is that many members of the general public simply do not trust dueling professionals to determine the truth. In fact, their skepticism is somewhat justified. The law is an adversarial process where winning, not science, is everything. Not surprisingly, many members of the general public view the insanity defense as a collaboration between patient, psychiatrist, and lawyer for the dishonest purpose of getting a criminal off easy after he or she committed a crime, or between psychiatrist and lawyer for the dishonest purposes of collecting big fees this time and keeping the referrals coming in the future.

A controversy that especially troubles the general public is about whether to incarcerate a mentally ill individual in a mental hospital or in a jail. While this focus has serious implications for the criminal, it is in a sense a distraction. What the general public is really worried about is that a person who commits a crime because he or she is mentally ill will be released after a short time when that mental illness subsides or is treated effectively to the point that he or she is no longer adjudged to be mentally ill and a danger to society. In such cases the general public, quite understandably, compares the apples of the therapeutic response to the medical treatment of someone who is both insane and has committed a crime to the oranges of the punishment that is indicated for a sane person who has committed the same crime. They compare the appropriate length of stay in a hospital as prescribed for a severe and often chronic mental illness to the appropriate length of confinement in a penitentiary for purposes of punishment (and—for the more charitable among them—rehabilitation.) The general public wants to be sure that criminally insane offenders are actually and sufficiently confined, that is, punished, in exactly the same way that they would have been if they were not adjudged criminally insane. Therefore they will only accept a sentence to treatment that is at least as long as the sentence to jail that the criminal would have gotten if he or she were not adjudged mentally ill.

A very serious problem exists in relationship to minor crimes committed by people who are subsequently adjudged insane. Theoretically, at least, and practically speaking as well, the man or woman who commits murder and is committed to a mental hospital on the grounds of insanity can be institutionalized for a shorter period of time than if he or she were treated strictly as a criminal. But in reality that does not happen very often. I believe that what does happen often is that a petty criminal adjudged not guilty by reason of insanity gets an unconscionably long sentence, if only to a mental hospital. A man who sets a small fire in front of someone's door to exorcise the devil inside is convicted of arson but committed to a mental institution on grounds of insanity. He stays much longer in a mental institution than he might stay if he were merely sentenced as a criminal for minor arson—a poignant example of our failure to balance punitive and therapeutic response, and issues of confinement and treatment, for those who appear to be, and are in fact adjudged, NGRI.

PART II

Cause

CHAPTER 9

The Roles Society and the Family Play in Causing Paranoia

In the following chapters I study the social-developmental, psychodynamic, interpersonal, and cognitive-behavioral causes of paranoia. This chapter, on the role that society and the family play in the development of paranoia, consists almost entirely of my personal observations and the collected impressions of experienced colleagues. While much of what follows is consensually validated, little of it is scientifically based.

THE ROLE OF SOCIETY

While society plays an important role in causing or facilitating individual paranoia, we should not necessarily blame social factors exclusively for the paranoia of any given individual. Doing that is itself paranoid when it becomes just another way to say, "You made me the way I am." However, our society does send its members four powerful paranoia-inducing, -condoning, and -enhancing messages. The first is that we should all be alert to and anticipate the worst, focus our energies on preparing for it, concentrate on adversaries presumed to be responsible for bringing it about, and deal with them preemptively, definitively, and triumphantly. The second is that we should not take responsibility for ourselves and for our actions. Instead, when confronted with our flaws and mistakes, we should blame others and make them entirely responsible for our deficits, errors, and fate. The third is that maintaining high self-esteem and a burnished self-image is appropriate even when our actual behavior belies the nature and extent of our self-congratulations. The fourth, which is related to the third, is that elevating our self-esteem is more important than creating warm, loving relationships, so that it does not matter at all if the method we choose to elevate our self-esteem involves lowering the self-esteem of others.

THE ROLE OF FAMILY

Parents play a critical role in helping to create and facilitate the development of paranoia in their children. Here are some examples of paranoiagenic parents.

Abusive, Traumatizing Parents

Bone and Oldham (1994) note that "Abuse is a common finding in the histories of paranoid patients. What might be seen by others as persecution is sometimes rationalized by the parent and child as appropriate disciplining or caretaking" (p. 8). However, as noted throughout, one must be careful to determine if the past abuse actually occurred as claimed, or if the patient claiming the past abuse, a patient who is, after all, diagnosably paranoid, is having persecutory fantasies about the past as well as about the present, so that he or she only thinks that he or she has been abused and traumatized. In such cases the traumatic memories would be not the cause, but rather the product, of the paranoid ideation.

Truly abused children often become paranoid because they expect the same abusive, humiliating, and demeaning treatment later in life from strangers that they became accustomed to early in life from their parents. They may also become paranoid because, having been unloved as children, they go through life hating themselves and anticipating that everyone will hate them too. In this connection we should recall what I emphasize throughout: that the paranoid complaint "you persecute me" can almost always be translated to mean in some significant respect that "you do not love me."

Excessively Critical Parents

Individuals who have been constantly and unfairly criticized as children often go through life criticizing themselves and expecting others to criticize them. They develop lifelong feelings of low self-esteem, which they then go on to explain in persecutory terms. Also, they model themselves after, that is, they identify with, their hostile critical parents and become extremely hostile and critical to others. Along these lines we should always remember that the delusion "you persecute me" is more than just a statement of "what I fear from others"; it is also a critical statement that says to others, "what I condemn you for."

For example, a patient remembers, "When I was three years old, my mother and I were walking side by side carrying the family cat in a carrier. When I happily checked in with the cat, my mother screamed at me, 'Don't stick your face into his,' then slapped me." Later in life the patient found it difficult to express any positive, and especially any positive sexual, feelings because he feared being brought up short by new mother figures. He also became extremely critical of others, squelching them in kind for their loving and sexual feelings. He criticized others the same way his mother used to criticize him, and did so to get there first—to humiliate them before they humiliated him.

Of course, destructive criticism with its serious pathogenic results can originate outside of the home—with teachers, bosses, and colleagues. However, destructive criticism often does not stick unless it locks into previous home-based criticisms. For example, after an older doctor expressed his opinion that the newer hypertensive medications were not necessarily better than the older ones, as an association, really as a reply, a colleague told him the story of how when Harvey first discovered circulation no one who was older than 40 believed him. The implication, of course, was clear: that the first man did not prefer to use the older medications, he was just too old to be able to learn how to use the newer ones. This criticism was devastating because it revived early parental criticism for being the dolt and retard his mother called him. He described his relationship with his mother, half seriously and half in jest: "She died at age 85, one day before she could pay me her first compliment. What I most hated about her was that she never gave me the benefit of the doubt. She even blamed me for my poor grades when the problem was my poor teachers. My whole life I felt just like a parishioner who lives in constant fear that his minister will focus only on his sins, oblivious to his good points, and quash his spontaneous sexual feelings, oblivious to his humanity." When his colleague criticized him he first got depressed. As he put it, "I began to live in fear of yet another bad review just as a child I lived in fear of having my mother devalue, disavow, and possibly even disown me." Soon he began to feel that all strangers put him down and were devaluing him, and that they were doing so not only to his face but also behind his back. Ultimately, he socked a stranger who was merely biting his lip because he thought that the stranger was signaling to him that he knew that he was a queer.

Unfair Parents

Parents contribute to later paranoia in their children not simply by criticizing and blaming them but by criticizing and blaming them *unfairly*. Typically they make the child responsible for doing something for which the parents are entirely at fault. Philosophically, spanking may or may not be an appropriate form of punishment, but it is certainly inappropriate when the parents have first provoked the child to misbehave and are therefore punishing the child when they should be changing themselves. One very young child was first provoked by being asked to do what he couldn't possibly do—remain silent on command for long periods of time—then spanked for not being able to do it. As with all children of his age, he simply did not have the kind of control that would have enabled him to remain silent for long periods of time. Besides, his babbling was a healthy thing, for he was, after all, just learning to talk. Therefore, when his mother told him, "Do not talk for two minutes because I am busy now," then blew up at him for disobeying her, she set in motion the process of creating a lifelong resentment in him of her, and that set the stage for his lifelong resentment of anyone in authority. Later in life he became extremely hostile to and potentially violent toward anyone he could conceivably parentalize. To illustrate, the following incident occurred when he became an adult and took a job as a transit worker. He told me, "Every time I go into my favorite donut store there is a long line. The last time I was there on my lunch hour my boss came in after me and asked me if I didn't have anything better to do than eat while I was working. It was hot, I was thirsty, I had worked very hard all day, and I had been waiting on line for an unconscionable period of time just to get something to eat, so he was being very unfair just by asking the question. So I started to drop-kick him. But at the last minute, and only at the last minute, I thought better of it and decided instead to keep my temper so that I could keep my job."

Paranoid Parents

For many paranoid adults the expression "the apple doesn't fall far from the tree" applies. Some have become paranoid later in life because they have the same genes that their paranoid parents have, and some have become paranoid later in life because their parents have effectively bred them in their own image by providing them with a ready-made model for how to be paranoid and encouraging them to follow their lead. Overheard fights between parents not directly involving the child, especially when these contain false paranoid accusations, can also lead to paranoia in the child as the child comes to view adversarial relationships as the norm. As Bone and Oldham (1994) suggest in another context, sadomasochistic relationships between parents where the main "concern [is] with attack and counterattack; with beating and being beaten [set the stage for perceiving all of life in terms of] provocation, insult, or injury" (p. 8). When children with such experiences grow up they tend to retool all interpersonal interactions to become the adversarial combatant situations with which they are most familiar. As one patient put it, "My whole life I act like I never got over my early combat training."

Hypermoralistic Parents

Sometimes paranoia in adults can be traced back to the child's having soaked up his or her parents' overly moralistic attitudes. Not surprisingly, hypermoralistic parents often make a special effort to see to it that their children are equally hypermoralistic and preachy. Predictably, as adults these children focus on the sins of others, and almost as predictably put a persecutory twist onto others' sinning—that is, they go from "you are a sinner" to "and you are sinning against me."

Overly Controlling Parents

Overly controlling parents sometimes lead their children to fear and to rebel against anyone in authority, then to fear the consequences of their rebelliousness. One student with such a background hated the general liberal arts curriculum he felt constrained to endure in college. He wanted to be an artist and therefore felt that he should not be forced to take courses in pedestrian subjects he disliked. He remembers suffering throughout course after course of subjects that he had no interest in or talent for and demanding, to no avail, a program tailored to him, not the same courses forced down his throat as were forced down everyone's throat. At first when he did not get what he wanted, he simply felt frustrated. Later he started cutting classes to avenge himself against those whom he believed responsible for forcing him into a mold. Next he suspected that his teachers were getting back at him by talking about him behind his back, condemning him for being lazy and stupid, and plotting to have him thrown out of school.

Parents Who Put Too Much Pressure on Their Children to Succeed

Children often respond with deep feelings of resentment to too much pressure to succeed and to do so in ways that are right for their parents, but not right for them. They often become rebellious individuals who, to get back at parents whom they believe to be intimidating them, deliberately fail at what they do, then blame others for their demise. Also, adolescents whose parents push them to be number one often feel that their parents by definition regard them as number two. Should they then go along with their parents but not get the good results that their parents expect from them and that they come to expect from themselves, they feel inadequate. They then blame their parents for setting them up to fail, and next blame the whole world for causing them to grow up to be big failures.

Parents Who Fail to Recognize and Respect a Sensitive Child's Complexes and Hang-ups

The usual rules of child-rearing do not necessarily apply to children who are potentially or actually paranoid. For example, telling a paranoid child the facts of life can backfire. A paranoid adolescent told his parents that, as far as he was concerned, "parents and sex don't mix." He was in fact informing his parents that he did not want to hear the facts of life from them because he felt that they were criticizing him for masturbating and for his homosexual leanings. Later in life he went on to develop the delusional idea that people who said hello to him were in fact saying, "too much sex."

Unempathic Parents

In the history of many children who grow up to be paranoid adults, we often find memories of legitimate needs not being understood or met. Children whose legitimate needs were neither understood nor met tend to become adults who react violently when later in life others act, or are perceived to act, in an equally insensitive, nongratifying way. I treated a number of veterans who described the homes in which they grew up as places where they were virtually ignored because they were one of a large number of children. A disproportionate number of these veterans were the last child in a big family and always thought of themselves as accidents. As adults they came very close to getting violent when the government, adding insult to injury, in effect ignored their legitimate needs by mishandling their cases, making them causes. For example, a patient with a suspected brain tumor on CAT scan became paranoid about the government after his doctor read him the positive test results, then did nothing except to tell him to come back in six months for a follow-up visit. This patient, and others like him, going beyond anger, became violent because he felt that important people in his life were treating him in a "who cares about you" fashion, compounding real medical neglect with the (perceived) personal message that "you are a big-nobody."

Erratic Parents

A number of observers have noted that paranoid patients often have had parents who were alcoholics, or who were unreliable for other reasons, and that many paranoiacs-to-be came from broken homes. Presumably basic trust is difficult to develop under such circumstances—because one never knows what to expect from the people one depends on the most.

Seductive Parents

Many clinicians have postulated that sexual seductiveness or overt sexual abuse often leads the child to conclude that adults cannot be trusted and therefore that one must be circumspect in what one shows them and therefore the world.

Parents Who Encourage Their Children to Act Out

Some parents actively encourage their children to act out the parents' paranoid fantasies for them. Some even encourage their children to be violent just to obtain vicarious satisfaction from watching the children hurt others.

In some of these cases the parents overlook the obvious—like bomb-making material around the house—because they do not see what they do not want to see. In one case, a child talked of nothing but making bombs, but his parents ignored his warnings using the transparent excuse, "I didn't really think he would actually make one." There are cases where parents lock up the guns but leave the keys in an obvious place because they want the child to find them. Some parents even become advocates for the child's right to be free not because they truly want to promote a child's healthy individual freedom, but because they want the child to be free to be the equivalent of the mad bomber that the parents themselves always longed to be.

Parents Who Spoil Their Children

Paranoia may not be solely the product of abusive parenting that leads the child to be wary of authority. It can also be the product of overly indulgent, overly permissive, and overly supportive parenting—that is, of spoiling. Children whose parents spoil them by doting on them can feel overwhelmed by all the attention. Later in life they may feel equally overwhelmed by everyone they meet, and cry out, "I want to be independent, but everyone gets on my case." Alternatively, too much doting can foster an atmosphere in which an absence of no-saying authority leads patients to expect that everyone will indulge them, to the point that they rage when someone appears to be reluctant to do that even in the slightest degree.

For example, a patient had overly permissive parents who excused his every temper tantrum as the product of fatigue properly handled by early bedtime, or as a sign of healthy self-expression. Partly as a result their son turned out to be an infant king who felt that he could act up and out whenever and wherever he chose without fear of reprisal. As an adult this man expected everyone to coddle him the same way his parents did, and he became angry when others did not oblige. He then treated them as if they were his enemies, deliberately out to spoil his life by depriving him of what he felt he needed.

A patient's parents were overly permissive due to a "my baby above all" mentality. They took their children to a restaurant where they first proudly showed them off to all the (disinterested) customers, then allowed them to loudly scream and play with *Star Wars* toys, oblivious to how they were bothering others. They also allowed their children to play on crowded city streets, not caring that the children were interfering with the flow of traffic. They installed a basketball hoop in the public hallway of the large apartment complex in which they lived, and when they moved to a side-by-side duplex home installed a backyard swing set that ran the length of the whole yard, though the yard was shared with the next-door neighbor. Should it come as a surprise, then, that after years of being allowed to get away with telling the neighbor's children, "That's my swing, get off it" in a very nasty tone, one of their children became a spoiled, violent adult who attacked anyone he imagined to be figuratively trying to "take my swing set away from me."

Paranoid grandiosity can certainly start with parental spoiling. A set of parents spoiled their son by treating him, an ordinary child, as if he were someone extraordinary. Later in life this son told anyone who would listen that it was his clever political maneuvering as an attorney that stopped a nuclear facility from being built in his backyard. As it turned out, he was not the prime mover but merely one member of a group of protesters who in concert were able to defeat the project. The eulogy at his funeral revealed something of the early origins of his latter-day grandiosity. His son reported during his funeral oration that as a child his father believed that he was instrumental in stopping World War II merely because it happened to be over on the very date (his birthday) he wished it to end. His parents then fixed that grandiose idea by showering him with kisses for being cute and precocious.

Paranoid dereality can also start with the kind of spoiling that involves seriously participating in childish unreality. A family hired a man to play Santa Claus. The actor visited late Christmas Eve, made noises that suggested he was descending via the chimney, and left presents behind, which of course the parents had bought. An uncle made the mistake of asking the parents, within the child's hearing, how much Santa Claus had cost, incurring the parents' undying wrath and enmity. Later the child stubbornly resisted anyone who tried to convince her to be realistic about things. That included her psychiatrist, whose every attempt to help her reality test she met with an angry retaliative tirade, figuratively along the lines of "you are trying to make me stop believing in Santa Claus."

Another young man proclaimed that he was going to be a musician. As his mother reported it, his great contribution to the musical world would be combining the popular with the classical—not exactly the first person to try that. This young man had no musical talent whatsoever. Still his parents wholeheartedly supported his plan, letting his grandiose fantasies go unchecked, thereby encouraging them to run wild. For example, they helped him choose and apply to colleges selected precisely for their strong music departments. Later in life he raged mightily at anyone who failed to buy completely into his craziest grandiose schemes. He had the delusional idea that he was a genius, and that like most geniuses he knew everything and everyone else knew nothing. He had started thinking about life the same irrationally grandiose way his parents thought about him: "I can do anything I want to if only I believe in myself."

For many spoiled children, the problem is that forbidden impulses too readily surface and are thoughtlessly acted on with decidedly negative consequences as guilt becomes a special problem. At first the child welcomes being free, but then he or she feels too free for his or her own good and comfort. Intense guilt over being selfish, self-centered, and self-gratifying can appear. The child can cope with this guilt in one of two ways. He or she may attribute his or her guilty feelings to the agency of others, convincing himself or herself that "you made me feel guilty, therefore you deserve to be condemned and punished." Or he or she may wash away his or her presumed guilt by attempting to cleanse others of their sins, becoming a proselytizer who silences his or her own aroused forbidden passions by going to extremes to silence what he or she believes to be like passions in others.

A woman with such a childhood could neither suppress the sexual feelings she had about her boss nor tolerate the guilt that these feelings aroused in her when they surfaced. She first felt extremely attracted to him, partly because he was like a father figure to her. She then dealt with her troublesome attraction by attributing her unwanted sexual feelings entirely to him, as if he were their agent. She blamed him for trying to seduce her, then sued him for sexual harassment to prove to herself and to others how unwelcome his approach was and how unacceptable the feelings he aroused in her were.

Guilty individuals like her often strike out at anyone whom they believe to be engaging them in actions that they feel guilty about. They think, "He is encouraging me to sin." Two men picked up a soldier when he was hitchhiking and alternated having sex with him in the back seat of the car as they were driving along the highway. After it was all over, he pulled out a knife and tried to kill them both for seducing him. His plan was to rid himself once and for all of the unacceptable sexual feelings the incident aroused. His reasoning went, "If I attempt to kill you it means that I do not desire you." Fortunately the incident was resolved peacefully when one of the men perceptively calmed him down by telling him to just not worry about what happened, chalk it up to experience, and enjoy the sex he just had guilt free, if only this one time.

Speaking in terms of prevention, children growing up should have just the right balance of control and freedom, criticism and congratulations. Too much suppression and they can become rigid individuals who repress their feelings and seek to repress the same feelings in others. Too little suppression and they can become guilty hedonists for whom at first the sky is the limit—until, as is predictable, they later pull back into controlling and condemning themselves because no one else will do it for them, and into condemning others for encouraging them to be freer than they can handle.

Unfortunately, the ideal balance between control and permissiveness, compliments and criticism can be very difficult to achieve. Parents disciplining children, and especially parents trying to discipline somewhat paranoid teenagers (most teenagers are somewhat paranoid), always wind up walking on eggshells. They are in that unavoidable bind inherent in the difficulty of disciplining without being overly controlling, and advising without being unduly critical. For their part, children and adolescents, most of whom already have a tendency to be difficult and rebellious, double-bind their parents, making it impossible for them to walk even on eggshells. They condemn lack of guidance on the part of their parents as disinterest in them, yet condemn appropriate legitimate guidance on the part of their parents as overcontrol.

Therefore, no matter what their parents do, some children feel unsupported and overcontrolled at one and the same time—setting the stage for the paranoid worldview that "nothing anyone does to or for me is ever exactly right" and then that "everyone is out to mess up my life."

In conclusion, there are no surefire ways society can avoid making others paranoid and parents can avoid bringing up a paranoid child. But there is a lot we can all do besides merely suppressing violent computer games to help reduce the incidence and prevalence of paranoia in today's society. (A case can even be made that violent computer games discharge violent tendencies safely, so that there is no build up of hostility and therefore ultimately no need for paranoid defenses meant to avert a violent explosion.) Society (and authority figures who represent society) needs to send sensible, balanced messages, and parents have to have reasonable expectations of their children and present a health-giving plan, which is one that the child can follow. A most important message for society to send is, "When indicated accept individual responsibility, and do not blame the devil whenever you do something wrong." And although the following advice is not science-based it appears to be central to me: parents should always try to maintain a desirable balance between overwhelming the child and ignoring and rejecting him; between supporting and coddling her, and between demanding that the child do too much—attempting to energize the child to do something that he or she is incapable of doing—and expecting too little from the child—discouraging him or her from achieving his or her true potential.

As much as possible, parents should avoid buying into one-size-fits-all advice on how to rear children and instead individualize the child's upbringing. Not all children are temperamentally alike. Some children like and do better with parents who are authoritarian. Others hate authoritarian parents and prefer to have parents who are more like friends. Even very young children have well-developed personalities that help determine what they need personally and what they will respond to positively and, perhaps more important, negatively.

This said, scientific studies of the developmental origins of paranoia are generally lacking in precision. For example, I cannot entirely satisfactorily answer the question, "Why does paranoia develop under two diverse circumstances: in abused children who grow up to think that everybody will abuse them the way their parents did, and in children whose only abuse was being loved to distraction, who grow up thinking that everybody will not love them as much as their parents did?" There are two possibilities here: different roads lead to Rome, or we just do not know enough about early childhood development and its sequelae to be able to predict what a child will be like when he or she grows up, because we simply do not understand how early childhood experiences develop into adult personality or into adult personality problems.

As suggested throughout, childhood experiences do not explain everything paranoid. There are important contributions to adult paranoia made by late adolescent and adult events such as drug usage, disappointments in love, and unfortunate, sometimes accidental, encounters with paranoiagenics such as hostile, demeaning schoolteachers, sexually abusive priests, and cruel army sergeants. Particularly destructive are later experiences that are simultaneously harsh in and of themselves, change the patient's status in some significant way, and revive childhood traumata. Two examples of such multiple highly disturbing life-changing incidents are being expelled from school and being fired from one's job for little or no reason and in a bad job market with no other job in sight. It is of crucial importance that those involved handle such pivotal situations in a way that avoids terrorizing the victim unnecessarily to the point that he or she gets so angry that he or she shoots up the school or returns to his or her former place of employment with guns blazing.

CHAPTER 10

Psychodynamic Causes

While some observers view paranoid ideation as unanalyzable, that is, as not further reducible into component parts, I believe that paranoid ideation can, like any other symptom, be understood dynamically as the product of primal contributing psychological forces, including prevailing character, early experience, and inner conflict. Therefore I believe that a symptom such as a delusion can sometimes be treated with verbal, psychodynamically oriented psychotherapy, much the same way that one can usually treat an obsession or many other psychological symptoms.

CHARACTEROLOGICAL UNDERPINNINGS

Like many other symptoms, paranoid symptoms including delusions often originate in and develop out of such personality traits as narcissism, grandiosity, sadomasochism, perfectionism, stubbornness, and rebelliousness. They are therefore understandable according to these antecedents in the person.

In the realm of narcissism, which may be severe and malignant, some paranoid individuals have become severely narcissistic because they were unduly deprived as children and are now trying to make up for that by getting and having it all. Others have become severely narcissistic because they were spoiled as children to the point that now they feel devastated by even the most minor setback. As an example, a paranoid patient, a wealthy woman who nevertheless suffered from delusions of poverty based on the equation that "if I do not have it all I have nothing," remembers an incident when as an eight-year-old child she got a toy for Christmas, only to find that one of the parts was missing. She threw a temper tantrum and threatened to kill her mother for being so stupid as to not check out the purchase before bringing it home. The mother, eager to make amends, the very next day, at considerable personal sacrifice, made a special trip to the toy store to return the defective gift and get a new one. As the mother put it, "If I didn't do that, my poor baby would have been completely devastated."

As adults, malignant narcissists have to have things always go their way, and they become easily disappointed and enraged when there is even a minor deprivation, which leads them to feel singled out as having been ignored and rejected. A paranoid pitchman who begged for money on the subway was a narcissist along such lines. His first cry was, "Help me out, you never know when you might need some help yourself." Then, when nobody gave, that piteous cry turned to a hostile one, "None of you ever smile, do you. I am not a bad but a good guy at heart, and at least *I* have a pleasant look on my face, not like the rest of you sourpusses."

Paranoid fanaticism can originate in malignant narcissism. When it does, the fanaticism can take the form of fanatic social protest, where the stated wish to cure society of its ills has little or nothing to do with social reform but instead originates extensively in an adversarial wish to perpetuate an image of oneself as someone who is more caring and concerned than thou.

Paranoid blaming is narcissistic in the sense that the overly negative view of others is associated with an overly positive view of oneself as the perpetually innocent victim, infinitely the butt of persecution and bad luck, who almost never produces any of his or her own problems or makes any of his or her own difficulties. Such a view is also narcissistic in the sense that it becomes a ready-made pretext for what is selfishly desired: seeking recompense or other forms of gratification or salvation, not by changing oneself but by getting that thing, individual, situation, or institution presumed to be the source of all one's problems—a wife's independence, a court's unfair verdict, or a government's so-called discriminatory policies—to change, and to do so for me, and along the lines I desire.

Grandiosity also plays a central role in the development of the paranoid process and in many of its specific symptoms. Grandiose traits contribute heavily to the paranoid individual's belief that "I am important enough to be the center of everyone's attention and concern, and the one selected out of all others to be victimized by being persecuted." They also contribute to the morally superior attitude certain paranoid individuals have that leads them to feel that they are in a position to criticize others. Too, they contribute to the above-detailed narcissistic paranoid rage that appears when excessive expectations go unmet, and are partly to blame for adding an angry litigious element to the paranoid picture, arising out of that grandiose sense of narcissistic entitlement that says, "When it comes to me, everything must go right, and if it doesn't, I'll see you in court."

Bone and Oldham (1994) emphasize the role played by characterological *sadomasochism* in the development of the paranoid process and of many of its symptoms (p. 3). Paranoid individuals are *masochists* in the sense that it is a desire to suffer that contributes to their need to conjure up adversarial relationships with others out of slim stuff. For example, a paranoid woman, self-destructively confounding a paramour's voting Republican with his being a totalitarian dictator, rashly dubbed the man, someone who loved her, as a hate-filled Nazi. Dynamically, delusions of persecution often express not only a fear of being mistreated but also a secret longing to be harmed—in order to salve one's conscience. So others in the paranoid individual's life often willingly oblige, which is why we hear, "lock him up and throw away the key" or other punitive expressions clearly, however unfortunately, provoked, at least to some extent, by the paranoid individual himself or herself.

Paranoid individuals are also *sadists* who desire to put down, defeat, hurt, harm, or maim others. In blaming and accusing others who are innocent, they become as hurtful to others as they imagine others to be hurtful to them. I have seen a number of cases in which members of the mental health professions agonize over how to handle a given paranoid patient, asking themselves, really torturing themselves, with questions without satisfactory answers, such as "should we medicate this person against her will" or even "should this person be sentenced to prison for his crime or be let off as not guilty by reason of insanity?" I have often suspected that the patient secretly relishes putting others through their paces, enjoying every minute of the intellectual confusion and real management uncertainty that surround being a difficult case.

Perfectionistic trends contribute heavily to paranoid blaming. In part paranoid blaming of others arises out of the need to view and present oneself as *completely* faultless—someone who never does anything wrong—a self-view markedly enhanced by viewing others as people who, compared to me, never do anything right.

Psychopathic trends contribute heavily to the paranoid tendency to be free with the truth. Some paranoid individuals get into the bad habit of reflexively, almost deliberately, distorting the past to justify the present, just as they willingly and consciously distort the present to justify something in the here and now. They distort the truth to prove their innocence, to achieve a specific worldly goal, or to settle old and new scores—as did the man who, after witnessing a crime, faked his eyewitnesses account to settle an old score with authority. For others there is truth in the assertion "I saw it with my own eyes." For him, a long history of problems with feeling persecuted by law enforcement personnel determined what he thought he saw, so that what he reported as having been observed differed from what his brain actually registered. Among those who distort the past for present gain are serial killers who blame their murderous rampages on an abusive upbringing so that they can be excused from taking any personal responsibility for their behavior. Among those who distort present reality for immediate advantage are, to use a term that is in itself paranoid, the usual suspects discussed throughout: politicians who deliberately paint a negative picture of a rival; wife-beaters who blame provocation so that they may continue to beat their wives both guilt- and consequence-free; employees who falsely accuse the boss of sexual harassment so that they may sue the company for money; and petty criminals who falsely blame the police for brutality in order to shift the focus from "what I did" to "what you did to me." I have treated many patients who lied and said that they were delusional and hallucinating when they were not in order to get what they wanted: a benzodiazepine, barbiturate, or opiate; a place to stay for the night; a lab test to satisfy their hypochondria; a doctor's note so that they did not have to pay for a vacation that they contracted for but now wanted out of because something better came up; or the like. These people were mainly out to save their own skin by acting insane, simply because there was something to be gained from the performance.

Victims must take stern measures to cope with psychopathic, manipulative paranoid individuals who incorporate them into their delusional lies for direct personal gain. The longer the victims let them go on, the more they will prevail and the harder it will be for a progressively weakened victim to do something corrective. Right from the start, innocent victims should refuse to feel guilty as accused and instead, anticipating and finessing all paranoid counterarguments, simply, directly, and continuously demand fairness, rationality, and justice.

ANGER ISSUES

As Bone and Oldham (1994) suggest, paranoid individuals are extremely and intensely aggressive people (p. 3) who as a group feel angrier and get nastier than most. Still, the causal role anger plays in paranoia is generally overlooked or downplayed. As Haroun (1999) says, "angry feeling states are minimally recognized in the DSM, either for judgmental reasons (i.e., it is not okay to be angry) or for science-based reasons (i.e., the neurotransmitters involved in depression may be better researched than those involved in anger)" (p. 335). Therapists hesitate to attribute angry motives to their patients, and laymen to their family or friends, out of fear of criticizing and offending them based on the belief of all concerned that anger is an emotion to be ashamed of. As a result, many people in referring to the angry paranoid individual speak in somewhat veiled tones. They favor all the familiar euphemisms that have evolved to describe angry paranoid people, such as *difficult people, assertive people, competitive people*, and *people who are professionally jealous*.

As discussed throughout, paranoid fantasies can be partly explained dynamically as a defense against, that is, as a way to disavow, unacceptable anger, the familiar "I am only angry with you because you persecute me." Anger also creates paranoid fantasies directly by distorting reality, for people who are angry usually do not assess reality accurately. Too, character traits like stubbornness that form the basis of the paranoid response are in turn themselves anger equivalents. In a typical sequence, the angrier a patient feels the more stubborn and therefore the more paranoid he or she becomes. I have long suspected that phenothiazines reduce paranoia in part by chemically disabling the anger mechanism (as well as by chemically reducing sexual pressures and so reducing the guilt associated with forbidden sexual desire).

However, many paranoid individuals tend not to get overtly angry or to have temper tantrums. They tend to at least start off by hiding their rage, which they often do passive-aggressively. For example, the complaint "I fear you are persecuting me" is inherently a passive-aggressive attack on one's presumed persecutors. Paranoid passive-aggressives often hide their anger behind a shield of professed concern. For example, a mercy-killer husband who in fact euthanized his sick wife because she was bothering him with her medical problems claimed that he did so not for his own good, but entirely for her benefit, that is, solely to spare her, not himself, from suffering.

EARLY ABUSE/TRAUMA

In some patients symptoms of delusional disorder are activated by new traumata that bring old traumata back to mind. Some patients have told me that they feel that intermittent retraumatization can be worse than retraumatization that is continuous. As an illustration, a patient told me, "Each morning I walk down by the river. Perhaps 1 out of 10 times I am attacked by a large vicious dog the neighbor lets loose. I am not prepared for any of those attacks, having forgotten about the last one by the time the next one comes along. If the trauma were continuous I would be ready for it, or stay away. But since it is intermittent I go back innocently over and over again, only to be taken by surprise and retraumatized each time. Now I have become completely gun-shy, to the point that I have stopped walking down to the river."

Keeping in mind that paranoid patients often traumatize others, and that others retaliate, we have to ask if in some cases and to some extent their so-called traumatization is not the cause but the product of their paranoia. Just recently I offered to treat a friend to lunch. She was someone who regularly complained that her parents had traumatized her. Instead of showing up, she called one hour after she was due to meet me and, though she knew that I was waiting in the restaurant, left a message on my home machine that she had forgotten our appointment and besides she was too busy to take the time out for our date. I asked myself, could it have been that she was such a difficult child that her parents found her as impossible to handle as I found her, to the point that they felt as traumatized by her as she felt traumatized by them—and so when they traumatized her they were at least partly only retaliating in kind out of frustration?

REPRESSED HOMOSEXUALITY

A number of observers, notably but not exclusively Freud, have commented on the relationship between repressed homosexuality and paranoia. (In the following discussion I refer to genitally oriented homosexuality and not to such gender-identity issues sometimes associated with homosexuality—in fantasy or in reality—as femininity or passivity.) Exactly how central and important homosexual conflicts are in creating paranoid symptoms is a subject of considerable debate. (This debate is one of the favorite, if not the favorite, subjects of Freud bashers—those contentious individuals who are somewhat paranoid themselves in their selective attention to where Freud went wrong, while completely overlooking anything at all that he might have been right about.) What is certain is that homosexual fantasies do produce some of the content of some of the delusions of some paranoid patients. Certain delusions like "the angel of suck is sitting on my shoulder," the belief that a girl's school is emitting computer rays and sending them into my vagina, or the belief that FBI agents have inserted a microchip into my penis have at least a manifest homosexual tinge to them. Conflicts about homosexual sex were almost certainly an issue for a patient who had to buy what was for him an unaffordable book on psychology because he just had to know what the people on the bus were saying about him. "In fact," he subsequently concluded, "I do not need that book because I already know what they are saying about me: they are saying . . . [here he quite dramatically gives himself the finger in a way that distinctly reminds of anal penetration]."

In my opinion, some paranoid phenomena can be explained dynamically at least in part as a defense against, that is, as a way to disavow, one's forbidden homosexual desires. As examples given throughout this text suggest, some paranoid delusions are at least in part the product of the projection of guilty homosexual wishes outward in an attempt to disavow homosexual leanings, along the lines of "I am a straight person; the problem is that everyone falsely accuses me of being queer." Gay-bashing is, at least in some cases, a not-me behavior geared to prove that "I am not a bad queer, see, I hate queers." The term *homosexual panic* refers to a clinical entity exemplified by the young man who, the morning after a night of close buddy contact accompanied by inhibition-releasing heavy drinking and substance abuse, developed an acute delusional and hallucinatory state in which he heard others accusing him of being queer and threatening to do him harm to punish him for his evil sexual thoughts of the night before, and maybe even for the pass he might have made at his friends, although he doesn't exactly recall having done that. It is of interest that patients suffering from alcoholic hallucinosis (an acute or chronic toxic-withdrawal state related to delirium tremens occurring in patients who drink heavily, with the most intense symptoms possibly, but not always, appearing during relative or absolute alcohol withdrawal) often hear voices calling them queer. Though this is pure speculation; their voices may be a product of unacceptable homosexual feelings aroused in a setting of years of drinking in the company of bar buddies who, rather than their wives and children, have now become their closest family.

Conflicts about heterosexuality also occur and in some cases can be of equal or greater importance than conflicts about homosexuality. For example, in erotomanic paranoid individuals, delusions of being sexually harassed that form in the absence of actual sexual harassment often originate in feelings of disgust with their heterosexuality. Such patients deny and project blame for their forbidden heterosexual desires onto others, developing delusions that say "I don't want to do it; you are trying to force me into it." One patient, after what—as she described it to me—was clearly consensual sex, said, "I didn't consent to it; he assaulted me." Often hiding this way behind a shield of professed innocence becomes insufficient. Now the individual goes on to become a litigious paranoid individual who publicly accuses his or her presumed victimizer of sexual assault in order to make his or her point clear and his or her position public and therefore more widely known, while simultaneously attempting to get others to share his or her delusion in order to gain consensual validation for the false accusations as well as support along the lines of "There, there, you are innocent, and you deserve justice, and recompense."

CONFLICT, DEFENSE, AND SYMPTOM FORMATION

As mentioned throughout, I view most paranoid symptoms, ranging from ideas of reference and overvalued ideas to delusions, as dynamic constructs that are created from the same building blocks of conflict, anxiety, and defense that go into making up all or almost all psychological symptoms, including character traits and obsessions. Therefore we would expect unacceptable hostile and sexual feelings to be prime movers in the formation of paranoid phenomena, and perhaps especially in the formation of persecutory delusions. As an illustration that anticipates my discussion of the relationship between *unacceptable sexuality* and persecutory delusions, an individual wrote a nasty e-mail message to demand that a television announcer stop beaming sexual innuendoes at him. He did this in response to feeling ashamed of his sexual desires—a feeling of shame that was set in motion by the announcer's saying that a certain company was creating "high performance input output solutions." A familiar example of the relationship between *unacceptable hostility* and persecutory delusions is to be found in those paranoid patients who deny how hate-filled they fundamentally are by blaming their hatred of others on the evil that all men, and all mankind, have done to them.

Projection is classically the defense paranoid individuals resort to. It is a complex defense mechanism that is actually made up of other, more primary defense mechanisms that interact and operate in concert:

Denial, repression, and reaction formation (the three are often indistinguishable and are used in concert). For example, hate is disavowed by being transformed into love, or the other way around.

Displacement and reattribution (the two are often indistinguishable and are used together). Here "me" is disavowed to become "not me, but you," as the person's own desires, fears, anxieties, and guilt feelings are attributed to another person or to an external impersonal agency such as "those mysterious forces" or "the influencing machine."

The specific results of displacement and reattribution include the familiar "not me" alibis that disavow self-blame by attributing aspects of "me" either to "you" or to a literal or figurative "them"—the latter referring in a general way to external forces beyond one's control—followed by an almost mechanical psychic boomeranging where one's own fears and wishes come back unchanged except in direction—a kind of psychic mirroring where aspects of the self are reflected, identical in size, shape, and substance, only in reverse.

Freud (1957), in tracing the transformations of a forbidden homosexual wish to become a delusional conviction (in the Schreber case), was probably one of the first to make not only a specific point about the relationship between homosexuality and paranoia, but perhaps an equally important and more sustainable general point that all sorts of self-disavowal is central to all forms of delusional formation, that is, that the basic cry of the deluded person is, "You, not me, are the one."

Blaming is central to the processes of displacement and reattribution. As Cooper (1994) says, projection not only "has to do with emptying the self of unacceptable contents" (p. 147); it also has to do with blaming. Someone to blame is a critical requirement for these patients. Others are blamed for epitomizing and provoking the patient's own unacceptable anger and sexual feelings. That helps explain why perceptive people often say that "behind every criticism of another is a self-criticism" and that "it takes one to know one."

Now instead of meting out presumably deserved punishment to and flagellating themselves for forbidden wishes, paranoid individuals blame others, make them the guilty ones, then go on to punish them for what they believe to be others' presumed bad behaviors, beating others in the way that they formerly felt that they themselves deserved to be beaten. Simultaneously they tell the world, "I am good, not bad like you, worthy not worthless, trusting not jealous, peaceful not aggressive, asexual not whorish—a saint to be beatified, not a sinner to be condemned."

Blaming is most obviously a component of those delusions of persecution that say, "I am not to be blamed for hating you; I only hate you because you hate me." It is also an obvious component of litigious delusions, as well as of erotomanic delusions that say, "I am not to blame for being attracted to you; you are to blame for trying to seduce me." It appears to be a secondary aspect of somatic and grandiose delusions.

Identification, where the distinction between me and you is blurred in a kind of pathological oneness involving an extreme fluidity, or complete loss, of boundaries. For example, a complete stranger sitting next to me, as I was editing this manuscript in a public place, created a connection to me that did not exist when he leaned over and whispered in my ear, "Mark 'em up, eh? Just like you, I find stupidity and lack of coordination in the newspapers all the time and cross out what is wrong." This process is sometimes referred to as *projective identification* because it says, usually with slim evidence to back it up, that "you and I are very much alike, which means that I have no trouble at all recognizing elements of me in you." Projective identification is strongly the product of hypertrophied empathy, that excessive resonating with others based on the conviction that "under the skin we are all *exactly* alike." Paranoid individuals who suffer from delusions of jealousy empathically identify with others when they assume that others' motivations are aligned with, and equal to, their own, as in "when it comes to sex, everyone is an animal just like me, so what else can you expect from people besides their always trying to seduce you?" When boundaries are blurred like this, making faint the differences between subject and object, between "me" and "you," the stage is set for what might be called projective confusion. As an example of such projective confusion, an artist, deciding that she had long enough drunk from cows, got into a trough in order to let the cows drink from her.

We also find *identification with the aggressor* that says, "You did it to me first, so I will, fighting fire with fire, become just like you, and do it you back." Patients thus get back in an eye-for-an-eye fashion by changing themselves around from the person attacked into a vengeful attacker similarly, and understandably, inclined.

Dissociation, which facilitates the other mechanisms by giving them an automatic, reflexive, spontaneous quality so that they take place unconsciously, that is, outside of full awareness. The defense of dissociation facilitates the projective process by lending it a spontaneous, automatic, unconscious quality. It also helps paranoid individuals win other people over to their unreal view of the world by throwing them off balance by virtue of the same sheer force of the paranoid individual's convictions and well-rehearsed arguments that challenge elementary principles that paranoid individuals use against themselves. The result is a kind of logical shock in others, not unlike the patient's own dissociative state, in which others fail to respond as rationally, and so as constructively, as they might. For example, an Israeli patient, an ordinarily vocal and intelligent man, was so cowed by a terrorist-type's threatening words that he was unable to even mutter a protest to her proclamation that "Israel as an apartheid state like South Africa should not be permitted to survive." Suckers are not necessarily born every minute. Some are born skeptical, but made suckers of the moment by a paranoid individual's clever persuasive manipulative thinking.

Rationalization, which justifies the other mechanisms by putting a good spin on a bad thing. Two familiar examples are "doesn't every husband worry that his wife is being unfaithful to him?" and the transparently overly self-congratulatory, old, presumptuous homophobic saw, "I hate the sin, but that is okay, because I love the sinner."

The projection process itself is set in motion by anxiety. As Shapiro (1994) says, "The . . . threat will be constructed [both] out of repudiated impulses and feelings [and] out of the particular anxieties generated in the rigid person by [these] repudiated impulses and feelings" (p. 55). Specifically, anxiety is the product of one or more of the following dynamisms:

- An inner conflict between a wish and a fear—that is, between (sexual and aggressive) instinct and guilt, or, put in what are perhaps more familiar terms, between desire (the ego) and regret. Regret comes from the ego ideal (e.g., I am not what I *want* to be) and the superego or conscience (e.g., I am not what I *ought* to be).

- A feeling that one is being flooded by strong impulses that threaten a loss of control of one's feelings, and so of oneself.

- Interpersonal and real-life stresses, particularly those that would call forth certain strong impulses as well as feelings of humiliation, dishonor, rejection, and abandonment in almost anyone.

In spite of its many negative aspects, projection improves the internal economy by reducing anxiety, which it does by allowing the patient to

- Lay the blame for forbidden and unacceptable tendencies on others' doorsteps.

- Deny the reality of personal weaknesses by attributing them to others' malevolence (Millon, 1981, p. 382).

- Conceal one's own flaws by condemning the same flaws as they are perceived to or actually exist in others (Millon, 1981, p. 388).

- Aggrandiz[e] the self (Millon, 1981, p. 382), helping maintain the illusion of adequacy and significance through fantasy (p. 382).

- Justify one's hatred of others, making it acceptable by viewing others as deserving of being hated.

- Get back on top and in control as the blaming, accusing, condemning, and hating person assumes the right to impose his or her standards on others, for example, put simply, to boss them around. Thus, "I am not queer; I hate queers" leads naturally into "If you must be queer, I accept that, but still I, as your newly self-appointed boss, command you to stop doing queer things."

In short, patients project in order to resolve their anxiety-laden conflicts between their true desires and their disappointments in themselves that have to do with their big ideas and self-expectations, their sacred ideals, and their guilt, often associated with moralistic schemata. Projection helps them convince themselves that they are not responsible for their failures, are innocent of feeling a certain way, and are therefore not responsible for the bad things they do. Though the cost is great, they at least reduce their anxiety by improving their self-image and salving their conscience, thus mitigating their disappointment in and hatred of themselves.

The generally defensive "not me" view of the world adopted by individuals who are paranoid is far more basic than any of its specific (persecutory, grandiose, erotomanic, litigious, or somatic) consequences, and in my opinion is what marks paranoia, stamping the disorder—in all its forms, trivial to serious, ranging from the paranoia of everyday life to delusional paranoia—with its most defining characteristic. This is the common thread that runs through the child's "you did it too, and first" knee-jerk response to criticism, the guilty criminal's response to being caught red-handed ("you are wrong to accuse me because I am innocent until proven guilty"), and the patient's delusional belief that "I am not guilty of anything, it is just that the FBI has collected false evidence against me by tapping my telephone."

As with any defense, the end product is a tribute to that which it is attempting to disguise. That helps explain why paranoid homophobes who gay bash in order to suppress their own homosexual desires always seem to manage to get close to and emotionally entangled with the objects of their supposed disdain. We can just imagine what a famous evangelist is thinking when he prays constantly for a new Supreme Court that this time will reaffirm the sodomy laws. The operative principle here may very well be the Freudian one: behind every professed fear lies a secret wish.

When the projective defense fails, the individual, paradoxically no longer paranoid enough, may go on to become rapacious, or violent to self or others. This can happen spontaneously or when poorly conceived treatment stirs a potentially paranoid individual up, producing a boil-over effect, which it can do in one of two ways:

- by exposing or overexposing, through uncovering psychotherapy, deep-seated sexuality, rage, and fear, leaving the individual literally defenseless in the face of the onslaught aroused from within
- by arousing sleeping instincts through prescribing speed-like antidepressants in the mistaken belief that the patient is not paranoid but depressed—a prescription that is especially dangerous for children and adolescents

However, it is an oversimplification to view the externalization process solely as a *defensive* one. Externalization also involves other, primarily non-defensive, mechanisms. It involves fantasies of being retaliated against, the not unreasonable fear that one is getting his or her comeuppance for prior thoughts and actions. A paradigm of this aspect of externalization is to be found in the instructions on the back of a voodoo doll that warn that the curse can backfire and result in bad things being worked against the practitioner. A patient told me that she feared that she had caused her cat to miss the litter box simply by telling the cat, "I hate you." She was certain that the cat picked up on that, in response became angry with her, and as an act of vengeance started urinating on the patient's bed.

Shapiro (1994) describes the process of externalization in *cognitive* terms, not as an extrusion of inner feelings but as the product of selective attention to external matters. He suggests that this selective attention makes the "struggle with [the self] . . . into an experience of conflict with an external antagonist" (p. 52). He suggests that a paranoid individual "searches only for signs of threat, not for an absence of such signs" (p. 54). In effect he describes a kind of opportunism as paranoid individuals look both for real-life situations whose qualities, and for others whose traits, meet their negative needs and pessimistic expectations.

Externalization can also be an almost conscious making of self-justifying excuses for oneself. There is a refusal to acknowledge the active role one plays in life. Instead one conveniently lets oneself off the hook by viewing oneself as a passive victim of others' blameworthy actions. A patient with AIDS told me that he had unprotected sex with someone he met at a sex club. Afterward the man he had sex with e-mailed him seeking reassurance that the patient was not HIV-positive. His response was, "Right, you idiot, how stupid can you be, thinking that you meet people who are HIV-negative at sex clubs?" The reasoning was, "If you don't take care of yourself, how can you expect me to take care of you"—that is, "don't blame me if I infected you; blame yourself for allowing yourself to be infected." Manipulative opportunism/self-gratification is another centerpiece of the plan when the goal of externalization is to make others feel guilty to the point that they comply with one's wishes and give one what is being demanded. For example, "I am not a thief if I steal Microsoft's programs without paying for them because I am just getting back at Bill Gates for stealing what little money I have."

The process of projection as a whole can also be viewed positively, as an *organizing force* put into place to manage an otherwise unfathomable sense of inner dissolution and explain troubling mysterious outer events. Projection gives patients comfort because it allows them to think the reassuring thought that "now I know, or at least I think I know, exactly who and what I am dealing with." In a way it is very reassuring to think, "I am not losing my mind; I know exactly what is happening and why" or, more specifically, "I am not losing my mind; you are confusing me by removing my thoughts and inserting yours into my head." As the case vignette of the man who bought a book to find out what others on the bus were saying about him illustrates, it can be comforting to no longer have to worry about what others *may* be up to because one has convinced oneself that "now I know *exactly* what they are thinking and doing."

Projective phenomena often have an existential component. They can be interpreted to reflect an expression of the basic distrust, insecurity, and low self-esteem that constitute one's worst fears or even one's fondest wishes. Delusions of jealousy often express the existential fear that "I am not good enough to hang on to you" and the existential worry that "you will humiliate me." Somatic delusions often express existential feelings of worthlessness in body language, not "I am not a big nobody," but "people think I smell." Grandiose delusions deny feelings of being criticized by concluding, "I am not bad; I am truly good" or feelings of danger directly by concluding not that "I fear you can harm me" but that "I am inviolable." The motivations of projection also involve some very positive existential human aspirations: to be important, central, heard, and loved. As examples, a goal of many people with litigious delusions is to prove their value to the world by suing those who appear to be challenging it, and a goal of those with erotomanic delusions is to prove that they are adored, not despised.

On another level, some modest delusions are simply the result of misunderstanding. As such they persist as long as no persuasive correction is forthcoming. For example, a man suspected that his neighbor hated him because he did not recognize him when he waved hello when walking by. The real reason the man did not wave back was that he was going blind.

Clinically it is noteworthy that the concrete, narrowed, oversimplified thinking associated with certain aspects of projection reminds us of similar thinking processes in patients whose IQs are low. To some extent, speaking in the vernacular, projection, and the delusions to which it gives rise, is a truly stupid way to think. Additionally, sociocultural and religious influences often contribute to the tendency to project and to become delusional, especially to develop shared delusions.

Finally, considering all the evil that actually occurs in the world, sometimes projection is just a matter of coincidence—the familiar "you are not paranoid; you have real enemies."

CHAPTER 11

Cognitive-Behavioral Causality

COGNITIVE CAUSALITY

General Principles

Eugen Bleuler, as Millon and Davis (1996) note, suggests that "paranoids make no more errors or misinterpretations of life events than [do] normal persons [with] the essential pathological feature . . . the 'fixity' of their errors" (p. 693). However, other observers note that paranoid patients do make more than the usual number of cognitive errors and that the cognitive errors they make are distinctive and form a pattern that contributes to the development of paranoid symptoms ranging from characterological suspiciousness to discrete delusions.

The cognitive errors that paranoid individuals make do not arise de novo. They do not, like primary delusions, just spring from the Earth. Rather, more like secondary delusions, they arise from, are activated by, and are therefore understandable in the context of, specific emotions and daily occurrences. It follows that these cognitive errors, and the symptomatic manifestations to which they give rise, can at least theoretically be reversed using verbal forms of psychotherapy meant to correct them intellectually and challenge them emotionally. As will be discussed further in chapter 13, these challenges can be either of a direct or of an indirect nature. In the realm of challenging (and reversing) cognitive errors *directly*, the therapist identifies and helps correct the patient's specific misinterpretations of the facts. In the realm of challenging (and reversing) cognitive errors *indirectly*, the therapist exposes their troubled origins in:

  Character and character pathology. Cognitive errors associated with *grandiosity* can originate in a *hypomanic* tendency to gloss over one's personal flaws. Cognitive errors associated with *persecutory feelings*, such as persecutory feelings of being wronged, can originate in such *narcissistic* tendencies as the tendency to personalize others' impersonal words and actions and in simple selfishness. As an illustration of the latter, a man decided that he was entitled to download CDs free from the Internet because "I wasn't screwing anyone; I was screwing them back." He arrived at his false premise after assessing reality through the lens of a passionate sense of narcissistic entitlement that can be summarized as "I am, therefore I deserve." He then went on to defend his original false premise, in an equally narcissistic self-serving way, by invoking the logic of selective abstraction in order to prove that he was as entitled to download CDs free as he thought. As he rationalized matters, "The manufacturers of CDs are stealing my money by overpricing their product, making it too expensive for me, or any average person, to afford. They charge their high prices though each CD only costs them 50 cents to make." He may or may not have been right about the 50 cents, but to arrive at the conclusion that he was the one who was being wronged, he had to overlook certain costs besides those related to manufacturing, such as the considerable outlay involved both in creating and in marketing the product.

Strong emotions. Faulty thinking is, according to Millon and Davis (1996), created from "heavily charged . . . emotion [which is why it so often comes to] dominate . . . the individual's psychic life" (p. 693). As Karg and Alford (1997) quoting Bentall suggest, projective cognitive errors are used to protect [from an awareness of unacceptable thoughts related to] negatively self-referent information" (p. 325). For example, a patient dealt with his guilt over being severely competitive toward people who were more successful than he by deciding that the real problem was that others were plotting against him to assure his failure. Rage and anxiety commonly make it difficult to think logically and so to be a good, nondistorting eyewitness to both past and present events.

Opportunism (making things happen). Paranoid individuals eager to manipulate others learn to do so by, as Millon and Davis (1996) suggest, "reason[ing] backward from preconceived ideas to the evidence" (p. 725). Politicians running for office do that, and so do dueling spouses in a divorce proceeding who attempt to get it all by painting the other spouse as the apotheosis of absolute evil.

Early experience. Early experience helps determine how one interprets, or misinterprets, current events. For example, it helps determine the faulty thinking that makes up the negative transference-like reactions paranoid individuals characteristically manifest toward others, including the therapist.

Currently stressful interpersonal events. An absence of needed emotional support from a significant other often precipitates or enhances the paranoid individual's tendency to develop overly pessimistic thoughts about life. To illustrate, a patient came out of the closet and announced to her husband that she planned to divorce him and marry her boss, a woman. A day after she came out, her new lover, her boss, told the patient that she could not join her in a gay pride march because she, the boss, already had a date with another woman. When the patient complained to her new lover that that made her feel alone, rejected, and abandoned, the new lover hurtfully warned her, "Never try to take over and devour me." The new lover at first refused to take her cruel statement back. However, a few days later she did give in and offered an apology of sorts. But it was not a full-bodied "I can see that I was making you jealous and I'm sorry," but a tepid "perhaps I misunderstood your intent, because I now see that you only wanted to tag along with us, not take over the proceedings completely." The patient, generalizing from the particular, now began to think, "I cannot trust anyone to treat me right." She became very morose and seriously withdrawn, and began to brood that "my boss is not the only one who hates me. In fact, everyone does."

Sensory deprivation. Paranoid individuals do not always think as logically as they might under situations of prolonged darkness ("winter paranoia") or when they are extremely isolated for long periods of time. In a particularly vicious cycle, paranoia induces interpersonal isolation, and the interpersonal isolation in turn induces more paranoia.

Toxic insults/organic disorder. Thinking can be negatively affected by such mental disorders as alcoholic hallucinosis and Alzheimer's disease—indeed, by any disorder that organically affects such parameters as perception and memory. Normal hypnogogic and hypnopompic delusions and hallucinations (phenomena that arise when one is just falling asleep or waking up) illustrate the relationship between the biological deficit state of incomplete alertness and faulty thinking. Obtundation due to being half asleep might have been part of the reason the woman described in the Introduction came to believe that every radio station on her clock radio was playing Polish music.

As previously suggested, once created and established, cognitive errors often become secondarily fixed by other, additional cognitive errors that justify and solidify the initial error and protect it from internal and external challenges. Rationalization and von Domarus thinking are two cognitive processes commonly used in this secondary fashion. Rationalization is discussed further below. As an example of the use of secondary justifying von Domarus thinking, a by-nature natively suspicious, jealous, and dependent gay patient decided emotionally that there was a good possibility that his lover was cheating on him. He thought that that must be the case because five nights in a row, when the lover came home from work, the lover mentioned the name of the same coworker. Using von Domarus illogic, the patient concluded, "people talk about people they are having sex with; he is talking about him constantly; therefore he is having sex with him." Of course, nothing untoward was going on: the lover was simply reporting the day's events, which the coworker by chance happened to figure in prominently five days in a row. Next, the patient, having established the false premise "you are cheating on me," solidified his belief that he was being cuckolded by using further von Domarus illogic: "I am older; people who are older are no longer as sexually appealing as they once were; therefore I must no longer be sexually appealing to you." Ultimately the patient became thoroughly convinced that his lover was regularly spending his lunch hour having sex with his coworker.

Specific Cognitive Deficiencies/Incapacities

The following, adapted from Karg and Alford (1997), is an overview of some specific cognitive deficiencies, or incapacities, that contribute to the making of cognitive errors commonly found in paranoid individuals. Remedies are implied here and discussed further in chapter 13.

There is an inability to take perspective on one's thoughts (Karg and Alford, 1997, p. 330). This is often associated with an inability, as Watts and colleagues suggest according to Karg and Alford (1999), to look for alternatives to and challenge evidence for a belief, leading to an inability to challenge the belief itself (p. 330). This is in turn associated with an inability to "view . . . one's thoughts or beliefs as constructions of reality rather than as reality itself" (pp. 330–331). Patients also pay attention "selectively . . . to redundant stimuli" (p. 324) leading to an inability to align their perceptions to make them consistent with the "true [nature and] meaning of . . . external stimuli" (p. 324). The latter process is central to the formation of illusions and hallucinations.

Additionally, there is an inability to, as Karg and Alford (1997) quoting Bentall and colleagues suggest, identify internal events (p. 325) without "attribut[ing them] to an external source" (p. 325), and therefore an inability to distinguish between what originates from within and what originates from without. This process is also central to the formation of delusions and hallucinations.

Finally, there is an inability to correct "misconceptions and unclarities regarding the identity of the self" (p. 326), leading to what Millon (1999) refers to as an inability to form rational "*self-schematas* that serve as a [proper] gauge for appraising and valuing aspects of the self" (p. 32), resulting in such thinking as catastrophic "I am all bad" thinking. This is often associated with an inability to distinguish oneself from another person, so that a person who is suspicious of everybody will instead think, "Everybody, being just like I am, is suspicious of me."

Specific Cognitive Errors

The following is a partial list of specific cognitive errors—sophistic logical distortions—that make up paranoid false beliefs and delusions. Because these errors resemble each other in significant ways there is considerable overlap, making the lines I draw between the different errors somewhat indistinct.

von Domarus errors. This form of faulty reasoning, also discussed above, can be a significant factor in creating the false expectations of disapproval, criticism, and attack behind paranoid pessimism and paranoid adversarial constructions. For example, a straight psychotherapist could never quite shake the conviction that all his patients thought he was queer because he lived in Greenwich Village in New York City. He reasoned as follows: my patients think, "You live in Greenwich Village; homosexuals live in Greenwich Village; therefore you are a homosexual." When he was offered an exceptional professional opportunity with significant financial benefits to relocate his office closer to his Greenwich Village home, he demurred, thinking, "I cannot relocate there because if I do, all my patients will become convinced that I am queer, and quit treatment." A patient had an aunt with a mole on her chin. Though the aunt was not a bad person, the patient thought, "You have a mole on your chin; witches have moles on their chins; therefore you are a witch."

Catastrophizing. The pessimism and negativity almost always associated with the paranoid view is also the product of a tendency to see the dark side of things after making a lot out of a little, specifically, after overemphasizing and overreacting to the dark aspects of a person or a situation that is both good and bad. Now paranoid individuals, unable to appreciate the good things in life, instead see only the bad things. They then become convinced that all is lost and develop depressive ideation that turns into persecutory misconception. This sequence helps explain the extensive clinical overlap between paranoia and depression.

Selective abstraction/attention. Selective abstraction involves rejecting facts that do not fit with one's primary intellectual or emotional bias. This process, central to forming delusions, is familiar to us from the paranoia of everyday life as found in the partisan editorial pages of newspapers, where reporters and editorial writers select one fact out of many in order to create a whole truth according to their personal needs and goals. As Shapiro (1994) describes the process as it occurs in more seriously troubled paranoid individuals, these people "satisfy [a] bias, regardless of [any] mitigating context" (p. 54). Teasing out one element from a complex skein of relevant, often contradictory facts in a given relationship, situation, or event, and simply disregarding anything that does not jibe with their need to see things in an adversarial light, paranoid individuals selectively overlook details of an incident or pertinent life event that conflict with a negative point they wish to make, such as the one that everyone is against them. As Shapiro notes, "they search . . . only for signs of threat, not for an absence of such signs" (p. 54). This process overlaps with what is familiarly called injustice collecting and with what, as previously mentioned, Karg and Alford (1997) call "selectively atten[ding] to redundant stimuli" (p. 324).

Typically paranoid individuals react negatively to compliments. After teasing out a remote, negative possibility in the compliment from other, more likely, more positive possibilities, they assign first priority to this secondary, less important, negative issue, and come to see only the negative implications in what are favorable statements. For example, a paranoid individual responded to being told "You look just like Marilyn Monroe" with "How dare you compare me to that troubled woman?" A man told a friend that he looked like a famous comedian only to have the friend think that he was being compared to a buffoon. In parallel fashion, these individuals view mixed motivation as all one-sided. They typically view others' motives, though both altruistic and self-centered, as all selfish. So they see only the profit motive in a doctor's charging a fair fee—as if he or she has no concern whatsoever for the well-being of the patient. Or they see their own and others' desire for success and achievement not at all as motivated by a desire for self-actualization, but purely as part of a plan to destroy a rival. They typically react pejoratively to displays of acceptable, ordinary human feeling. They view anger, others' as well as their own, not as a normal and even constructive emotion but as an entirely destructive one, and condemn sexual instincts as being entirely base, so that to them sex is not at all natural, pleasurable, and procreative but "just dirty."

Paranoid individuals think too narrowly as they tease out a passing remark, a Freudian slip, or a little joke from the flow and take that much too seriously and too much to heart, in the process overlooking overall intent. For example, a man became incensed simply because a friend joked that the man's daughter did not just borrow her father's laptop computer; she actually adopted it. Or they think narrowly as they overlook unconscious motivation and instead treat statements and actions as entirely purposeful and conscious. Or, they do the reverse—after overlooking conscious motivation they see statements and actions as entirely unconsciously motivated, thereby uncovering secret underground evil where nothing of the sort was intended or, if it were intended, was only part of the picture and not meant to shine through. As a result, they might see a deliberate rejection in every unavoidable cancellation of a date, or purely hostile intent in unavoidable lateness.

In the related process of splitting, the paranoid individual divides people into all good and all bad and focuses entirely on the bad. For example, a patient saw to it that, as far as he was concerned, his therapist could do no right. The patient had misinterpreted his therapist's good advice about what he might profitably become in life as a criticism for his having already failed to become much of anything. He also savaged his therapist unmercifully for suggesting that he settle down domestically, complaining, "You are completely devaluing me as a single man," and for suggesting that if he wanted to find Ms. Right it might be a good idea to become less outlandish and go mainstream, which, as the therapist put it, is "where all the fish are biting." In response, the patient could do no better than to complain, "You are taking my outlandishness away from me and by doing that you are robbing me of my individuality."

Schadenfreude provides the general public with a way to gratify its hostile, jealous competitive needs by fantasizing negative whole images created out of presumably defective parts split off from positive aspects of a person or situation. As an example, I cite the gleeful defiling of then-president Gerald Ford, whom some of the general public dubbed completely defective because once he tripped and another time hit someone in the head with a golf ball.

A more positive aspect of selectively abstracting and splitting is that it helps organize one's thinking—however much the organization comes at the expense of correct perception of reality. As Millon and Davis (1996) suggest, individuals who selectively abstract narrow "the natural complexities of [the] social world . . . to signify one or two persistent and all-embracing ideas [so that they] can effectively deal with . . . problems . . . by 'knowing' that everything represents basically one or two variants of the same thing" (p. 709).

In overgeneralization, a companion process to selective abstraction and splitting, patients, disregarding the qualifier *some*, expand *some* to become *all*, so that a few things become everything. Persecutory ideas and delusions of persecution are often the product of the distortive belief that the normal animosity people hold even to those they basically love is necessarily representative of their true feelings in entirety, and therefore constitutes their firm, unyielding, and unalloyed negative interpersonal positional statement. Grandiose delusions can be the result of the same process in reverse: a failure to recognize negative feedback when it exists, leading to the belief that *no one* is against me, overlooking how in fact almost everyone has at least *some* detractors, if not enemies, who at the very least see them in a negative light, and at worst hate them completely.

Retrospective distortion. Paranoid individuals often rewrite their personal history after the fact in order to make past events fit presently desirable adversarial schemata. In a common scenario they become false witnesses to the past to prove their contention that they were and are still being mistreated, emotionally and physically, by their parents, by their community, or by society in general. Not surprisingly, others with a stake in the outcome find it easy and profitable to buy into their already-made distortions and even to convince them—already poised as they are to imagine, or currently imagining, negative things that did not happen—to give false testimony against someone who is in fact innocent as charged. When this happens it is a good idea to consider reclassifying a so-called case of posttraumatic stress disorder due to child abuse as a true case of paranoia due to delusional misinterpretation of the events of the past.

Personalization. Personalization is a primary cognitive error consisting of an egocentric approach to life that catalogs random events as somehow meaningful to the individual. Personalization is a central component of ideas of reference and most persecutory delusions. It is also found in narcissistic grandiose imaginations of centrality and is an element in the deep resentment of paranoid individuals who become litigious after taking impersonal events personally, as when they view a massive layoff at their place of employment that affects and concerns them, but is in no way directed to them individually, as a personal slight.

Rationalization. Paranoid individuals who on one level suspect that their paranoid beliefs are ridiculous use rationalizations to deny the falsity of these beliefs and to legitimize the cognitive errors that go into creating and maintaining them. They make, warmly embrace, and actively advocate excuses, or alibis, for their distorting processes. A common form of rationalization is *universalizing.* Here there is an attempt to convince oneself that everyone sees things the same way, and so unjustified concerns are justified because "we are all alike: we all suspect that a wife or husband is being unfaithful."

The seeking of consensual validation is an important aspect of the process of rationalization. Paranoid individuals need to draw the unwary into their illogic in an attempt to get others to side with them to support and thereby to justify their false beliefs and misguided actions. With this in mind they use the same sophistic logic that they use so successfully to validate their paranoid ideas and to justify their paranoid behavior to themselves, here in an effort to achieve the same results with others. Usually the chosen validators are third parties, but patients sometimes demand a degree of acceptance even from their victims. In either case, the persons called on are in a difficult position, for to agree with a paranoid individual is impossible while to challenge a paranoid individual both makes him or her more anxious and is likely to be interpreted as siding with the enemy. Enhancing their ability to put others into a state of logical shock, and make them believe, is a false reluctance, where they attempt to convince others that their conclusions were arrived at against their better judgment and in spite of their fervent desire to think otherwise.

Actually changing reality is an integral part of the process of rationalization. Paranoid individuals can easily find ways to antagonize enough people to change reality itself so that they eventually can plausibly say, "I told you so. See, I was right all along." The paranoid premise is seemingly validated by circumstances, but it in fact remains invalid because their pessimistic predictions are made to come true by changing the circumstances along desired lines (and by making the pessimistic predictions often enough so that some of them almost have to materialize by chance alone). Changing reality supports the delusional view that the world is a place strictly populated by others who by their actions or inactions have given offense and done harm, and so deserve the retaliative victimization that awaits them at the hands of a justifiably vengeful person who acts—however much with reluctance—responsibly, inevitably, and correctly.

BEHAVIORAL CAUSALITY (PARANOIAGENESIS)

Cooper (1994) has suggested that "paranoia . . . is not a constant, but is a quality that appears under specific conditions of conflict for that patient"

(p. 141). Otto Kernberg (1994) notes specifically that paranoia typically appears or intensifies as a response to the provocative actions of another. He gives the name *paranoiagenesis* (p. 61) to the process whereby the provocative actions of another lead to an individual's paranoid response. By implication, and as discussed throughout, speaking therapeutically, knowing what stirs paranoid individuals up can form the basis for valid but often overlooked interpersonal remedies that are as readily available to the general public as they are to psychotherapists. A wife who understands paranoiagenesis can avoid provoking an already paranoid husband, one who, like most paranoid individuals, cannot tolerate what other people might overlook. Similarly, all of us can identify those individuals who are hypersensitive and prone to hair-trigger anger so that we can avoid incurring their wrath by poking them where it hurts. For example, we can avoid challenging their need to always be right and dominant by not arguing with them, especially about unimportant matters. We can avoid tweaking their readiness to be too easily shamed and humiliated by not doing anything to embarrass them. We can avoid bestirring their problems with feeling controlled, and not play into the serious problems they often have with both dependency gratified and dependency thwarted, by making a correct distancing decision with them so that we neither abandon nor devour them. By being neither too remote nor too friendly, neither too seductive nor too close, we can avoid arousing more anxiety and guilt about their forbidden, unacceptable homosexual or heterosexual sexual impulses than they can comfortably tolerate and handle.

Individuals who are themselves paranoid have two jobs to do. First, they should restrain their paranoia so that they can avoid antagonizing people with their suspiciousness and their distrustfulness. Second, they should be very careful where they go, what they do, and whom they do it with. They should avoid people who, as Cooper (1994) puts it in another context, predictably bring "out prominent paranoid defenses that were otherwise well contained" (p. 144). They should learn to choose their partners wisely. They should learn to seek people who want to have open honest relationships with them and avoid people with hidden agendas that might prove to be disturbing. They should learn to avoid partners who give them a real reason to be suspicious, such as people who cheat on them sexually. They should avoid covertly angry passive-aggressive individuals who infuriate them, then deny that they did it, leaving their victims feeling that they are the ones at fault.

All of us—caretakers of paranoid individuals, victims of paranoid individuals, and paranoid individuals themselves—should remember the following principle: when dealing with paranoia—one's own or that of others—the margin of error is very narrow, while the consequences of making even the slightest mistake are extremely broad.

PART III

Therapy

CHAPTER 12

Psychodynamic/ Interpersonal Approaches

INTRODUCTION

As mentioned throughout, I do not believe that paranoia is invariably a fixed process for which we have little to offer beyond pharmacotherapy. Instead I believe that the widespread conviction that paranoid patients always do poorly in verbal insight-oriented psychotherapy is a myth. Therefore I offer an integrated method for treating paranoia using a combination of psychodynamic (uncovering), interpersonal, cognitive-behavioral, and pharmacotherapeutic techniques.

However, there is no denying that the myth that paranoid patients are unresponsive to verbal psychotherapy has rational underpinnings. It is true that paranoid individuals are generally reluctant to see a psychiatrist, tending rather to seek help, if they seek help at all, from other professionals, such as chiropractors and herbalists. For example, they might consult a massage therapist for a bodily symptom that is in fact a manifestation of paranoia, such as a somatic delusion of neck pain that is the product of a secretly held belief that "rays are penetrating my spine." Unfortunately, on their part, therapists tend to have wide gaps in their understanding of and knowledge about what they can do for paranoid patients, having for years arbitrarily excluded anyone who is paranoid from studies of psychotherapy as well as from psychotherapy itself. Also, therapists tend to be overly pessimistic about the outcome of therapy with patients with a paranoid diagnosis because they diagnose only the most obvious and sicker people as paranoid, and so base their outcome studies exclusively on the results obtained with the least healthy paranoid people, and therefore on those with the worst prognosis.

Such interpersonal theorists as Harry Stack Sullivan (1953) and Frieda Fromm-Reichmann (1960) have described a number of cases of delusional patients responding positively to verbal psychotherapeutic intervention, and Oldham and Andrew E. Skodol (1994) have implied that psychoanalyses can help some paranoid patients: "Paranoia in the form of paranoid personality disorder does not seem to be a contraindication for psychoanalysis" (p. 164). As previously outlined in chapter 11, Karg and Alford (1997) describe sophisticated cognitive therapeutic approaches for successfully managing psychotic states. Information I gleaned from chat groups on the Internet also suggests that, able to speak anonymously, many people recognize that they are unduly suspicious, admit that their suspicions are ruining their lives and the lives of others they are close to, and say how desperate they are to discover what exactly it is that is bothering them, why it troubles them, and what they can do about it. Finally, I have personally treated some paranoid individuals who were sufficiently insightful to know that they might be paranoid and sufficiently curious to undertake an in-depth review of their paranoid beliefs in an attempt to see things differently. Their delusional thinking was not 100 percent fixed and immutable, but was rather subject to correction. Not only were these individuals aware that they were ill, and not only did they have a great deal of curiosity about their illness, but they were also sufficiently intact outside of the delusional process to be able to view their delusions from afar and to question them. For example, using once-a-week psychotherapy I was able to help the patient who believed that an analyst was a Martian spying on her get to the point that she could at least focus away from her paranoid fantasies and instead focus on solving her real problems with everyday living.

Therefore, when it comes to treating individuals who are paranoid, pessimism is an inaccurate generalization that seems at odds with certain data that strongly suggest that verbal psychotherapy has a great deal to offer paranoid patients, and that those who believe otherwise are being unjustifiably fatalistic. That is why I suggest that therapists at least try to treat some paranoid individuals essentially the same way that they treat anyone else with an emotional disorder. Of course, certain modifications are indicated. As we will see, it is necessary to take into account the paranoid individual's special needs and to avoid trampling on his or her special sensitivities, thereby creating undue anxiety and overt hostility, causing the patient to leave treatment, act in or out dangerously, or decompensate into paranoid schizophrenia.

In this and the next few chapters I describe an eclectic treatment approach that consists of the psychodynamic approach with interpersonal focus I describe in this chapter, combined with the cognitive-behavioral approach I describe in chapter 13, modified by the affirmative methods I describe in chapter 14, and sometimes combined with pharmacotherapy as I describe that in chapter 15.

THE PSYCHODYNAMIC/INTERPERSONAL APPROACH

The psychodynamic/interpersonal approach to psychotherapy with paranoid patients emphasizes amelioration though understanding. For some paranoid individuals, understanding is too intellectually difficult or too emotionally trying. For others it is both doable and helpful. The latter group can benefit from replacing emotional and therefore inaccurate and unrealistic thinking with logical and therefore accurate and realistic thinking by

- identifying their delusional thinking/frank delusions
- isolating their delusional constructs and viewing them dispassionately from afar
- understanding the intrapsychic and experiential factors that help explain why they think delusionally—thereby translating their delusions into human terms to become phenomena understandable in the light of past developments and present interpersonal interactions

In terms of past developments, as Lorna Smith Benjamin (1996) suggests, the therapist helps the patient remember early pathogenic experiences that led to present-day "expectations of attack and abusive control" (p. 336) and to recognize that while these expectations are understandable, they are "not always appropriate because not every environment is the same" (p. 336). In terms of present interactions, the patient benefits from identifying the interpersonal context in which his or her delusional thinking appears. As Benjamin suggests, a patient "alerted to how his or her [paranoid] patterns are worse with contact with the persons or situations similar to those in which the patterns were generated" (p. 337) learns to "not read his or her own fearful affect as proof that others have attacking intent" (p. 337). Also, as Benjamin suggests, the patient needs to learn that "hostility begets hostility . . . attack and alienation" (p. 336). In the most favorable outcome the patient no longer thinks delusionally. In a less favorable outcome the delusions persist in some form, but they no longer negatively affect the patient's personal life and professional activity, at least to the same extent as formerly.

As with other patients, some of the beneficial effects of therapy can be the result of what is in effect a transference cure. This can come about simply from patients allying themselves with the therapist as someone who treats them like a human being with hope, not as a pathological entity to be described, classified, and then drugged to the point of submissive recanting.

However, therapists should almost certainly not treat *seriously* ill paranoid patients, delusional or nondelusional, with psychoanalysis done with the patient lying on a couch. Seriously ill paranoid patients already turn the whole world into a blank screen. They therefore do not need a therapist who deliberately assumes that posture. That does not mean that psychoanalytically oriented techniques are not suitable for treating specific delusions or delusional thinking in general. It does, however, mean that for patients who are seriously paranoid these techniques must be adapted for less invasive face-to-face therapy.

When doing face-to-face therapy, the therapist must especially avoid

- Uncovering too much too soon, especially dredging up too many old, painful childhood memories prematurely—before the patient trusts the therapist, and before he or she feels up to reexperiencing the original terror associated with early traumatic experiences.

- Challenging and arguing with the patient, especially with the patient's delusions. However, though I mention this caveat repeatedly, I believe that as a cautionary statement it is somewhat overdone, because there are some patients who are up to, and do not mind, such challenges. Paranoid individuals do, after all, tend to enjoy arguing. Of course, it is unwise to disabuse the patient of his or her central protective notions too directly and too soon. Therefore, as Karg and Alford (1997) recommend, it is often a good idea to start by modifying "those beliefs that are the least strongly held" (p. 330).

- Being overly critical, especially when that involves humiliating the patient about sensitive matters such as latent homosexuality.

- Kidding the patient. These are essentially humorless individuals who do not take kindly to being joshed about anything, no matter how trivial the topic and minor its import.

Here is a step-by-step approach I follow when doing psychodynamic psychotherapy with paranoid patients. I first establish that the patient's problem is one of being paranoid. I next tell the patient that I believe that his or her paranoia does not appear in a vacuum, but is rather a human condition that occurs in the context of specific interactions, particularly those that arouse anxiety-laden conflicts by stirring up wishes that are unacceptable because they make the patient feel guilty and ashamed. I ask my patients to be alert to possible anxiety-laden conflicts within themselves, to identify the nature and manifestations of those conflicts, including their manifestations in the transference, and to work with me to bring these conflicts to a better resolution, one that at the very least falls short of requiring a serious distortion of reality.

To illustrate, some years ago a formerly hospitalized patient with almost no friends or even acquaintances bought dirty movies in Times Square, then, convinced that the board of the cooperative apartment in which he lived would find out that he had them and evict him from his apartment, deposited them out of sight in his safe deposit vault, only to later sneak back to get them, then once again redeposit them in the vault, and so on—doing this literally for days on end. I explained that he appeared to be in conflict between his sexuality and an overly rigid morality, and while he should have been resolving this conflict he was instead expressing it exactly, by first watching dirty movies, then cleaning up after himself by locking up the evidence. I then suggested that we attempt to resolve his conflict by reducing his guilt, that is, by resolving his conflict on the side of the superego. I said that I thought that in a general way he was being unduly hard on himself and reminded him that "you are human just like the rest of us. No one is as bad as you think you are. Besides, I believe that you fear and internalize others' criticisms of you because you forget that those who criticize other people almost always have their own problems, and personal, often hidden, agendas." After some weeks of this approach, he became able to watch his movies without having to conceal the evidence soon afterwards. A few weeks after that he completely lost interest in watching them because as they became less forbidden they also became less intriguing.

It would have been too much to expect that his guilty sexual fantasies would simply go away completely. Instead, more or less as anticipated, they shifted over to involve me. This was a fortuitous development, since the shift provided me with transference material that I could use to show him how his paranoid mind worked. For example, he said that he wanted to quit therapy because he feared that I was trying to seduce him, which he knew to be the case because once he caught me looking at his crotch. I helped him change his mind about that by showing him that he was projecting, making me the repository of his own guilty sexual wishes and turning his self-criticisms into criticisms of me, condemning me for having the same forbidden sexual desires toward him that he condemned in himself. I then suggested that he apply what we just learned to his daily life and relationships. Ultimately, he was able to stop thinking that others were being difficult when they were in fact being supportive. He was even able to attend a cooking class where he developed a few friendships, one of which led to an actual romance.

In another case, a new patient, a psychologist, upon entering my office for the first time asked me which of two chairs he should sit in, an in-reality grossly inappropriate question since the location of my chair was obvious because it was a swivel chair clearly meant to be situated behind my desk. I said nothing, but the patient, realizing his mistake, said he thought he saw a disapproving look on my face. Shortly afterward he decided to rent an office for his own practice right across the street from mine. He then felt guilty about competing with me and expressed that guilt in the first words he spoke to me upon entering my office the session after he signed the new lease: "You are angry with me for trying to muscle in on your territory." First I pointed out, "You are clearly projecting, for to be angry with you I would have to be a mind reader, because until you just told me about it I didn't even know that you had a new office." Then we learned that confusion about chairs and guilt about leasing suitable office space represented his forbidden desire to overthrow me, ultimately an oedipal wish, expressed and gratified symbolically but with a great deal of shame. He then spoke of how he had a history of competing with authority. He had always tried to be number one, yet he always pulled back at the last minute because he became guiltily self-critical, and because he became highly anxious due to a fear that authority would retaliate and strike back by criticizing, rejecting, and in effect castrating him. After about a year's worth of discussions of various aspects of this topic, it finally dawned on him emotionally that he responded this way over and over again, and how as a result at every turn he stalled his professional career and strangled his personal relationships just to obtain an illusory sense of personal comfort.

When analyzing paranoid phenomena as they appear in the transference, I often extend reassurances to the patient as I go along to help him or her avoid disorganizing anxiety/fall in self-esteem. For example, after explaining projection I might add, "We all project to some extent." I am also selective in choosing what transference clarifications I offer. I have found that discussions of issues of dependency, control, and competitiveness are likely to produce a lot less anxiety than discussions of sexualized and angry feelings toward the therapist.

Therapists should be very careful to wait until the patient is ready (if the patient is ever ready) before uncovering conflicts about homosexuality. Patients can usually accept their forbidden heterosexuality better than they can accept their forbidden homosexuality. It is usually easier for a bisexual man to accept that he condemns his wife for cheating on him with another man because he is projecting onto her his forbidden desire to cheat on her with another woman, than it is for a man to accept that he condemns his wife for cheating on him with another man because he is projecting onto her his own forbidden desire to cheat on her with her male lover.

Raw anger is almost always best left unexposed. Most therapists recognize that paranoia is a product of rage. But most also recognize the wisdom of doing nothing to further arouse that rage, or, if the rage is already aroused, of not trying to bring it to the surface and get it all out. Therapists should not tell paranoid patients to "get your anger out of your system, it's good for you." Instead defenses against anger should be thoroughly respected and some healthy ones, like sublimation ("punch a punching bag if you feel you are losing control and cannot sit tight"), if not encouraged then at least not countermanded.

In my experience, I have had even sicker, difficult-to-analyze paranoid patients respond satisfactorily to Benjamin's technique of illuminating the specific interpersonal and social context in which their paranoid thinking appears and intensifies. These highly delusional patients have benefited from learning, as Cooper (1994) says, how their "Paranoia is not a constant but is a quality that appears under specific conditions of conflict for [them]" (p. 141). I have found it especially useful to help paranoid individuals identify and manage their pet peeves—people and situations that they find especially stressful. Not all paranoid individuals have the same ones. A careful history, an understanding of the role played by character pathology, for example, an identification of the narcissistic element that leads a patient to feel that "no one criticizes me and gets away with it," along with insightful transference interpretations have helped determine what interpersonal peeves bother paranoid individuals the most and ultimately what specific coping mechanisms are available for the person. Thus an individual whose paranoia is fired by feeling abandoned will likely become paranoid under very different circumstances than an individual whose paranoia is fired by any hint of the arousal of dependency wishes and with those the possibility of being taken over and devoured. In the news recently was a case of a man who walked over to a young woman and asked her if she were working as a call girl. She replied to this obvious (to me) attempt at a sexual contact by laughing at him. He then, apparently taking offense, slashed her with a knife around the face and head. For this man a specific troublesome situation, or landmine, might have been "being rebuffed and criticized for your sexual desires." For other paranoid individuals other specific interpersonal interactions are more of a threat. Paranoid individuals who learn specifically what triggers their paranoia seem to be able to remain calmer by circumventing or avoiding certain specific stressful interpersonal contacts, at least as much as their reality permits.

What is Joe's trigger?!

Unfortunately, these difficult patients almost always provoke negative countertransference responses in the most patient and well-meaning therapist. Therapists who find the constricted, preoccupied thinking of paranoid patients boring or off-putting and who cannot hide their impatience with or dislike of them should consider referring these patients on. Should serious negative countertransference responses occur in spite of all precautions, therapists should not try to hide them, because paranoid patients almost always seem to correctly divine (although in distorted form) the negative things that their therapist is thinking and feeling. As Benjamin (1996) notes, "Because the PAR [paranoid individual] probably has a history of indirect condemnation in the family, any therapist discomfort is best disclosed discreetly and constructively" (p. 337). As an example, she offers the following interchange. If the patient has a temper tantrum, then asks, "Were you frightened by me?" the therapist should say something like, "Yes, [and] if that happens again, we will have to terminate the session immediately, and find a way to work differently with this. Perhaps I will have to bring in a colleague to help and maybe we will need to meet in a different location" (pp. 337–338). (As I mention several times in this text, therapists should never do therapy in a place where the patient feels uncomfortable, such as some out-of-the-way spot where the patient, isolated from the mainstream, is likely to think, "It's just me and you, and who knows what will come of that.")

However, there is a fine line to be walked here too. When therapists confess, in favorable cases patients appreciate the honesty of the response and can theoretically at least learn how others react to them and so how to behave differently. But in unfavorable cases patients see the therapist as weak and vulnerable, and feel disdainful. Or they feel so threatened by learning of the newly detailed effects of their own behavior that they quit therapy, giving reasons for doing so other than the most pressing one, which remains hidden and generally goes unrecognized—to protect the therapist from themselves.

CHAPTER 13

Cognitive-Behavioral Therapy

AN OVERVIEW

Cognitive therapists, working, like most therapists, in a setting of building rapport and offering emotional support, focus on changing illogical thinking that negatively affects behavior, anticipating one of two possible outcomes. In the more favorable outcome, patients are helped to think less delusionally. In the less favorable outcome, patients continue to think delusionally (and even continue to hallucinate), but they now view their delusions (and hallucinations) from afar and respond to them in a less disruptive way.

According to Karg and Alford (1997), speaking of cognitive-behavioral therapy for patients who are psychotic in terms that are equally applicable to paranoid individuals who are not psychotic, cognitive-behavioral therapy involves a "collaborative enterprise between the patient and the therapist" (p. 327). In the following discussion I first describe a dedicated cognitive-behavioral collaborative enterprise, then discuss a wider eclectic approach that combines cognitive and behavioral methods with other therapeutic modalities.

COGNITIVE METHODS

General Considerations

First, cognitive therapists should avoid confronting the patient with his or her erroneous thinking in an unsupportive way, imparting negative meanings concerning the self by challenging the patient's delusional thinking abrasively, thus conveying an attitude that is antithetical to the patient's positive self-view. As Karg and Alford (1997) suggest, to correct delusional thinking without imparting "negative reactions" (p. 324), cognitive therapists should *test*, not *challenge*, the patients' beliefs (p. 335). Thus, maladaptive interpretations and conclusions should be viewed not as misguided ideas but as hypotheses that may or may not be capable of being validated scientifically.

Second, cognitive therapists should consider helping the patient eliminate cognitive errors in the context in which they actually arise, that is, in the field, by giving the patient homework assignments. For example, cognitive-behavioral therapists often ask their patients to keep a journal, recording specific instances when negative thoughts arise along with possible alternative, more positive interpretations of a given incident.

As discussed in chapter 11, one can correct specific cognitive errors that form a component of paranoid cognition both *indirectly* and *directly*.

Correcting specific cognitive errors can be done *indirectly* by focusing on their troubled origin, particularly by helping reduce the emotional component of the irrational thinking. For example, many paranoid patients think negatively and pessimistically after overresponding catastrophically to insignificant negative cues. These patients can catastrophize less if they recognize and do not overlook the positive ameliorating context in which others' negativity is embedded.

Correcting specific cognitive errors can be done *directly* by in effect showing paranoid individuals how to think more clearly, precisely, and realistically. As Karg and Alford (1997) suggest, patients should be asked to view their thoughts and beliefs as "constructions of reality rather than as reality itself" (p. 331). As Millon and Davis (1996) suggest, goals include directly modifying basic assumptions and "core beliefs and schemas that others cannot be trusted and will intentionally try to hurt" (p 725). In a virtuous cycle, that approach helps "diminish hypersensitivity to social evaluation" (p. 725), which in turn helps patients "let go of [their] rigid defensive structure" (p. 726), and that in turn can "free up energy to use to acquire more satisfying interpersonal relationships" (p. 726).

Specific Techniques

Karg and Alford (1997) suggest that patients start off by challenging only those beliefs that are the least strongly held. Millon and Davis (1996) suggest focusing on exploring "alternative explanations. . . to shift the weight of probability . . . to . . . alternative hypotheses [with the goal of] introduce[ing] an element of doubt" (p. 725) about the old false hypotheses and so-called proofs. Karg and Alford sometimes ask their patients to challenge "the evidence for [a] belief, as opposed to the belief itself" (p. 330), and sometimes to subject the beliefs themselves to methods of "empirical investigation, reality testing, and problem-solving" (p. 323). They have patients rationally distance themselves from their irrational thoughts by playing the part of the "practical scientist" (p. 327), exploring and modifying unrealistic or unreasonable dysfunctional interpretations (p. 327) that distort the external situation.

Millon and Davis (1996) encourage patients to gather additional information from the environment so that they may explore how "closely [their] conclusions match the available evidence" (p. 726) and so that they can "reevaluate . . . assumptions about others [so that] the use of self-protective withdrawals may decrease" (p. 723) after patients "see that most fears are imaginary and invalid" (p. 723). Karg and Alford (1997) also suggest that patients "support . . . more adaptive beliefs" (p. 324) by paying more attention to whether others agree or disagree with their interpretations of events. As Millon and Davis suggest, patients should be specifically asked to relinquish the tendency to "counter the efforts of others to correct or otherwise influence their misinterpretation of events" (p. 693).

Millon and Davis also ask patients to "review . . . their past experiences" (p. 725) so that they can understand how maladaptive it is to view a current situation strictly in terms of past experience and so that they can see that "past beliefs of danger have not . . . proven true" (p. 725).

Finally, as mentioned in chapter 11, Karg and Alford (1997) suggest that therapists correct their patients' faulty self-concepts by helping them revise "misconceptions and unclarities regarding the identity of the self" (p. 326) ranging from "somatic perceptual distortions" (p. 326) to the inability to "distinguish [oneself] from another person" (p. 326), leading to merging with associated loss of boundaries and identity.

Here are some positive consequences of correcting specific cognitive errors.

Of Correcting Dichotomous Thinking

Paranoid individuals who learn to stop thinking dichotomously along the lines of "If I am not all good then I am all bad" or "If he or she does not completely approve of me that means that he or she completely disapproves of me" will be less likely to feel impelled to go to extremes to prove that they are not bad people. Therefore, they will be less likely to have to twist things around to convince themselves that they are good people. So they will be less likely to deal with their self-condemnatory thoughts and actions by seeing and condemning these thoughts and actions in others, and less likely to deal with their low self-esteem by overshooting to the point that they become grandiose in order to convince themselves that they are not worse but better than everyone else.

Of Correcting von Domarus Thinking

Paranoid individuals who relinquish von Domarus thinking—for example, "I am English; George Frederic Handel was English; therefore I am the composer of *The Messiah*"—will be less likely to develop delusions of grandeur.

Of Correcting the Tendency to Personalize

Paranoid individuals who personalize less will be less likely to develop ideas of reference characterized by the belief that neutral parties—people who do not care about them one way or the other—are saying bad things about them. They will not follow the example of the patient who, because it was freezing outside, made a stylistic exception and wore a cheap polyester pullover to an elegant restaurant just to keep out the cold, then spent the entire meal unable to eat because he could not shake the intrusive thought that the people at the next table had him in their sights and were pointing him out, staring and laughing at him.

Of Correcting Part-to-Whole Errors/Errors of Selective Abstraction

Paranoid individuals who make fewer part-to-whole logical errors and selectively abstract less will be better able to trust more because they will be less likely to see only the destructive aspects of a relationship and more likely to see and fully appreciate the whole relationship, including its constructive aspects.

Of Correcting Similar Equals the Same Thing Errors

Paranoid individuals who recognize that similar things are not the same thing will be less inclined to make invidious comparisons that result in troubled relationships. They will be less likely to become like the reviewer who compared me to a Nazi because I suggested that there was a genetic basis to behavior, which to him meant not that I was thinking about genetics but that I was advocating Hitler-style eugenics.

BEHAVIORAL METHODS

In selected cases, I recommend reducing anxiety and defensiveness using significant protective removal. I recommend different degrees of protective removal for different patients, depending on the nature and extent of their interpersonal anxiety and whether they are currently involved in specific interpersonal relationships that are either making them paranoid or are making their paranoia worse.

I discovered that some of my paranoid patients could not cope with their paranoia successfully unless they stayed away from most or all of the difficult people in their lives. This was the only way that they could feel adequately protected from their own unacceptable feelings and from having others criticize them for having those feelings. So they became difficult remote people who, so to speak, traveled alone. True, they become mountain men, living in shacks in the hills, sprouting long beards, wearing dirty overalls, and carrying shotguns. But at least they stayed out of the mental hospital.

Paranoid states that are part of a folie à deux (induced or shared paranoia)—where the so-called paranoia of one is predominantly a reaction of a highly suggestible individual to the actual paranoia of another, due to blindly buying into the paranoid pronouncements of a persuasive friend or family member, a charismatic cultist, or a mesmerizing, grandiosely delusional politician, then unthinkingly following along—usually require complete or almost complete distancing from the slick but sick companion or leader. In some cases children and adolescents who refuse to voluntarily remove themselves from such a pathological interaction need to be forcefully recaptured by their parents or by someone the parents hire to do that job for them.

However, in many cases adequate healing can still take place if patients merely constrict their relationships. They can still relate to one close friend only, or to only a few family members, while avoiding the most difficult people in their lives, such as people who are passive-aggressive or who cheat on them sexually.

This said, many paranoid individuals who want to relate and are potentially capable of relating can get better while continuing to relate widely. Such individuals can often benefit from learning how to act healthy even though they remain paranoid. They can learn to first identify their delusions, then put them on the back burner with the goal of acting well even though they remain ill. Now, instead of acting angry or suspicious or otherwise living out delusions or hallucinations, they can at least maintain a semblance of getting along with other people professionally, personally, and socially. As a paradigm, many years ago in Boston a number of hospitalized patients who were actively hallucinating were given evening passes to leave the hospital grounds to attend the symphony. There was but one proviso: during the concert they were asked to hear out their voices silently and postpone responding to them until after the final chord had sounded. Whether we are aware of it or not, many of us handle our own paranoia just this way—by training ourselves to remain calm on the outside and to behave in an acceptable social manner even in anxiety-provoking and paranoia-inducing situations. We accomplish this by using a little bit of insight and a great deal of self-control. To illustrate, I have had friends as well as patients who suspected their spouses of being unfaithful, yet wondered if they were imagining it. So on their own they decided to sleep on their fantasies before saying anything about or acting on them, and often wound up saying and doing nothing at all—that way keeping the peace and maintaining the relationship.

As Karg and Alford (1997) suggest, this group of patients tends to benefit a great deal from "us[ing] behavioral experiments . . . to examine alternative interpretations and to generate contradictory evidence that supports more adaptive beliefs" (pp. 323–324). Role-playing can help them correct their cognitive errors by putting the errors to a kind of controlled field test, providing feedback. As Benjamin (1996) suggests, role-playing can supply "excursions into the social world to test the idea that friendly approaches elicit friendly reactions" (p. 341). As Millon and Davis (1996) suggest, role-playing can help patients "explore the benefits of being alone versus having intimate relationships . . . [getting them to] accept that interactions with others may actually have something positive to offer" (p. 725). Role-playing can help paranoid individuals eliminate inappropriate behaviors by helping them discover, as Karg and Alford (1997) put it, "which particular verbalizations and behavior are appropriate [and which are inappropriate] for a particular situation" (p. 331), that is, by helping them determine if they are or are not behaving in a maladaptive, off-putting manner incompatible with satisfactory, rewarding interpersonal relationships. It can also help foster a more empathic attitude, as patients, as Millon and Davis (1996) quoting Benjamin suggest, "recall how it felt to be abused" (p. 725)—part of "anticipat[ing] the impact of . . . actions on others and . . . imagin[ing] what it would feel like to be in their shoes" (p. 726). It can also help patients, as Millon and Davis suggest, to become "less defensive and to inhibit expressions of hostility" (p. 727). In effect, patients who role-play effectively learn what paranoid attitudes and ideation to hide, how and when to hide them, and sensible alternatives to expressing them.

To illustrate, at the gym a patient, without any more provocation than the other man's saying "good morning" to him, told the other man that obviously he envied the patient because all the girls spoke to the patient and none to him. I asked the patient, "How would you feel if someone treated you that way," in preparation for telling him that "if you cannot say anything nice, you should not say anything at all." The patient, realizing what I was getting at, was subsequently able to push a number of his minor antagonisms aside, though he still had them, and to decide, to great personal and social benefit, that "from now on I will at least not act so paranoid."

Direct educational methods can also help. As Millon and Davis (1996) suggest, when "appropriate skills to contend with the situation are lacking, interventions that cultivate coping skills [can be offered to] increase self-efficacy" (p. 725). For example, because paranoid individuals generally "overestimate the threat posed by [a] situation [and] underestimate their capacity to solve the problem" (p. 725), it is often therapeutic to "promote a more realistic appraisal of coping ability [to] increase sense of self-efficacy" (p. 725). I suggested that the patient I just described recognize that his complaints that others disliked him were partly reality-based, a product of his having gotten quite a bad reputation around town for his difficult and strange behavior. I went on to detail what I thought that was and to reassure him that and show him how he could do something about it. I suggested that he stop preaching at others—strongly reminding him that other people resented being criticized for supposed defects no matter how lofty his reasons and how correct his negative presumptions. I asked him to stop broadcasting his paranoia by carrying a big black umbrella on sunny days and by looking around suspiciously to see who was watching him as he strolled along, fearful that his hips were swinging so much that others might think that he was queer. I suggested that he stop shrinking in horror from people because he believed that any approach on their part was an attempt to touch his genitals, so that he first flinched then haughtily stepped back when others came near. I asked him to censor what came to his mind, not to say everything he thought. For example, he once left a message on his brother's answering machine: "Call me with the plumber's phone number. I don't want to ask mother for it; she will only pick on me, and don't call me on my personal phone either—leave your message on my wife's business phone." I suggested that instead he simply tell his brother where to leave the message and stop right there.

AN ECLECTIC APPROACH

David P. Bernstein (2002) describes a form of eclectic therapy he calls "schematherapy." This is, as Bernstein suggests, "an integrative form of treatment that combines cognitive, psychodynamic, experiential/humanistic, and behavioral techniques" (p. 627). It starts with an assessment and "case conceptualization [which is] shared with the patient" (p. 627) "Cognitive restructuring [is then employed to] counter distorted beliefs regarding unworthiness, deprivation, mistrust, and other schemas; imagery exercises to release emotions and counter faulty inferences regarding [past] experiences [are employed and] homework assignments [are given to] counter avoidance and isolation, and to provide more effective means of self-soothing" (p. 627). The therapeutic relationship "with limited reparenting [provides the patient with a] corrective emotional experience within appropriate boundaries" (p. 627). Also "empathic confrontation [is used where the therapist] point[s] out the patient's self-defeating or destructive behavior while maintaining an attitude of acceptance toward the patient" (p. 627). Additionally, patients are asked to be responsible for changing their behaviors by "institut[ing] healthier forms of coping" (p. 628).

COGNITIVE-BEHAVIORAL APPROACHES ADAPTED FOR CARETAKERS

As we will see in chapter 18 on the caretaking of individuals who are paranoid, victims who understand how paranoid individuals distort cognitively and recognize that they have a great deal of difficulty doing any better will be better positioned to cope successfully and will be less likely to respond counteraggressively in an unnecessarily hostile fashion. For one thing, caretakers who recognize paranoid ideation and behavior as the specific product of a disturbed mind can take paranoid distortions less personally and instead quietly disregard them as they would disregard anything else obviously irrational. That way they can avoid getting angry with paranoid individuals, in turn provoking them to become even angrier and more defensive than before.

Caretakers can themselves do a form of behavior therapy with the paranoid people in their lives. For example, they can give the patient what I call the "positive silent treatment." This method avoids starting and perpetuating vicious cycles of progressively intensifying paranoia by restraining one's tendency to lash out in response to being provoked, instead stifling the temptation to reply in an angry way to various paranoid provocations. Caretakers can also learn to act in a helpfully supportive, reassuring way with paranoid individuals in distortive crises. I know of many cases where a spouse helped a paranoid person get over acute delusions of jealousy by reassuring him or her verbally, over and over again until it stuck, that "you have nothing to worry about," then backing that up, as one spouse did, by being easily traceable all day long or, when roaming, by offering 100 percent accountability for those unavoidably paranoiagenic temporary moments of separation that still made her husband suspicious, even though the husband recognized that they were both necessary and desirable and that it was incorrect for him to feel as if his wife were up to something bad just because she was out of touch with him for more than a few minutes.

CHAPTER 14

Affirmative Psychotherapy

Many authors have noted that paranoid patients are generally reluctant to see mental health practitioners, particularly psychiatrists. In my opinion, paranoid patients are reluctant not only, as is often charged, because of their illness-related reticence, shyness, and suspiciousness, but also because they know—from what they have heard from other patients or from personal experience—exactly what awaits them. Unfortunately, it is true that when it comes to treating paranoid patients, professionals partly deserve their bad reputation. In fact, when it comes to treating paranoid patients, mental health practitioners have a distressingly bad track record. Not fully understanding what paranoid individuals want and need, professionals have dealt with them improperly, confirming their worst fears about seeking and undergoing therapy. Then, in their own true paranoid fashion, professionals have added insult to injury by blaming their patients' unfavorable therapeutic responses not on therapy itself but on the patients' presumed refusal to accept treatment or, when they have accepted it, on their presumed inability to use it properly.

Partly the bad track record is due to the nonaffirmative nature of the psychotherapy that therapists have offered their paranoid patients. As a remedy I propose treating paranoid patients using a form of therapy called affirmative therapy. This form of therapy was originally popularized as a method for treating gay men and lesbians. It has two major goals. One is, according to Graz Kowszun and Maeve Malley (1996), avoiding reinforcing negativity with "highly damning psychoanalytic and medical explanations" (p. 175). Another is, according to Carlton Cornett (1993), focusing away from "psychotherapy as a neutral or interpretative enterprise [and instead focusing onto psychotherapy's] capacity to affirm the patient" (pp. xii–xiii). I believe that, the antiestablishment tone in the first of these formulations aside, affirmative therapy is potentially as helpful for paranoid patients as it is for gays and lesbians. It works well for paranoid patients partly because most of them come for treatment in a state of personal deaffirmation. Therefore, they are likely to benefit a great deal from a form of treatment that, as much as possible, bypasses the critical and controlling elements inherent in classic psychotherapy (elements that are invariably present in such therapy, however well-meaning the therapist) and instead offers the patient as wholly positive an experience as is possible in a legitimate psychotherapeutic setting, as Benjamin (1996) suggests, "support[ing] and affirm[ing] the PAR for quite a while" (p. 332) and "offering the patient understanding . . . when he or she is embattled" (p. 336).

The therapist offers the patient a positive experience by

- Simply agreeing to see the patient in therapy, sending the powerful message, "I accept you."

- Offering regular therapeutic sessions that act as an antidote to the loneliness that plagues so many paranoid individuals and leads them to conclude that "if I am lonely it must be because no one wants me." For example, one lonely patient's delusion that his neighbors were spying on him was in fact his way to express a hidden desire to be the center of their attention, as if he had a family "looking out for him." His delusional thinking diminished when his therapist offered him ongoing, minimally threatening, noncritical, once-a-month contact. That helped diminish his sense of isolation in part because it meant that there was at least one person in the world who did not devalue, diminish, reject, or desire to abandon him. In a parallel case, a neighbor savaged the child next door for looking at the birds in her feeder, telling her, in no uncertain terms, to "stop looking at *my* birds." What the neighbor was really complaining about was that the child was almost physically "sucking up" what little the neighbor could call her own and had left in life. A steady regular therapeutic relationship helped the neighbor tolerate the child's "competing with me for my birds," to the point that she welcomed the child's sharing and even encouraged the child to share "her" birds with her.

- Not buying into negative myths, particularly the one that says that "because this person is crazy, nothing I do makes a difference." A paranoid patient, like anyone else with an emotional disorder, should not be made to feel that he or she is now, and will be for the rest of his or her life, just another classic textbook case who can never get better and is even doomed to get worse.

- Offering positive feedback unalloyed by too much of anything that can be perceived to be confronting, critical, humiliating, blaming, or demeaning and instead offering what Benjamin (1996) calls "tender, noncoercive holding" (p. 336), which includes "accurate empathy, [and] genuine affirmation of accomplishments" (p. 336), recognizing assets over liabilities, abilities over disabilities, and positive over negative characteristics.

- Offering a corrective emotional experience—enveloping the patient in a noncritical, supportive, therapeutic holding environment, what Benjamin (1996) refers to as a "soothing" (p. 336) milieu.

- Relieving the low self-esteem that is characteristically found in paranoid individuals. This low self-esteem is both the cause and the product of the paranoid individual's sensitivity and vulnerability to criticism, humiliation, and rejection, and leads to one of the worst problems paranoid patients have—as Benjamin notes, "the PAR's need to be affirmed by [his or her] abusers [so that when] the PAR is degraded and extruded, he or she [fails] to recognize it for what it is and [instead] 'take[s] it to heart'" (p. 339). Relief comes not only from determining and isolating the early experiences that have left the patient feeling put down, but also from offering the paranoid individual a direct antidote in the form of a new, expert, professional reassessment of the patient's true personal worth. Enhanced self-esteem in turn leads to progressively developing self-confidence, increased by real personal and professional successes, however small to start, that have in turn become possible because of the patient's enhanced self-pride and newly developing willingness to take emotional and practical chances.

SOME AFFIRMATIVE TECHNIQUES

A cardinal rule of affirmative therapy is that all reality testing must be done gently, without blaming, without getting into an argument or into a contest of wills, and without appearing to be checking up or spying on the patient. Most (but not all) paranoid individuals view reality testing as disagreeing with, challenging, and thereby symbolically rejecting them. That bruises their narcissism, diminishes their positive sense of self, and increases their feelings of loneliness and isolation as they come to view the therapist as just another one of their evil eyes. Therefore, in the very beginning, before full rapport is established, I often respond to delusional ideation in a noncommittal way, by saying, "We will see," in effect saying, "Right or wrong is yet to be determined." That calms the patient down at least temporarily, while still leaving the door open for what will sooner or later become the necessary review of the patient's distortive notions, with the goal of helping him or her think more rationally and logically. I then leave it up to the patient to decide when he or she is ready to do some serious reality testing. I might say, "Let's not discuss these ideas of yours any further now. You are not yet ready for that. When you feel ready let me know. When the time is right we can start reviewing your conclusions, but we won't do that until you say that you feel up to it."

When direct reality testing does eventually take place, it should proceed slowly, cautiously, and in a stepwise fashion, keeping in mind that with paranoid individuals, the timing of what the therapist says is often as important as the content. I often find it helpful to go about reality testing indirectly. I carefully avoid saying or implying "You are wrong about that," as in "It is incorrect to think that everyone has you in their sights." That only says to the patient, "Your ideas and you are silly, and your fears are nonsensical." Instead I accomplish essentially the same thing by the back door of offering reassurance. I reassure the patient that "in my opinion, as you describe them, the actual circumstances do not seem to be as dangerous as you imagine them to be, so that things are not as bad as they might at first appear. Therefore, you can stop being so defensive and instead just sit back and relax." In like manner, instead of criticizing the patient for always imagining danger I reassure him or her that "you are safe" and that "you do not have to worry so much because people aren't as antagonistic to you as you might think." Instead of saying, "You are just imagining that he is your enemy," I say reassuringly, "Even the people you believe dislike you the most are probably just too wrapped up in themselves to think about harming you." Instead of telling patients that their suspicions of others are overblown and unjustified, I reassure them that their alarms are unnecessary and to a great extent originate with the feeling that they deserve the mistreatment that they believe that they are getting. Helping things along considerably are transference reassurances such as, "I'm not singling you out by telling you this, for we are all somewhat sensitive to criticism, and we all fear not being loved." Specific, alternative, more positive explanations for what the patient views as adversarial situations can also be helpfully reassuring. Is someone who reads an article in the *New York Times*, then says with a degree of surprise, "It says just what you said," really devaluing you by only taking you seriously after he or she finds out that the experts agree, or is he or she just impressed by the consensus? Did that policeman deliberately try to brutalize you, or did he or she just make an innocent mistake? Does complimenting you for one thing really mean subtly criticizing you for another? Is someone being critical of you or simply offering you good advice—that is, does advising you to do something imply that you are being condemned for not having done it, or for planning to do something stupid? As Benjamin (1996) puts it, therapists can be reassuring if they "Highlight . . . benevolent . . . behaviors [of others], so that the PAR cannot simply dismiss or ignore them as he or she is inclined to do" (p. 336).

Affirmative therapists must be especially vigilant about not belittling or humiliating their patients with gentle kidding. The day a patient arrived home from a year-long trip, he asked his neighbor to return a lock the neighbor had borrowed before the patient went away. The patient had brooded all year long about whether the neighbor would give him the lock back. The therapist kidded the patient for being such an alarmist and for having nothing better to worry about than a lock. As a result of this interchange the patient felt belittled. This patient already knew that he was being suspicious and hypersensitive and was ashamed of himself, but was unable to control himself. So he saw the therapist's comments as validating his own negative self-view and perceived the therapist as his enemy. How much better it might have been if the therapist had been perceptive enough to avoid all semblance of confrontation disguised as humor. Instead the therapist might have been sympathetic. That could have been done very simply by saying, "Many people tend to brood about losing small things, even though they aren't worth much."

Some affirmative therapists find it helpful to compliment the patient directly. Because paranoid patients, no matter how grandiose they appear to be, at bottom hate themselves, occasional compliments, as long as they are not exploitative or insincere, can go at least some of the way toward reducing the feelings of inadequacy that plague these individuals and lead them to blame and criticize others as a defense mechanism put into place so that they themselves can feel less inadequate. For example, I might say something like, "There are some good things about your paranoia. Your hypersensitivity makes you a good detective (lawyer, psychoanalyst, writer, politician), doesn't it?"

Affirmative therapists recognize that most paranoid individuals are so sensitive that one mistake with them is too many. Therefore, affirmative therapists recognize that it is a bad idea to be too spontaneous with them and that it is a good idea to think twice before saying something that afterwards the therapist might regret having said. The affirmative therapist simply accepts that with these patients you cannot say the first thing that comes to mind but must instead screen your thoughts before passing them on. A patient quit therapy for the following, in reality, trivial reason that, however, held a great deal of meaning for this particular individual. Her therapist called to leave a message that an appointment hour had to be changed. When the patient did not return the phone call immediately, the therapist called her back and left her another message, gently chiding her for not calling to confirm. Therapists must even be cautious when attempting to be supportive of paranoid patients. Even comments meant to be empathic and otherwise positive can provoke a strong negative response in these hypersensitive individuals. For example, a patient took it the wrong way when her therapist, assuming that he was offering her desirable sympathy, said, "You must be very worried." All she heard was a statement that she had something to be very worried about. She would have felt much more reassured if he had instead said, "Stop worrying about nothing."

Affirmative therapists work hard to build basic trust between themselves and their patients. The trust-building process can take a long time in, just as it can outside of, the therapy situation. Trust-building is dedicated work, and not every therapist has the inclination or personality for it. It is most likely to be successful with paranoid individuals who become temporarily paranoid about one thing in particular, brood about it for a day or two, then get over it. A patient's experience with his real estate agent exemplifies the trust-building process with patients who are temporarily paranoid about something specific. This patient was looking for property in a rehabilitation zone in a New Jersey town. Each day he went to the area and checked on its progress. When he saw none, he believed that his agent was trying to put one over on him, and called the agent up to find out "what is going on." The agent, a sensitive woman who had a native ability to recognize a paranoid individual when she saw one, was each time able to talk him down by reassuring him that things were progressing nicely, although for now behind the scenes.

Eventually he came to trust the agent and stopped grilling her every two days or so to find out if he was being scammed. In contrast, the trust-building process can take a long time or even fail with individuals with fixed paranoid notions. A gay man's experience with his lover illustrates how trust-building can be a prolonged process. This gay man was pathologically jealous for the first twenty years of their relationship. It took his lover all this time to calm him down using constant support and reassurance, and even that only worked because as the years passed by the lover, like many other people, paranoid or not, had become older and wiser.

Therapists attempting to build basic trust should avoid giving patients a stake of reality to support the vines that keep their paranoia growing full and erect. It is just common sense to recognize that, in therapy or out, getting along with paranoid individuals means giving them little or nothing to be paranoid about. As a paradigm, therapists should not be deceitful, doing the equivalent of what one gay man did with his lover. After years of reassuring his lover that he and a gay coworker had very little contact, when he saw the coworker at a party that all three were attending the gay man rushed over to greet him as if he were greeting a long-lost relative. His lover noted this, recognized that "we have very little to do with each other" was a fiction, and became suspicious, not without some justification, about what was going on between the two men. A therapist attempting to build basic trust should be particularly on the alert not to upset the patient with threatening actions of a nonverbal sort. It is always wise to set the therapeutic stage in a way and place that reassures both therapist and patient that both are safe. It is an especially bad idea to see the patient in a remotely located office in an empty building after hours, causing the patient to become anxious due to a fear that he or she might lose control of aggressive impulses. One way to be reassuring is to sit behind a desk that acts as a barrier between therapist and patient—an especially sensible precaution to take with patients who are potentially dangerous. Another way is to have a visible alarm system for summoning help. That reassures the patient that both patient and therapist will have some protection should the patient feel, or actually become, violent.

SOME CAVEATS

Therapists who remember that paranoid individuals are always alert to the possibility of being dissed behind their backs will avoid discussing a patient in the patient's absence. When revealing anything at all about the patient to others—certainly when speaking to the patient's boss, and possibly even when speaking to the patient's other doctors—they will take special care to obtain permission, oral or in writing (depending on the degree of paranoia and the specific situation). In fact, outside contacts between the therapist and others in the patient's life should, whenever possible, be kept to a minimum. When these must take place it is usually wise to tell the patient in advance what will and what will not be said, and afterwards what exactly was discussed.

Because paranoid individuals are rejection-sensitive, and because delusions that say "you persecute me" can be translated to mean, in part, "you reject me," the therapeutic relationship should be one of steady, predictable involvement. The therapist should be clear from the start about what the patient can expect from the therapeutic relationship. That way, unpleasant surprises can be avoided. A therapist who cancels too many appointments, is always late for sessions, and even suggests termination before the patient is ready (if such a patient is ever ready) predictably makes the patient anxious and afraid. A delusional patient of mine did very well when I was seeing her once a week on a regular basis. But after I terminated, feeling she had reached maximum therapeutic potential, she attempted suicide—exactly one year to the date of our ending treatment. The implication for the general public is clear: if you have a paranoid family member, friend, lover, or spouse, do not make promises you cannot keep. Friends, family, and lovers should never be less than open, honest, and predictable about what the paranoid individual can expect from them. They should certainly decide in advance what level of commitment they are prepared to offer, and stick with that. They should never threaten to walk out on a paranoid individual (unless they mean it, in which case they should follow through) or actually suddenly walk out on him or her one day without warning.

It is especially nonaffirmative to become overly ambitious about completely normalizing a paranoid patient's personal relationships and professional activities. Because of their difficult personalities and rigid defenses, these patients are often limited in what they can accomplish in life, particularly in how far they can go in becoming resocialized. In many cases accepting the patient's obvious limitations is best. In contrast, pushing the patient too hard to succeed can create bad feelings toward the therapist. Therefore the therapeutic goals for these patients often have to be somewhat limited. Sometimes social remission is the best that these individuals can manage. Patients in social remission still think delusionally but learn to be less fearful of their delusions and even to encapsulate them to the point that they become less disruptive of their lives. Therapists have to be especially cautious about not attempting to completely resocialize patients suffering from paranoid personality disorders or delusional disorders in the mistaken belief that the patients are suffering from avoidant personality disorders or social phobias. Some paranoid patients tempt the therapist to use exposure techniques (slowly, slowly meeting more and more people, progressively taking on and mastering more and more anxiety) to help them resocialize. However, these techniques, while potentially suitable for the patient with an avoidant personality disorder and for one suffering from social phobia, are not nearly so useful for, and may be distressing and harmful to, the paranoid patient. The therapist who insists on resocializing such patients should at least consider giving them antianxiety medication to reduce their social anxiety, or even low-dose antipsychotic medication to help reduce the paranoid thoughts that are likely to be creating the social withdrawal in the first place, and that will probably increase in duration and intensity when they attempt to take on more and more anxiety-inducing projects. Too much resocialization can easily intensify the turmoil that leads to defensive paranoia. Sometimes Zen Buddhist approaches can be a much better idea. As Benjamin (1996) suggests, "Buddhist meditation [can] help . . . dissipate intense anger" (p. 340) and "teach . . . empathy and other pro-social attitudes" (p. 340).

DOWNSIDES OF AFFIRMATIVE THERAPY

Of course, affirmative therapy, like any other form of therapy, is not without its problems and lacks. For one thing, affirmative approaches are rarely enough by themselves to bring about full positive change. They are mainly useful to mollify and enhance uncovering, interpersonal, cognitive-behavioral, and pharmacotherapeutic approaches. Excessive affirmation can be much too threatening for paranoid patients and exacerbate paranoia should it turn into a love duet with intimations of seduction that overwhelm and threaten—a special risk for paranoid patients who have significant fears of passivity and closeness. It is also possible for a therapist to be so affirmative that he or she seems to agree with or to condone the patient's paranoid ideas, affirming a patient who needs instead to be constructively criticized and selectively brought up short. As Benjamin (1996) puts it, "Finding the vital balance between needed affirmation and iatrogenic enabling is difficult" (p. 337). An important caveat always holds: the healing companionship that can be derived from the therapeutic relationship must not be spoiled by crossing boundaries.

In conclusion, by reputation affirmative therapy is usually deemed valuable only for, and so held in reserve for, gays and lesbians. However, affirmative techniques, when used not by themselves but as part of a therapeutic armamentarium, can be very helpful for paranoid patients as well. There is an implication for the general public too: we can all help repair the paranoid individual's damaged self by acting positively (in a controlled way) and avoiding acting negatively toward these individuals. These are sensitive, hyper-reactive, alarmist people with low self-esteem. Almost all of them can potentially benefit a great deal from positive interpersonal approaches that help them reduce anxiety and guilt and that simultaneously enhance self-esteem and the feeling that they are liked and loved. In turn, that can help them trust more, be less hostile to and more accepting of others in their lives, and begin to fit into society as society comes to accept them better because now they are acting better toward society.

CHAPTER 15

Pharmacotherapy

Which paranoid individuals can benefit from pharmacotherapy is a source of much controversy within the mental health professions. The following are my practice guidelines, not the only or final word on the subject.

Low-dose or moderate-dose antipsychotic medication is often appropriate for patients with delusional disorders, especially for individuals who are nonverbal, noninsightful, extremely angry, very remote, or acutely decompensating. Munro (1999) has suggested low-dose pimozide for patients with delusional disorders, and others have had a degree of success with the atypical antipsychotics such as clozapine and risperidone. When depression and anxiety are present, clinicians should consider treating these using indicated agents.

I have personally had some success treating adults who are suffering from mild delusional disorders with low-dose pharmacotherapy combined with psychotherapy. In the absence of serious symptoms such as preoccupying delusions and marked hallucinations, and in the absence of imminently dangerous behavior such as potential or actual violent behavior, I was able to leisurely start with a low dose of phenothiazines and raise the dose later should that be indicated. Starting with a low dose avoids unpleasant side effects that tempt patients to go off the medication. Less medication is also cheaper and easier to take.

Some patients with severe paranoid personality disorders may also benefit from pharmacotherapy. They may benefit from the use of anxiolytics to reduce social anxiety and/or from the use of low-dose antipsychotic medication to reduce their hostile suspiciousness. However, many patients suffering from paranoid personality disorders, especially those who are verbal, motivated, and insightful, are appropriately treated with psychotherapy alone.

MAKING A CORRECT DIFFERENTIAL DIAGNOSIS

Before prescribing medication, pharmacotherapists must first make a correct differential diagnosis between the following.

Attention Deficit Hyperactivity Disorder and Paranoia

The inability to concentrate due to attention deficit hyperactivity disorder must be differentiated from the inability to concentrate due to paranoid delusions and hallucinations. Ritalin, sometimes indicated for the treatment of attention deficit hyperactivity disorder, is not an acceptable primary treatment for paranoia because it has the potential for activating the patient to the point that he or she becomes more delusional or pays full attention to the delusions and hallucinations that he or she was formerly able to ignore.

Social Phobia, Avoidant Personality Disorder, and Paranoia

The shyness due to social phobia and avoidant personality disorder must be differentiated from the remoteness due to paranoia. Patients with social phobia and avoidant personality disorder avoid others because they fear getting close and committing, while paranoid individuals avoid others because they fear being attacked. Antianxiety agents used alone can be helpful for treating social phobia and avoidant personality disorder but are inadequate for treating severe paranoid states.

Posttraumatic Stress Disorder and Paranoia

Patients with posttraumatic stress disorder are reliving one or more traumas that are real. In contrast, paranoid patients are reliving one or more traumas that are at least partly imagined. Also, the flashbacks of paranoid patients are less true flashbacks, even when they are to some extent reruns of earlier traumata, than they are attacks on individuals falsely presumed to have placed the patient in harm's way. Antidepressants useful for treating posttraumatic stress disorder may enhance a paranoid individual's anger and so his or her tendency to feel traumatized by, and to traumatize, others. Some veterans I have treated reported having recurrent flashbacks to their wartime experiences in terms that convinced me that they were extremely but inappropriately angry at their superiors for deliberately singling them out for mistreatment. When treated with antidepressants alone, these veterans became even angrier. Now they became more resentful of their presumed or actual past mistreatment, to the point that they began to focus on a quest for vengeance against those who had presumably mistreated them.

Obsessive-Compulsive Disorder and Paranoia

Obsessive-compulsive worry differs from delusional conviction. A fear of being accidentally contaminated is different phenomenologically from a conviction of having been deliberately poisoned. Antidepressants or antianxiety agents alone or together, while potentially useful for treating obsessive-compulsive disorder, are inadequate for treating, and even have the potential to intensify, delusional states.

Depression and Paranoia

The withdrawal, sadness, and despair due to depression must be differentiated from the withdrawal, sadness, and despair due to paranoid suspiciousness or other forms of irrational paranoid thinking. In depression the belief that "others are persecuting me" to a great extent reflects the belief that nobody loves me, while in paranoia the belief that "others are persecuting me" mostly reflects the belief that people are after and out to get me. Antidepressants alone can, of course, be useful for treating patients who are depressed. But as the experience of people abusing cocaine and other stimulants has amply demonstrated, the speed-like effect that antidepressant medication can have in paranoid individuals can lead to increased hallucinations and delusions and other forms of psychotic ideation. This seems especially true for paranoid adolescents, who seem to be in particular danger of becoming suicidal or violent when misdiagnosed as depressed and treated with antidepressants alone.

To illustrate, a doctor's colleagues thought that he was depressed because he got an unlisted phone number so that people did not call him up to harass him. He did this even though he was assigned to be on call and needed to be reached if there were an emergency. They reasoned, "He is overworked and that is getting him down," and started treatment with an antidepressant. In fact, he got the unlisted phone number because he was suspicious of the motives of the people who were calling him up. He believed that they were calling him up to open up circuits so that they would have a functioning venue for spying on him. This man was not too depressed to do his work. He was too paranoid to be able to function either alone or as part of a team. Not surprisingly, he responded to the antidepressants by becoming even more agitated, suspicious, and isolated than formerly.

I am regularly troubled when I read about certain cases in the news of adolescent men on antidepressants who go postal, then shoot up the school, and about adult men on antidepressants who go postal, then shoot up their places of work. When it comes to representing the person described, the reports may or may not be accurate. When it comes to presenting a picture of what in my clinical experience can happen in real life when paranoia is treated with antidepressants, these reports, in spite of possible internal inaccuracies, are certainly chilling. I found one Associated Press news report (2003) particularly alerting. It told of a worker who "sat in a meeting with managers at his factory job, listening to them explain the importance of being honest and responsible in the workplace [and of] getting along with coworkers, regardless of their sex or race. . . . But at some point during the meeting he had heard enough. He walked out of the room . . . [and] minutes later . . . returned with a shotgun and a rifle [saying] 'I told you about (expletive) with me.'. . .[He] had undergone counseling at least once in the past couple of years, frustrated because he thought black people had a leg up in society [and because he] had been passed over for promotion. [He was said to keep] 'score' on whoever he thought was offending him. Fellow employees also described him as a hothead who had used racial epithets and made threats against blacks. . . . He admitted he had a temper and underwent two weeks of 'anger management.' [Recently he] wore a white covering over his head that resembled clothing worn by Ku Klux Klansmen. . . . [Once he had threatened]: 'one of these days, they're going to (expletive) me off and I'm going to come here and shoot some people.' Later [a friend said] that [this person] took medication for depression."

Bipolar Disorder and Paranoia (and Paranoid Schizophrenia)

Pharmacotherapists who fail to differentiate bipolar disorder from paranoia may prescribe lithium or other mood-stabilizing medication alone. These medications are suitable for treating affective disorders, but inadequate when used by themselves for the treatment of severe paranoid states. Or they may prescribe antidepressants alone, which, as mentioned throughout, can increase paranoid thinking even to the point that the patient attempts suicide or becomes violent to others. Or, more likely, they may prescribe both together, which is either overkill for patients with paranoid personality disorders or somewhat wide of the mark for patients with delusional disorders or paranoid schizophrenia.

Sometimes the motives of such practitioners are admirable. They want to avoid giving their patients what many perceive to be an unfavorable, critical, humiliating, and shameful diagnosis, to spare them a grim prognosis, and to be able to offer them medications (antidepressants and mood stabilizers) that they (rightly) believe to be better tolerated and far less productive of severe side effects than the phenothiazines generally used for treating major paranoid states. At other times the motives of these practitioners are somewhat misguided. Some a bit presumptuously think themselves true scientists just because they speak of what they deem to be such highly technical matters as the

chemical imbalances and genetic proclivities supposedly associated with affective disorder (although no definitive gene or chemical has to date been
isolated and found entirely culpable). Some are simply poor diagnosticians,
reminding me of the television psychiatrist who was scripted to say, somewhat
confusedly, "This patient suffers from epilepsy, bipolar disorders, and manic
schizophrenia." Some give mood-stabilizing agents and/or antidepressants because these are what a drug detail man or the "freebies" that come in the mail
happen to be pushing. Sometimes the problem is that a practitioner's own
affective disorder replicates itself in every diagnosis the practitioner makes,
along the lines of "to know one it takes one." Such practitioners put themselves in the patient's place, and the other way around, in part for narcissistic
reasons and in part to normalize the patient by reasoning, "How bad can your
problem be if I have it too?" Sometimes the problem arises because the practitioner has failed to challenge the diagnosis the patient has given to himself
or herself. In my experience, patients predictably dislike being diagnosed as
suffering from paranoia or paranoid schizophrenia. They much prefer to view
themselves as suffering from bipolar disorder. Indeed many patients, following
the principles of von Domarus, see being manic-depressive as an asset, along
the lines of "George Frederic Handel was manic; George Frederic Handel
was great; I am manic; therefore I am great." Some such patients demand
(and get) antimanic agents for their paranoia, much as some patients with
colds demand antibiotics for their sore throats. Of course, practical-minded
physicians are aware that patients gravitate to doctors who give them the
diagnoses they prefer to have and the medications they tolerate well. Finally,
some younger psychiatrists, and those who want to act more youthful than
they actually are, are part of a fairly recent trend to reclassify most or even
all cases of schizophrenia as affective disorders. These psychiatrists view making affective diagnoses vis à vis making schizophrenic diagnoses as the latest,
most modern thing—a phenomenon many observers are in effect referring
to when they note that in America in modern times there has been a tendency
to overdiagnose schizophrenia. Thinking of themselves as young Turks, these
would-be-pioneers view those who make schizophrenic diagnoses as old fo-
gies, while they, on the other hand, proudly bear the antiestablishment banner
of the new, under-forty generation who have the word—that what looks to
"the backward clinician" like schizophrenia is really an affective disorder.
While the intergenerational battles like the one that took place between the
late romantic Richard Wagner and the impressionist Claude Debussy are acceptable and fun in the world of music, they are entirely unacceptable in the
world of science. Here controlled studies make better guides than oedipal
rivalry.

   At the time of this writing, a new generation of psychiatrists is just emerging
with its own word, based partly on its own need to relegate the last generation
of so-called affectophiles to the past, along the lines of "they didn't know what
they were talking about back then." Fashions have once again changed some-

what, and now there seems to be a newly increasing acceptance of a schizo-phrenic diagnosis on the part of at least some mental health practitioners, if still not on the part of most patients. A few decades ago it was fashionable to diagnose early schizophrenia by identifying subtle thought disorder, for ex-ample, circumstantiality, tangentiality, or minimally loose associations such as non sequiturs. While that went out of fashion in more recent times, it is coming back again in a newly emergent school of thought that believes that identifying schizophrenia early and treating it actively before it becomes overt and subchronic can help keep patients from becoming lifelong mental pa-tients. Some modern-thinking practitioners do not even like to wait the six months the *DSM-IV* prescribes before being certain that the diagnosis is schizophrenia. They feel that doing so just involves letting serious illness go untreated for a very long time. So now, once again, practitioners are identi-fying subtle thought disorder, including subtle cognitive errors that are not part of the classic mental status examination and that do not appear in most of the textbooks, and diagnosing accordingly. I feel that this is an exciting "new" approach. (The specific cognitive errors in question are discussed in detail in chapter 11 and chapter 13.)

It is crucial to distinguish negative effects of medication that are the product of *adverse side effects of the right medication* and negative effects of medication that are the product of *adverse consequences of giving the wrong medication*. Ex-amples of adverse side effects of the right medication include the hyperexci-tablity that can be an untoward but sometimes unavoidable consequence of antidepressants properly prescribed for depression, and retardation that can be an untoward but sometimes unavoidable consequence of phenothiazines properly prescribed for paranoid schizophrenia. An example of adverse con-sequences of giving the wrong medication—and, as my discussions through-out clearly imply, the one that most concerns me—is the appearance of violence to oneself (suicidality) and to others (homicidal behavior) in patients, especially children and adolescent patients, given Paxil or other related sub-stances alone for a paranoid disorder after misdiagnosis of the paranoid dis-order as a depression. While these reports specifically warn against giving certain antidepressants to adolescents *who are depressed*, as if the effect is an adverse effect of the right medication, they tend to skip over the possibility that what we are seeing is an adverse consequence of the wrong medication given after a misdiagnosis. The violence that is a side effect of medication properly prescribed for depression could not have been easily predicted and perhaps not even prevented, while the violence that is an adverse effect of antidepressant medication improperly prescribed for patients who look de-pressed but are in fact paranoid could at least sometimes have been predicted and prevented by making the right diagnosis and giving antiparanoid medi-cation alone or in combination with the antidepressant. (While it is also a bad idea to treat depression as if it were paranoia, at least it is not as dangerous to society as it is to treat paranoia as if it were depression. For when depression is treated as if it were paranoia it is the patient alone who suffers unnecessarily, from such side effects of phenothiazines as tardive dyskinesia, enhanced depressive withdrawal, and possibly even increased suicidality. But while that is bad enough, at least the rest of us tend to be spared.)

I recall two cases I followed up on where the rules were broken and paranoid schizophrenics were given antidepressant medication alone with either potentially or actually disastrous consequences. The paranoid patient who thought that Hunter College, a woman's college in New York City, was deliberately sending out rays to penetrate her vagina was at first diagnosed as depressed because of what appeared to be a primary problem with existential hopelessness related to low self-esteem. Treated with antidepressants alone, her condition, being a paranoid one, worsened, to the point that she began to speak of her plans to bomb the school to stop the rays from coming at her. The patient who believed that the images of a mural were talking to him, really cursing him out, said that he was (and in fact looked and probably was) somewhat depressed, claiming that his self-esteem dropped after hearing all the mean things the painting said about him. He was prescribed antidepressants and lithium alone. Unfortunately, being paranoid, he got worse to the point that his next move was to slash the painting to stop it from cursing him out as well as to get back at it for what it had already said to and about him.

Paranoid individuals prescribed antidepressants alone have another problem. They go off the medication because they do not like its activating speed-like effect. Paranoid patients prescribed a combination of antidepressants plus lithium or another mood-stabilizing medication alone sometimes complain of an *increased* inability to control their anger. This is because their anger, being not only affective but also ideational, persists, and they have difficulty containing it because now they feel spaced out by the medication combination. Often when such patients stop taking their medication they are accused of being perverse, stubborn, and uncooperative. Not only is that not a helpful corrective approach and wrong, it also sets up an adversarial relationship between psychiatrist and patient, one that is bound to carry over to all future contacts with psychiatrists and psychological treatment.

As implied in the above discussion, the differential diagnosis between depression and paranoia is particularly hard to make in adolescents. Not only is it difficult to make the diagnosis in the first place, but having made it, it is difficult to medicate the patient properly. Adolescents are predictably unpredictable in their response to almost all psychiatric medications. This is in part because they are constantly in flux emotionally, making it difficult for any prescribed medicine to catch up with, and so be right for, the psychological problem in current ascendancy. Also, adolescents frequently use other (illicit) substances along with the prescribed medication. Expectedly, the former nullify the good and intensify the negative effects of the latter.

Paranoid Personality Disorder and Other Personality Disorders

Some severe personality disorders require and respond to pharmacotherapy. The pharmacotherapy (if any) of the following personality disorders, which are often confused with paranoid personality disorder, is different from the pharmacotherapy of paranoid personality disorder in ways that are beyond the scope of this text.

- borderline personality disorder, where others are routinely feared and condemned both for getting too close and for staying too far away, that is, where others are first put in an impossible position then viewed as impossible people

- psychopathic personality disorder, manipulative paranoid type, where paranoid ideation is used almost consciously and deliberately for purposes of immediate or long-term gain—for example, in negative political ads that deliberately set out to reduce an adversary to a cartoon-like bumbler in much the same way that the paranoid schizophrenic melodramatically reduces all FBI agents to my persecutors

- narcissistic personality disorder (Pollyanna paranoia), where rage and a desire for vengeance follow upon unmet, excessively high, and often selfish expectations that the world must be perfect, or else I will be totally disappointed

- passive-aggressive personality disorder, with its characteristic hostile raging around a misperception of what others have in mind and should be subtly excoriated for thinking and doing

- mixed personality disorder, defined by Arnold Cooper (1994) as a "mixture of paranoid, narcissistic, masochistic, and obsessional features" (p. 145), an entity that is, according to Cooper, a "common presentation of analytic patients" (p. 145)

Toxic-Organic States

The treatment of the organic paranoid aspects of alcohol hallucinosis, delirium tremens, and other alcohol-related toxic and withdrawal states, as well as the treatment of Alzheimer's disease, can differ markedly from the treatment of functional paranoia. For example, phenothiazines once were but are no longer the treatment of choice for the delusions and hallucinations of delirium tremens.

Normalcy and Paranoia

A number of observers have noted that we all think like paranoid individuals, but only true paranoid individuals are focused on their paranoid ideation, and it is that focus that turns the paranoia of everyday life into a recognizable syndrome. Therefore, not everyone who thinks in a paranoid mode needs pharmacotherapy.

THE USE OF DRUG COCKTAILS

In recent years it has become the unfortunate practice of some psychiatrists to give the same drug cocktail to most or all their patients. These psychiatrists reason that everyone is comorbid with everything and that all bases have to be covered. So they give mood stabilizers to normalize affect, benzodiazepines to induce calm, antidepressants to activate, phenothiazines to reduce psychotic symptoms, and anticholenergics to counter the side effects of the phenothiazines. They either start with all these medications at once or they build up to the whole cocktail gradually, adding a second, third, and fourth medication should the first seem inadequate. Some do this even though the patient needs more (or sometimes less) of a given medication, or not more or less medication but an entirely new approach to being medicated, for example, with a more modern medication such as an atypical antipsychotic. Unfortunately, once the patient is on high-dose combination medication he or she tends to stay there. Inertia is a powerful force regulating some physicians' behavior. Also the dangers (for example, relapse) of reducing or stopping medication already prescribed are mostly greater than the dangers of continuing to give the same amount of, or even more, medication, which, with the exception of tardive dyskinesia, are often "no more serious" than increased lethargy, reversible Parkinsonism, or a fine tremor of the hand. Therefore, many psychiatrists are reluctant to reduce medication once started, at least for their outpatients. If they are willing to reduce medication at all, they are only willing to do so after hospitalizing the patient. Since that is often both practically and financially infeasible, leaving the patient on the same medication or giving extra medication, not reducing or stopping medication already prescribed, is almost always the path taken, because it is almost always the one of least resistance and greatest physician comfort and safety.

PSYCHOTHERAPY AND PHARMACOTHERAPY COMBINED

Proper and sufficient psychotherapy should generally accompany proper pharmacotherapy. In managed care settings patients often go off their medication because the therapist has failed to address their underlying resistance to receiving pharmacotherapy. Many paranoid patients do not take their medication properly, or stop it completely, because they develop destructive, distorted views of the medication and of the doctor giving it, and cannot correct their views because they are not given the opportunity to discuss them with the doctor or therapist.

In some cases lack of improvement, decompensation, or violence seems to have occurred in relation to a common clinical practice of splitting the psychotherapy and pharmacotherapy between doctors and nonmedical therapists. Often a nonmedical therapist such as a social worker or psychologist does the psychotherapy and a doctor, either a psychiatrist, a general practitioner, or an internist, does the pharmacotherapy. In some of these cases any lack of improvement, decompensation, or violence that occurs can be at least partly the product of a lack of coordination between treating personnel. The medical doctor might be unaware of changes in the psychological status of the patient—changes that require alteration of the drug regimen—because the nonmedical therapist, unaware of the indications for dose adjustment, does not report these to the doctor. Or the doctor, believing that "my only job is to medicate," is unresponsive to important psychological cues or, feeling that "doctor is boss," is unwilling to listen to a nonmedical therapist's psychological formulations because the latter doesn't have an MD degree. Also the competition, or infighting, between therapists can, and often does, put any patient, and especially a patient who is paranoid, in a difficult position. Paranoid individuals are rarely comforted by the specter of real adversarial relationships in the world around them. Such adversarial relationships tend to replicate their own struggles with the world, thus seeming to prove the paranoid contention, one that they intended to prove all along, that the world is in fact a dangerous place populated by people who do not get along with each other and moreover are likely to turn on them at any moment in exactly the same way they turn on each other.

However, sometimes what looks like an external problem is in fact an internal one due to the patient's distortions of reality—that is, the patient's response is not a product of the actual situation but of the patient's relationship to the situation. Patients receiving therapy from two therapists generally parentalize both in a typical way. Often the patient makes one, for example, the social worker, mommy, and the other, for example, the psychiatrist, daddy, or the other way around, as part of his or her attempt to go home again to his or her dysfunctional family. Chaos erupts when the patient starts pitting one against the other in order to go back to the old days and the old ways when the only thing he or she knew, and so got used to and is therefore reproducing in today's world, was family feuding and fighting.

In conclusion, therapists sometimes prescribe the wrong medication for paranoid patients who are misdiagnosed as having one of a number of other disorders, especially depression. That can lead to ineffective treatment or treatment that is contraindicated, possibly resulting in a worsening of delusions and hallucinations, and perhaps even resulting in decompensation into suicidality or violence.

Antidepressants alone are generally contraindicated for treating paranoia, while mood stabilizing or antianxiety medication alone, and even mood stabilizing medication combined with antidepressants and antianxiety medication, are generally insufficient for treating paranoia. While many patients who have been diagnosed as paranoid when they were actually suffering from an affective disorder have seemed to, and almost certainly did, benefit from changing to either or both mood-stabilizing medication and antidepressants, many patients who have been diagnosed with an affective disorder when they were actually suffering from paranoia have gotten worse with these regimens due to the neglect and/or mistreatment of an existent underlying condition.

When paranoid patients are mistreated pharmacotherapeutically, any violence that occurs is not the product of such often-cited sociocultural or interpersonal influences as the easy availability of firearms, or the result of the patient's having identified with the killing depicted in the media or in computer games. In these cases the violence is promoted or even caused by the treating physician, that is, it is iatrogenic. As such it is potentially avoidable, with a little diagnostic acumen followed by a lot of proper, rational, scientific, medical care.

CHAPTER 16

Therapeutic Cautions, Caveats, and Errors

Therapists treating paranoid patients psychotherapeutically need to recognize that these are critical people who readily perceive their therapists to be adversaries—not friends out to help, but enemies out to deprive, criticize, seduce, and control. They therefore, as Benjamin (1996) suggests, show an ever-present tendency to become "deeply injured" (p. 332) and quit therapy in a huff. To avoid such an outcome therapists should avoid the following.

OVERLY AMBITIOUS, OVERLY CONFRONTATIONAL REALITY TESTING

As noted throughout, therapists should avoid testing reality in a way that effectively amounts to arguing with favored emotional complexes and proffered theoretical positions. Instead, therapists should use an affirmative approach that maintains or, in more unfavorable cases, restores, the patient's confidence, trust in, and comfort with the therapist. However, being affirmative does not mean permitting paranoid ideas to run unchecked. Delusional thinking is a symptom that must be treated, and if it is to be treated it must be first challenged. To illustrate, it was simply not possible to completely ignore a patient's assertion that two of her neighbors—a father and daughter—had put "three six-inch long gray striped mice in her yard because they wanted to be veterinarians and they wanted to be veterinarians because they wanted to put her dog to sleep." Also, even those paranoid individuals who view reality testing as an unwelcome intrusion into their fantasy lives do not necessarily appreciate a therapist's being too accepting of their distortive views. Instead they secretly long to have limits set on their wild fantasizing that has spun out of control. So while therapists should not argue with or challenge these patients' delusional ideas in an abrasive way, they should still subject them to scientific scrutiny.

As mentioned in chapter 13, cognitive therapists follow two rules when it comes to reality testing a patient's delusions. First, they start with a kind of practice run, in the beginning scrutinizing peripheral and relatively unimportant rather than central and relatively important beliefs. Second, they ask the patient to focus on testing not the beliefs themselves but the evidence for the beliefs. In the above case vignette, the therapist asked exactly what the patient found and how exactly she determined that they were striped mice, what evidence she had that her neighbors had put them there, and what exactly led her to believe that they had done so because they planned to become veterinarians to put her dog to sleep. She ultimately considered the possibility that what she found were baby squirrels that had died, or even just old plant life that she had mistaken for dead animals.

DEFLATING WHAT LITTLE REMAINS OF A PARANOID INDIVIDUAL'S POSITIVE SENSE OF SELF

Therapists who recognize that a paranoid individual's delusional thinking is a way to maintain his or her positive sense of self will do what they can to avoid discussions that diminish this positive sense, particularly discussions on topics that elicit and so increase a patient's feelings of guilt. For example, a paranoid patient shopped for and purchased many suits, only to wear the same suit over and over again, even after he wore it out. The excuse he gave to himself for never changing his suit was that he was afraid that if he wore a new suit a passer-by would hit the fabric with a lighted cigarette and burn a hole in it. But an important reason that he did not change his suit was that he wanted to look seedy and threadbare because that way he thought he could avoid any possibility that others might think that he was publicly broadcasting his perverse sexuality and easy carnal availability. My just mentioning his unacceptable sexual wishes had the effect of making him feel guilty about being simply human, intensifying his self-criticisms and so his delusional avoidance. A more effective approach involved encouraging him in a general way to be a little kinder to himself and to at least try to enjoy his life more.

THE OVERASSIDUOUS USE OF BEHAVIORAL EXPOSURE TECHNIQUES

As mentioned throughout, with patients who are in fact suffering from paranoid personality disorders or other paranoid states, therapists must be cautious about employing the interpersonal exposure techniques that work so well for patients with social phobias or avoidant personality disorders. Paranoid patients pushed to socialize regularly respond with an intensified fear of closeness and commitment, and come to suspect that the therapist is forcing them into something—trying to control, humiliate, corner, attack, envelop, devour, and mutilate them. That is, they suspect that the therapist is trying to dissolve the boundary lines that they have so carefully set up to protect themselves from incursions by others, is trying to take their identity away from them, and ultimately is trying to get rid of them. I once had a patient who said that he was manifestly uncomfortable in his isolation and therefore desperately wanted to meet a woman to marry. However, though he thought about all the possible ways he could meet women, he never actually tried to meet one. The only time in his life he had even a dinner date with a woman he became intensely angry at her because he felt that she ordered an expensive appetizer just to bankrupt him. Then he spent the rest of the meal thinking about killing her and afterwards refused to speak to her ever again. I got very ambitious when he turned 60. His mother, the only family member he was still speaking to, was dying, and I was leaving private practice, so I tried to get him to meet someone before she and I left, hoping that he would have something going for him and not be all alone when we both departed. Instead of welcoming my effort he saw me as trying to uproot him from his comfortable spot. So instead of trying to meet someone he became even more isolated to avoid entering the world full of the potential and actual adversaries he believed I was trying to force down his throat. Additionally, he became suspicious of my exact motives. He began to think that I was pushing him to socialize so that I could have a successful result that would make me look good with my colleagues, and wanted to foist him off on some woman just so that I could leave him behind guilt-free. As a result, he became paranoid of me, and not entirely without justification. So one day, after years of therapy, he called me up, out of the blue, to tell me that he no longer wished to continue treatment.

COUCH THERAPY

As previously mentioned, therapists should not treat extremely paranoid patients on the couch, but should use face-to-face therapy instead. Treatment on the couch promotes sensory deprivation, and sensory deprivation in turn promotes fantasy, making it more difficult for the patient to keep a toehold in reality. One paranoid patient compared his experience on the couch to a disorienting trip he made to a clinic built on a cliff, so that instead of the usual procedure of entering on the lowest floor and going up, he had to enter on a higher floor and go down. While most people who went there found that merely a bit confusing, this patient found it intensely disturbing. He also compared his experience on the couch to the time that a gay man picked him up and brought him home to an apartment where abstract paintings hung on the wall with "Rorschach-like blots that disturbed me intensely because they reminded me of bloody insides just lying there exposed."

ANALYTIC-STYLE NEUTRALITY

Therapists treating paranoid patients must avoid wearing a cloak of mystery, one that paranoid patients, like most patients, readily misinterpret as hostility and rejection. Therapy that amounts to little more than the silent treatment is especially frightening to paranoid patients. They find any form of prolonged mutism on the part of the therapist quite intimidating and disapproving, as they think, "My therapist, too shocked for words, is refusing to reply to what I said because it is so disgusting, or is not saying anything to me because he is too busy reading my mind."

REGRESSION AND VENTILATION THERAPY

Forms of therapy that are relatively or absolutely contraindicated for paranoid patients include regression and ventilation therapy, especially when both are combined, as in primal scream therapy. These have the potential to break down the patient's defenses and release truly frightening material, possibly creating severe problems with emotional dyscontrol and disorganization of thinking.

While encouraging depressed patients to ventilate their rage can sometimes be helpful for those depressed patients who are not in the first place too guilty about feeling and getting angry to tolerate expressing anger, encouraging paranoid patients to ventilate their rage "because it's good for you to get your anger out of your system" often causes them to become more paranoid. This is because, as Pat Potter-Ephron and Ron Potter-Ephron (1995) suggest, paranoid people think, "You're not supposed to get angry. That's not acceptable. You might get punished. No aggression allowed" (p. 46). Therefore they feel guilty about being angry, then begin to hate themselves even more than formerly. Next they deal with their guilty self-hatred by blaming others for making them feel angry. As a result they get even angrier—now with the world. Ultimately the escalating anger undermines their self-control in a general way by in effect drawing everything into its vortex. Now they become more agitated than formerly and possibly even suicidal or assaultive to others.

Encouraging paranoid patients to talk in detail about sexual (and other embarrassing) fantasies prematurely, or at all, can also create intolerable guilt, leading to defensive projection of guilt in the form of blaming, and sometimes killing, the messenger—that is, the therapist. Especially vulnerable in this regard are paranoid individuals who view sex as immoral and on that account become angry with, and are tempted to harm, therapists they believe are leading them into carnal sin just by bringing up the topic.

CROSSING THE PATIENT

Many paranoid patients like to be coddled. For example, they hate to be kept waiting for their appointments to start, for reasons that go way beyond the actual trouble they were put to. Predictably they become furious with a therapist who does not begin his or her sessions on time. They view him or her as insensitive and selfish, and their being kept waiting as a personal statement on the therapist's part that they are not highly valued or eagerly sought—that is, they think, "You hate me." Therefore, therapists should at least try to be on time for their sessions and whenever possible avoid canceling appointments, especially at the last minute.

Also, most paranoid patients hate it when others say no to them about anything. Therefore *no* should never be the first word out of the therapist's mouth. Unless presented with an outlandish request that must be immediately denied, such as a request to see the patient at odd hours on demand, at the very least therapists should avoid the arbitrary reflexive no and instead say, "Let me think about it."

SURPRISING THE PATIENT

Paranoid patients generally dislike being surprised or, as they often put it, "jumped." Surprising them makes them feel as if a dangerous enemy is charging them from behind. Therefore, therapists should lead in gradually to all emotionally charged topics, carefully preparing the patient to avoid hitting a nerve. To illustrate, a therapist needed to give a patient he at first did not know was a lesbian medication that could conceivably interfere with the normal growth and development of the fetus. Rather bluntly and without preparation he asked her, "How do I know that you won't get pregnant on me?" This angered her because she felt that he was an ignorant man who should have recognized, but was instead overlooking, her specialness and individuality. In parallel fashion a therapist angered a gay paranoid patient by asking him, without lead-in, questions about his sexuality and sexual activity. The therapist had failed to make it clear that he knew that this was a sensitive topic and that he was merely collecting information, not criticizing his patient for being homosexual or promiscuous. A doctor frightened a patient because, without explaining the reasons for and the necessity of gradually increasing the dosage of her antidepressant medication, he restarted her on a much lower dose after she had gone off her high maintenance dose. In the doctor's view this was simply something that made sense medically. In her view this was her punishment for having defied him. The therapist was unknowingly working at cross purposes with this paranoid individual. A simple explanation could easily have resolved what turned out to be a misunderstanding that was nearly fatal to the relationship.

ACTING SEDUCTIVELY

Therapists, both male and female, especially therapists who are themselves physically attractive, must be especially careful to avoid acting seductively both to their male and to their female paranoid patients. I once had a male paranoid patient who felt that I was getting too close to him. I had intended to talk about his everyday activities as a way to foster our therapeutic bond, but he thought that I was trying to get to know him just a little bit too well. He saw my trying too hard to help him, which I perhaps was, as being too nice to him for reasons of my own, which I was not, and became highly suspicious about what I was up to. He then announced that I was incompetent, and moreover that I was spending entirely too much time in a space I obviously had chosen because it was small and cramped enough to bring us close together. So he started to attack me physically, but fortunately settled for calling me names and for merely making threats against my person. Therapists working in small closed rooms in remote areas should be especially alert to signs of discomfort in their patients. Should the patient become extremely restless or seem to be shrinking into the corner, the therapist should take immediate steps to put as much distance as possible between himself or herself and the patient, for example, by opening the door of the examination room or by promptly terminating the interview.

SHARING TOO MANY PERSONAL EXPERIENCES

Therapists should be cautious about sharing personal experiences with their paranoid patients. Some patients like hearing about a therapist's personal experiences. They find it enlightening and supportive. Learning that we are all alike helps them feel a sense of relief over not being different or especially abnormal. But many paranoid individuals have a tendency to misinterpret a therapist's experience-sharing. They feel that "you are talking about you, and I am here to talk about me" or, worse, come to believe that professional boundaries are being violated.

ACTING TOO MUCH THE PART OF A SUBSTITUTE GOOD PARENT

On the surface at least it would appear that it could only be supportive for therapists to offer themselves up as a substitute good parent to help undo a patient's lifetime of abuse and abandonment from an uncaring family and a hostile society. Indeed, as discussed in the section on affirmative therapy, therapists who provide lonely patients, paranoid or not, with a form of substitute relationship can temporarily tide them over and even sustain them for years to come. But though affirmative in the short run, in the long run parenting a patient can make him or her feel uncomfortably dependent on the therapist and suspicious of the therapist's intent. Patients who for the moment like being supported and coddled often later come to feel threatened sexually, fear being made dependent, or fear being taken advantage of financially by a therapist who, as they assume, plans to treat them indefinitely so that he or she can in effect use them as his or her substitute family or, worse, as an annuity. Needless to say, those few cases where a professional has gotten too close to someone to the point of actually taking him or her under his or her wing and, even worse, home, only to be murdered for his or her rescue efforts, illustrate all too well the folly of assuming that loving and curing the patient are one and the same thing. Of course, too much distance can be as bad as too much closeness, maintaining too-rigid boundaries as bad as crossing too many—just another reason why with these patients therapists, like everyone else, have to do a balancing act and avoid going to extremes.

TAKING TOO MUCH RESPONSIBILITY ON ONESELF FOR A PATIENT'S TREATMENT

It is unwise to view paranoid patients as passive objects entirely unwilling and unable to actively participate in their therapy. This is the philosophy behind some pharmacotherapy-only treatment approaches offered up under the false assumption that all paranoid patients have insufficient insight to know that they have problems and are too stubborn and uncooperative to listen to, and be swayed by, a therapist attempting to convince them that they are wrong about some things. As noted throughout, in my experience many paranoid people are interested in their paranoia and motivated to explore what is going on inside themselves. Besides, taking over tells paranoid individuals, "I expect very little of you." Patients, paranoid or not, should instead be asked to participate actively in and accept responsibility for the outcome of their therapy the same way that they should be asked to participate actively in and accept responsibility for the outcome of their lives. Here are some responsibilities they have to take in therapy:

- to drop the "only a fool is honest and open with authority" attitude and instead to speak frankly and disclose completely, divulging all important information—with a possible exception of material that is for the moment just too frightening or too embarrassing to face and handle

- to drop their "not me but my therapist" attitude that replicates their overall view of themselves as innocent victims who blame the therapist for their not getting better the same way they blame everyone else but themselves for everything that goes wrong in their lives—the media, the gun lobby, abusive parenting, or any other external agency

- to not allow anger, perversity, stubbornness, hurtfulness, and other undesirable personality traits over which they have some control to take over and become an excuse for "why my therapy went bad" and so a reason for keeping their illness or leaving treatment

- to not allow their angry, illogical, negative transference to snowball to the point that a few minor transient nascent delusional ideas, especially those related to medication, lead to their becoming entirely uncooperative and even to their no longer coming in for sessions

I have seen the latter, particularly unfortunate, process occur over and over again with patients receiving depot (injectable, long-lasting) medication. Theoretically it is an excellent idea to give the paranoid patient who is noncompliant with medication a monthly shot to replace the daily pills he or she will not take. But practically speaking that often just means that the patient becomes noncompliant once a month instead of three times a day. A patient started developing a few unrealistic ideas about his injectable medication. Ultimately he worked himself up to the point of viewing his medication as a mind-controlling poison, and the shots necessary to give it as part of a planned assault on his person, and moreover one with sexual overtones. So he stopped coming in for his shots. Six months after going off his medication he gouged out his mother's eyes, then killed her. His therapist was unable to protect his mother because he was not able to convince the patient to come in for his sessions or to talk him into taking his medication, no matter how hard the therapist tried. Nor was the therapist able to convince his mother to stay away from the patient. She felt that he needed her and that therefore staying away from him would only make matters worse. Also the therapist was unable to arrange for involuntary hospitalization, for when he asked the patient a few key questions to uncover any potential for violence, the patient simply denied being a danger to himself or others. Since there was no relevant past history or present indication of actual or potential trouble, there was no entirely satisfactory way to proceed.

However, therapists have to walk the fine line between insisting that their patients participate actively in their therapy and making their patients feel completely responsible for any therapeutic failure that might occur. When one therapist continuously insisted that a paranoid patient take the entire responsibility for the outcome of her therapy upon her shoulders, the patient went on to develop migraine headaches whose head-pounding she interpreted as reflecting "what I would like to do to my psychiatrist." Should the patient complain that "my therapy isn't working," the therapist should not reflexively become defensive and start blaming the patient. Instead he or she should take the complaint seriously and ask the patient if there is something that the therapist has done wrong and some way the therapist can do better.

KEEPING THE PATIENT OUT OF THE HOSPITAL AT ALL COSTS

Therapists should not fail to hospitalize a patient when indicated. The adolescent who is passing out Nazi literature, using other people's credit cards to make Internet purchases, calling the neighbors dickheads and the like, and threatening to blow up the school possibly needs more than a suspension from school and a recommendation to go see a therapist for anger management. He or she needs to be evaluated professionally and possibly to be hospitalized. There should be both follow-through and follow-up. After discharge the therapist should continue to see the patient, or arrange to have him or her seen, check back on a regular basis to make certain that all recommendations are being followed, and be available to step in somehow if the patient seems to be tracing a downhill course. Therapists should consider actively recontacting patients who quit therapy prematurely, even, or perhaps especially, those who do so in a huff, to see how they are doing and if they need and want to come back. For both medicolegal and humane reasons, the therapist should consider writing letters and possibly sending them via certified mail to recidivistic patients, especially those who are adjudged to be potentially a danger to themselves and others. When appropriate these letters should inform the patient, sometimes the family, and possibly other individuals or agencies responsible for the patient's care that continuing therapy is needed, and alert all concerned to the consequences of ignoring that advice.

SIDING WITH THE REAL ENEMY

Therapists should never refuse to take the paranoid individual's side when the paranoid individual is right and others (which sometimes includes the therapist) are wrong. Therapists should not assume that a patient's adversarial beliefs are always and entirely unjustified. They should always remember that even for patients who are paranoid there are two sides to every story, and that sometimes what we call delusions are in fact appropriate complaints. However, this works both ways. A paranoid patient in a cooperative building complained that the building was deliberately withholding heat to save money and threatened to sue. The therapist completely fell for the patient's version of events— until he happened to learn, by accident, that the patient had torn down walls to redecorate, removing some radiators along the way, and had replaced the functional radiators that remained with antique ones that looked better but gave out little heat.

This said, bad outcomes in treating paranoid individuals may be due not to therapeutic errors but rather to the real difficulties involved in managing and treating individuals who are paranoid. For one thing, some paranoid individuals are unpleasant people. Some of them are violent individuals who can even become violent toward their psychiatrists. For example, a patient of mine threatened to kill me if I reported him to a child protection agency for punishing his son by throwing him against the wall. I feared for my own life if I crossed this patient, and I feared for his child's life if I did not. (Eventually administration took over, and the problem was handled in an impersonal way, leaving me out of it.) We speak of outpatient commitment for the violent patient, but it can be difficult to find professionals comfortable with getting involved.

It is especially difficult to treat paranoid patients who are not motivated to change or capable of changing. Like manic patients who enjoy being over-productive, paranoid individuals often enjoy being overly suspicious. They feel that suspiciousness keeps them on their toes and is protective. Also some paranoid individuals are by nature evil people. As such they are not struggling with their hostility. Rather they want to be mean. Therefore, they do not take kindly to anyone who suggests that they turn over a new leaf, reconsider their negative attitudes, and think twice before living them out.

Also, as many observers have noted, these patients can be difficult to sit through a full session with. They tend to be individuals who, spending much of their psychic energy denying what is going on within, reveal little about themselves and even appear to be empty. Those who are rigid, controlled, and fearful of opening almost any new door do not do much that is interesting, and therefore have few fascinating tales to tell. So, when asked to talk about themselves, they often have little to say. This leads some therapists to complain that they dread 50 minutes with them because they are at best silent, and at worst repetitive.

At other times the problem is not one of too little but of too much material, that is, the problem is one of overinclusiveness. Many paranoid individuals are so intent on proving that they are being misunderstood, violated, or harmed that to make their case they mention every little detail about what happened in their past lives and about what is happening to them now. Many of them start at the beginning of a story and slowly, too slowly, fearful of leaving anything out, wend their way toward an end that they approach but never seem to reach. Only therapists prepared to listen to a slow-motion tale that never seems to get to the point, and the same thing day in and day out, and willing to pay attention to stalled, circumstantial, or tangential thinking hour after hour should take such patients on in long-term therapy. Therapists who must always have closed-end, meaningful stories that hang together and make a point, and precise fascinating details that come tumbling out day after day, will feel uncomfortable with, or even hate, treating some of these patients.

Therapists must also be willing to accept limited goals with many of these patients. Therapists who are looking for ongoing progress and growth as the product of daily eureka insights and breakthroughs, leading to newly developing networks of socialization, rapidly progressing to a long-term satisfying monogamous marriage, leading to the birth of children and grandchildren are likely to be seriously disappointed in the progress of such patients. Therapists who cannot accept that with some of these patients the goal is less personal growth than adequate functioning outside of a hospital without gross symptoms should consider referring these patients on, without, of course, appearing to be in any way rejecting them.

CHAPTER 17

Prognosis

While this chapter is nominally devoted to discussing prognosis, the reader will note that many of the positive prognostic determinants to follow can be profitably read as helpful therapeutic suggestions for patients, caretakers, and therapists alike to pursue.

What is the ultimate outlook for patients with paranoid personality disorders? I can find no good statistics, but anecdotal evidence suggests that many get better, and that they do so through various means and in various ways. Some get better on their own after working their paranoia through implicitly, that is, after thinking their problems through in their minds, in effect lifting themselves up by their own bootstraps, without much or any outside help. Others get better with nonprofessional assistance from concerned and supportive friends, family members, and spouses, and from the good advice they obtain from self-help books on such topics as how to overcome personality problems and how to deal with difficult people. Some get better simply because they get older. With increasing age their passions subside and with them the pathological constructs that are the product of their earlier turbulent emotionality. Some try therapy and benefit.

However, some stay the same, but not all of those function poorly, and indeed some function very well, and even extraordinarily effectively, sometimes as the direct result of their paranoia. Unfortunately, even with treatment, some progress to the full-blown paranoid imagery of delusional disorder or decompensate into paranoid schizophrenia. In a typical sequence some patients at first only manifest paranoid overvalued ideas, but these progress to full-fledged persecutory delusions. However, while again exact numbers are not available, I believe that the deteriorating paranoid patient who develops fixed delusions and along with those becomes more and more isolated, unapproachable, and dysfunctional as time goes by represents only the tip of the iceberg of a widespread disorder with many sufferers, only some of whom become seriously ill and go on to trace a downhill course.

Insofar as one can be clear about the difference, the prognosis is improved and treatment most successful in those patients whose delusions are secondary rather than primary, that is, in patients whose delusions are the product of intellectual and emotional currents that the patient can identify and understand as arising in specific contexts. This is particularly true for patients whose paranoid ideation originates as a response to specific, identifiable interpersonal and situational stress, and who are both willing and in a position to take steps to reduce that stress—by finding new jobs, getting new friends, or just not asking too much of themselves and instead taking on less responsibility and becoming more realistic about their goals and their prospects of attaining them. Also, paranoid individuals who, instead of insisting that they must function at an unrealistically high level or else, are willing to just accept their disability and with it some degree of impairment—settling for remote or no relationships, or seeking quiet work in a pet shop dealing only with animals, or in the post office sorting mail away from stressful human contact—can often look forward to at least a social recovery.

In contrast, grandiose megalomanic paranoid individuals without much artistic talent who try to be number one at all times, no matter what, and insist on making a living from writing or painting, only to become bitter with the world when they fail professionally, may do quite poorly. Not surprisingly, such people begin to chain think that "no one appreciates me, therefore no one respects me, therefore no one loves me, therefore everyone hates me, therefore everyone is my enemy." An especially negative fate awaits extremely narcissistic individuals whose sense of entitlement makes it inevitable that, at the first sign of any deprivation whatsoever, they will become angrily demanding in a way that puts people off. For example, I once wrote a book on finding loving relationships. A man contacted me by e-mail to tell me how unhappy he was with his love life and to ask me for specific advice about a problem with a lover, which of course I couldn't give him over the Internet. He told me that he liked my book but that he could not afford to buy it. Sensing his neediness I offered to send him a free copy, and did so, autographed. Following the principle that when it comes to narcissists, paranoid or not, no offer of a hand goes without their taking an arm, his response was not to thank me but to demand, via an intrusive series of e-mail and instant messages, becoming more and more frantic and hostile when I did not immediately reply, that for my next charitable act I send out another copy of my book—gratis—to his ex-boyfriend!

That does not mean that all paranoid people should give up on having serious, committed relationships or on aspiring to become rich and famous. I know of many, and have personally treated some, patients whose paranoia even provided the fodder for a life of great personal and professional achievement, including (or especially) artistic achievement. Many artists, dancers, lawyers, and other professionals are able to work not only around, but also with and from, their paranoia. But for those paranoid individuals who simultaneously lack talent, intelligence, luck, and opportunity, when it comes to choice of profession and to a lesser extent relationships, the motto might profitably be, "Better safe than sorry."

Patients who are motivated to develop and capable of developing insight into the paranoid process to the point that they are willing, eager, and able to look for evidence of paranoia in themselves in preparation for attempting to understand specifically what it is that makes them paranoid have a better prognosis than patients who do not spot their paranoia or who, after spotting it, have little or no desire to learn and then to do anything about it. As an example, an improved prognosis awaited a patient who was eager to discover when and why he was being irrational, and was then willing to try to talk himself out of his irrational beliefs. This patient was a man with delusional sexual jealousy who spotted that he was being "foolish for being jealous," saw that he was "getting paranoid over nothing" because he was projecting his own guilty sexual desires onto his wife, then went on to at least try to think differently each time he found his suspicions aroused. In fact, some observers even reclassify the symptom of delusional sexual jealousy as (the less serious) symptom of obsessive jealously based on the ability to spot distortions of reality as revealed in the patient's saying "I am worried about" rather than "I am convinced of" a partner's infidelity. We hear two expressions all the time that reflect the patient's ability to step back from and study his or her paranoia from afar. The first is "I *guess* I am being paranoid about it," and the second is "I feel *as if* everyone is out to get me." However, the extent to which either or both of these expressions actually reveal deep, useful insight is not always clear.

Particularly positive prognostically is the ability to understand the interpersonal dynamic basis of specific counterproductive motives, defenses, and illogical cognitions. A paranoid individual improved after discovering that she could not meet anyone sincerely interested in marrying her not because, as she previously thought, of who and what people were falsely accusing her of being and doing, but because of what she actually thought and did. She recognized that she went through life suspiciously questioning everyone's intentions toward her to the point that she thought that any man she met was either married and only interested in sex, or a gold digger only interested in her money. A big breakthrough came when she learned that "I have intense separation anxiety, and I handle that by not getting deeply involved with other people in the first place or, when I do get involved, by coming up with one excuse after another to become suspicious of and push the other person away." In like manner, the coffee shop man discussed throughout stopped running his coffee shop into the ground when he stopped blaming his business problem on the gay men in the community ganging up on him, a straight man, to see to it that he failed, and started realizing that his self-destructive emotional lability, his tendency to be critical of all patrons, and his refusal to stay a few minutes late if a guest had not yet finished eating at closing time were the real reasons he was about to go out of business.

Contrast these two individuals with the patient who was not open to questioning his delusions about the *New York Times*, but insisted on the rationality of his assertion that the *New York Times*'s crossword-puzzle makers were responsible for causing his mother to get Alzheimer's disease. He explained his reasoning as follows: "Doing crossword puzzles has recently been shown to help the brain stay active and healthy. But the ones in the *New York Times* are so hard that my mother could not do them. That is why her Alzheimer's started and progressed."

The prognosis certainly improves when the patient is able and willing to identify, understand, and master such of his or her protoparanoid characterological traits as stubbornness, masochism, and sadism. Patients who become less stubborn adopt less of an "I know it all, and don't argue with me" view of the world and hence a less "my (delusional) theories are the only correct ones" approach to interpersonal relationships and to life itself. Patients who become less masochistic benefit considerably from no longer needing to see fortune as misfortune in order to have a reason to suffer emotionally, as well as from not actually creating their own misfortune in order to have something that they can go on to complain about.

The prognosis also improves for those paranoid individuals who are at least willing to try to live with and around those delusions and hallucinations that they cannot dispel one way or the other. More paranoid people than we think are strong-willed individuals who can effectively teach themselves to ignore delusions and hallucinations that they cannot completely get rid of. I know of one patient who discovered that he had the ability to blot out some of his hallucinations by wearing a personal stereo and playing tapes of others talking on talk shows he had previously recorded. It is also a good thing when patients who cannot ignore or dispel their delusions and hallucinations entirely can at least learn to stop responding to and acting on them. I once saw a patient who had hallucinations that actually helped him ignore his delusions—hallucinations that consisted of a running commentary that told him, "That is a stupid idea; disregard it."

Prognosis also improves when a patient finds ways to replace a negative with a positive behavior, as when a patient learns to turn hypersensitivity into empathy. Empathic patients can further reduce their paranoia by roleplaying—putting themselves in another's place in order to seek alternative, nonadversarial explanations for the negative things that they at first believe friends and families are saying about and doing to them. That way they can avoid taking everything so personally and negatively and instead give others the benefit of the doubt. A paranoid patient, after putting herself in a friend's place, understood that her friend practically hung up on her when she called not because of any personal animosity toward her but because he was on his way out the door, in a rush to get to work, and the call was holding him back. A man confronted by a rusted dump truck parked in a neighbor's driveway threatened to report the eyesore to the authorities, and if that failed to beat the truck's owner up. He finally saw his way clear to putting himself in the truck owner's place and accepting the explanation that his wife patiently offered him: "He is not dumping on you personally, he just doesn't have anywhere else to store the vehicle while he is trying to sell it."

Paranoid individuals who retain their senses of humor about themselves and their foibles can do especially well. A personal willingness to lighten up and to be less serious about everything, especially about minor things of little or no real import, is a good prognostic sign. In contrast, patients who remain too intense, idealistic, serious, easily humiliated, and overly ready to feel devalued, who are in some respects still like adolescents who take everything too much to heart and in the wrong way, are especially vulnerable to rage reactions that can lead to delusional thinking and violent behavior.

Finally, prognosis depends to a great extent on what other people in the patient's life say and do. If a paranoid person is lucky enough to have a spouse who is willing to act in a therapeutic fashion with him or her, that is a good thing. As mentioned throughout, paranoid individuals do very poorly with passive-aggressive spouses who provoke them, then blame them for feeling provoked, an especially paranoiagenic attitude because it throws paranoid patients into a state of logical shock, forcing them to come up with emergency (paranoid) defenses. Cheating mates are also very difficult for paranoid individuals to handle. I can never completely suppress my suspicion that the composer Robert Schumann was driven to paranoid insanity in part because he could not handle his wife Clara Schumann's perhaps excessively close relationship with another man, the composer Johannes Brahms. It is a particularly hopeful sign when a spouse is willing to help a paranoid mate save a marriage threatened by the spouse's paranoia. A gay man accused his lover of a kind of infidelity for using the showers at the gym. "That's okay for straight but not for gay men," he said. The lover at first became incensed at being accused of cheating, and denied that he was even looking. Then the gay man, seeing that he had gone too far, begged for forgiveness, saying, "Please cut me some slack; you know how I am." The lover responded positively, and together the two rescued the hour and the relationship by understanding each others' needs and sensitivities, thus moving on to the higher plane of a relationship newly marked by true and basic trust.

PART IV

Self-Help

CHAPTER 18

Ways Caretakers Can Deal Effectively and Supportively with the Paranoid Individuals in Their Lives

In this chapter I suggest ways caretakers can help paranoid individuals feel better and avoid making them feel worse, while simultaneously coping with and protecting themselves from victimization by the paranoid individuals in their lives. This chapter is profitably read in conjunction with chapter 16, which describes therapeutic errors psychotherapists commonly make with paranoid patients, and in conjunction with chapter 19, which describes things all of us, laypersons as well as therapists, should avoid doing with paranoid acquaintances, friends, and family.

UNDERSTANDING

The interrelated processes of helping, coping, and self-protecting start with understanding that paranoia is an emotional disorder that can, like any other emotional disorder, be conceptualized in human terms and that therefore can, like most other things human, be positively influenced using psychological methods. These methods can be used not only by a therapist treating a patient but also by a sophisticated layperson attempting to help out a friend, lover, or member of the family.

Caretakers need to realize first when the actions of someone who is paranoid are attributable to either the paranoia of everyday life or to pathological paranoia, and second the wisdom of not responding in an abrasive manner to individuals who are paranoid—not getting into an argument with someone who is just looking for a fight—and instead responding productively, for example by counting to 10, in effect taking a time out in order to hold a meaningful conversation with oneself about the best way to react. Thus drivers who see the everyday paranoid individuals with whom they come into contact for what they are, and also understand the wisdom of not arguing with a paranoid person, will know why when they get the finger on the highway they should not give the finger back, but should instead avoid making eye contact, look the other way, and keep going after holding the following conversation with themselves. "Why is that man behind me blowing his horn at me constantly? Where does he want me to go? And what should I do about him? Aha! I know the answer. He thinks that I am his enemy because he is responding to imagined slights, having blown this unimportant interaction up way out of proportion and to the point that he takes his so-called plight much too seriously and personally, while seeing it much too narrowly. He is blaming me entirely not only for what is happening now but also for everything bad that has happened to him in his whole life, reducing his entire complex troubled existence to the narrow cognition of 'that idiot in front of me is going too slowly.'"

Here are representative examples of behaviors that may be attributable to paranoia and that should be understood as such and managed accordingly. A woman bumped into someone due to her own carelessness, then instead of apologizing, snapped at him, "Watch where you are walking." In parallel fashion when she did not see her cat lying there and stepped on its tail, instead of saying "I should have been more careful," she railed against the cat for being a "dumb animal who always has to lie where I can walk on it."

The proprietor of the coffee shop mentioned throughout was trying to get his business off the ground. Next door to his coffee shop was a busy restaurant that did not take reservations, yet had no place set aside for the patrons to comfortably wait for a table. So people gravitated to his coffee shop to wait there while their table was being made ready. Although this crowd would only order coffee or a soda, there was still a profit to be made. However, the proprietor did not like this crowd because he believed that they were treating him as second best. Therefore, when they came into his shop and ordered only coffee or a soda, he threw them out, telling them that no one used him that way and, adding insult to injury, confronting them with how stupid they were for eating in a place with bad food while his was better. When I suggested that he use the situation as an opportunity to build up his own business, he in essence replied, "Don't tell me what to do. Don't tell me how to run my business, and don't ever tell me to accept being used." His was a paranoid attitude first because he had elaborated a minor negative component of a potentially mutually beneficial arrangement to become an all bad and even an adversarial situation, and second because while I was simply a friend meaning to advise him, he saw me as an enemy attempting to control him.

A patient prone to road rage was an immature, impulsive individual prone to minipsychotic paranoid breaks. When driving he was less interested in getting someplace than in maligning and humiliating the other people on the road, whom he believed were keeping him from getting there. So, he would come up from behind and tailgate them, giving his car gas and blowing his horn to razz them and to tell them, "Eat my dust, you hog." Then he would pass them at high speed, and often on the right—not to make time, but to make a statement, to tell the other driver, "You are a wimp for going too slowly, and I'll show you what a real man is."

It follows that

- Wives who recognize that they are being abused because their husbands are paranoid, and perhaps delusionally so, will be less apt to react in ways that feed into their husbands' distortive thinking.

- Lovers who understand that a lover's pathological jealously borders on the delusional can make a more informed decision to either rework that relationship along healthier lines or to get out before it is too late.

- Voters who see that the negative campaigning of politicians is as paranoid as the negative view of paranoid patients who make a benign world into a dangerous place will be better able to sort the reality from the distortion and so less likely to automatically buy into what they hear and instead recognize that the candidates are using paranoid ideation opportunistically in order to sway the vote. Now they can look to and vote for those candidates who are less manipulative and more realistic, honest, and trustworthy.

- Dieters who understand the delusional premises behind fad diets will be better able to see the need to stick with or go back to diets that are scientifically sound, just as anyone who sorts quack from real medicine will be in a better position to protect both their health and their pocketbooks.

- Mental health workers who diagnose paranoia correctly and understand it through and through can better decide which of their patients are harmless and which they should restrict and lock up because they are dangerous.

- Sociologists who understand paranoid recidivism can make more informed decisions about whether the death penalty will deter paranoid individuals from committing horrific crimes or will be just another example of how futile it can be to argue with and threaten some people who are delusional.

- Parents who spot and understand paranoia and that some widespread myths are paranoid constructions can feel comfortable having their children vaccinated for polio without worrying that it will make their children sterile. They can also better protect their children by more effectively screening people they hire to babysit or help around the house, and can better decide whether to let a child stay in a cult run by a quasi-religious, grandiose dictatorial leader or whether to pull the child out against his or her will. Also, they can make more informed decisions about how to raise their young and adolescent children, most of whom are normally somewhat paranoid. For example, they can recognize and simply accept that to some extent parenting most children involves the same principles as managing and coping with some paranoid adults. That means walking certain fine lines between being too critical and too accepting of them; between giving them enough freedom to express themselves adequately and not so much freedom that they permit and encourage them to act destructively; between imposing their own adult ideals on them, pressuring them to blindly conform, and allowing them to develop a personal set of ideals on their own, running the risk that they will become victims of their immaturity or fall under the spell and influence of bad companions; and between not pushing them at all to succeed in life, allowing them to flounder, and being too ambitious for them to the point that they send them off on journeys that they do not want to take, that they are unlikely to complete, or that they are ill-equipped to survive.

- Teachers who spot and understand paranoia can recognize that their adolescent charges in many ways resemble brittle paranoid individuals in their tendency to see all authority as the enemy—effective preparation for not giving their charges reason to strike out by behaving in a way that turns teacher into a member of the hated establishment. With this in mind they will avoid acting like arbitrary "teacher-knows-best" authority, while not completely abdicating their responsibility to educate and strengthen those who, however much they protest, basically need and seek their guidance. Teachers can also, taking a page from the books of therapists using diagnostic and therapeutic methods worked out over the years by the best thinkers in the field, identify paranoid previolent students in preparation for properly handling therapeutically the sensitive, suspicious, withdrawn people these children and adolescents mostly are—perhaps not unlike the rest of us.

In short, those who spot someone who is paranoid will understand how to avoid provoking them, or provoking them further, by responding in a way that contributes to and becomes part of the problem. Instead when they see that someone is paranoid, they will understand the importance of acting in a calming fashion by not saying or doing anything to cause passions to flare. They will see that the operative principle for caretakers of paranoid individuals is to do nothing to rile the paranoid individual up, but instead to do everything to talk the paranoid individual down.

Understanding the specific psychodynamic, developmental, cognitive, interpersonal, and social dynamics of a given paranoid response also helps considerably by enabling caretakers to hone their own responses so that they are replies not to the superficial ideation and behavior involved but (a more helpful response) to the deep meaning of what is being communicated—the hidden message behind the manifest words and deeds. An operative principle here is that, to develop highly effective mechanisms for helping, coping with, and self-protecting from paranoid individuals, it is necessary to identify, speak to, and respect a paranoid individual's specific vulnerabilities and personal idiosyncrasies. That means recognizing and speaking to the paranoid individual's specific complexes, and that in turn requires recognizing the specific underlying personality structure and personality problems, particularly those involving issues of narcissism and dependency, that lead to the paranoid individual's special discomforts and fears.

Most paranoid individuals are sufficiently *narcissistic* to dislike being told that their concerns about the CIA are unjustified because the CIA has other things to think about. These are grandiose people whose delusions are more like bragging than they are like complaining, who are telling us, "How smart I am to know the truth; don't you realize it?" and who are secretly enjoying being the center of attention and in the spotlight. Therefore caretakers who tell them to "relax, because no one is spying on you" are likely to make them feel angry and disappointed about no longer being in the public eye and the center of things. So, caretakers should instead encourage them to satisfy their needs for status and affirmation, and to get into the spotlight, in ways other then through pure fantasy.

Many paranoid individuals seem to be independent people who fear getting close. These are the familiar individuals—often misdiagnosed as suffering from social phobias or avoidant personality disorders—who both figuratively and literally prefer cats to people. One such individual told her lover, "When I get home from work, I expect you to go into the bedroom, shut the door, and not say anything at all to me for an hour." Among such people are those who like to celebrate the holidays alone. Often they wander geographically so that they can avoid making close friends and seeing their relatives, whom they predictably feel stuck with. As employees and coworkers they are more likely than average people to see sexual harassment in overtures of friendship because these overtures stir up unacceptable sexual wishes, which they then integrate and master by extrojecting them to become "I don't want sex with you; you are trying to seduce, really force, me into having it." The person may even start a lawsuit meant to impress the world with his or her innocence, to get the message out by announcing to all, in no uncertain terms, "I will not put up with such behavior, and to prove it, I am going to court to sue, and make sure that my suit gets into the newspapers so that everyone knows how displeased I am with what you are doing."

But, it is important to understand that underneath many of these individuals' seemingly independent exteriors are hidden secret dependency longings. In this regard Benjamin's (1996) words ring true: some of these "PARs can become very dependent and show *inordinate* trust. To those few who are seen as 'on their side,' PAR's can maintain blind, even inappropriate loyalty" (p. 320). Their complaint "you persecute me" is then a cover for the complaint "you do not love me and are going to abandon me." They deal with their fear of abandonment by staying away from others to avoid having others stay away from them. They actively arrange to be hated so that they can avoid passively—suddenly, without warning, and without time to make preparations—finding themselves unloved. They are fundamentally oral dependent people always ready to attack a fantasized mother figure for withdrawing the breast before they feel completely sated [a rough approximation of Melanie Klein's (Kernberg 1985) "paranoid position"]. It follows that these individuals, perceiving any pullback at all as complete abandonment, respond quite negatively to any hint of withdrawal of affection, doing so especially with those who lead them first to expect long-term constancy they can count on only to suddenly withhold or withdraw their love. Indeed, some of the worst cases of spousal abuse have occurred when a spouse threatened separation or divorce in the midst of a fight or, worse still, actually walked out in a huff and without warning. For that reason, caretakers should not be too remote with such paranoid individuals, and they should not respond in turn to their apparent coldness and removal by feeling rejected themselves and then acting in a retaliative way. They should be especially careful not to surprise paranoid individuals with unexpected rejection. That can only lead to a reflexive response that resembles that of wild animals in the jungle who, when people sneak up on them, in favorable cases run away or in less favorable cases turn around and bite. Instead caretakers should try to engage these individuals personally—while, of course, walking the fine line between overgratifying their dependency needs and crossing their carefully established, overly rigid boundaries. That means making a correct relationship distance decision with them, one that involves

- Deciding how close and how remote to be—striking a balance between being warm and friendly without being overly seductive, between being reassuringly remote and being openly and frighteningly rejecting, and between getting friendly and getting too friendly and failing to respect boundaries.
- Assisting and encouraging them without appearing to be controlling them. This was especially necessary for a paranoid man who saw all advice as control and counted as enemies those who responded to his tales of woe with suggestions about what to do, then felt hurt when he did not take them. To be his friend it was only necessary to hear his problems out without comment, that is, to offer him support and sympathy without telling him what to do, then ordering him to do it.
- Offering support without being pathologically enabling by being too affirmative and permissive.

Finally caretakers also need to spot and understand a paranoid individual's cognitive errors. Those who are aware of the mechanics of the paranoid individual's distortive thinking will be less likely to buy into his or her delusional constructs and take them personally to the point of getting steamed up and responding in an angry, vindictive, counterproductive fashion to what has been said and done. Now they will be better able to focus on the positive aspects of the person and the valuable aspects of the relationship.

ALWAYS SAYING THE RIGHT THING

Being supportive starts with saying (and doing) the right thing and not saying or doing the wrong thing. Caretakers should not expect paranoid individuals to cut them any slack if they fail to watch what they say, as did the man who in a locker room at the gym set one of my paranoid patients off by responding to his attempt to exchange a few pleasantries by pulling out a bottle of mouthwash and gargling. With paranoid individuals complete honesty is not always the best policy. It is often better to censor one's remarks—correcting for a paranoid individual's hypersensitivity by speaking less than the whole truth. Caretakers should also not speak vaguely, expecting that a paranoid individual will fill in the gaps right. More likely, the paranoid individual will misread between the lines and insert a negative meaning that was not intended, or pick up on a negative meaning that was intended but was not intended to be quite so clearly broadcast and received. Caretakers should be especially careful not to say things that can be interpreted in two ways, one negative and the other positive. To illustrate with a paradigm from clinical psychology, some examiners still ask patients to define the proverbs "a rolling stone gathers no moss" and "a friend in need is a friend indeed," then go on to use the response to make or rule out a psychotic diagnosis. A patient who does not give what the examiner believes to be a proper definition of the proverbs but instead interprets them too literally is diagnosed as having a thinking disorder marked by an inability to abstract. Therefore, the patient is considered to be possibly suffering from a form of schizophrenia. Unfortunately, nobody knows for certain what these proverbs mean. Is it good or bad to "gather moss," that is, is gathering moss settling down and becoming established (good), or is it getting silted up to the point of not being functional (bad)? Also, what about that friend in need? If he is your friend when *you* need *him*, that is good; if she is your friend only when *she* needs *you*, that is bad. Vague communications like this creep into our everyday speech all the time. With individuals who are not paranoid they are of relatively little importance. But with those who are paranoid they can arouse a great deal of unnecessary anxiety and antipathy. In particular, caretakers who choose to tell a paranoid individual that he or she can do better should do so in a way that avoids any possibility of being misinterpreted as devaluing what has already been done.

RESPECTING

Caretakers should be very respectful of paranoid individuals and avoid shaming or otherwise inducing guilt, or more guilt, in them. Paranoid individuals feel disrespected over very little. It takes hardly anything for them to feel as if they have been dissed. They do not favor rigid, intolerant people who criticize them for every little thing. Rather, as Oldham and Lois B. Morris (1995) put it, they mostly hate confrontations and arguments (p. 179), especially when those involve putting them down and making them feel guilty. A somewhat paranoid neighbor let her few-months-old baby play naked in the public courtyard of the building in which she lived. She was brought up short by the other members of the cooperative association, who censured her in the cruelest possible fashion—by putting her indiscretions in the building's monthly minutes. She felt guilty, and predictably dealt with her guilt by offering not an apology but an attack, in the form of a lawsuit that was her response to having become convinced that "they are all out to get me." This paranoid response could have easily been avoided by taking her aside and simply asking her to clothe her child. A spouse has a minor accident or loses something insignificant, like an umbrella. A guilt-inducing response might be, "You are even clumsier than I thought." In contrast a supportive response might be, "Everyone spills coffee and loses things of little value." Of course, it is not paranoid to respond negatively to actually having been dissed—as in the following example. I recently asked an agency nurse what her next assignment would be. Her husband did the answering for her: "Alaska General, I hope."

Since putting paranoid individuals down virtually assures that they will feel more paranoid, it follows that it often helps to compliment them. But they should only be complimented when they deserve the compliment. Most paranoid individuals characteristically look askance on insincere compliments. They recognize that they do not deserve them and that those paying them the compliments have a secret agenda. They predictably wonder what others have in mind, think that they are up to something, and soon enough come up with their own distortive view about what exactly that might be. We now hear negative responses ranging from "you are a phony" to "the only explanation I can give myself for your saying all these nice things to me is that you want my money, or my body."

SETTING APPROPRIATE LIMITS

Caretakers can help support paranoid individuals by setting appropriate limits on them, especially when the paranoid individuals are actually doing others real harm. Of course, caretakers should always set these limits carefully and judiciously and only on those deemed not dangerous and without an arsenal at home. Many paranoid individuals respond in a surprisingly acceptable fashion to appropriate limits set for good and rational reasons. For example, a man properly and effectively restrained his wife from living out her germ paranoia and misusing her position as a practical nurse to get and give their children antibiotics for colds while simultaneously arranging for them to have medical workups for other imagined infectious diseases. Conversely, setting too few limits on potentially dangerous paranoid individuals can possibly lead to their becoming more dangerous. One patient, complaining that I failed to set appropriate limits on his chastising me, compared himself to the blackbirds in his backyard (and me to the crows): "I watch the crows being attacked by the much smaller blackbirds. The crows are extremely accommodating. Though they are bigger and stronger, they are the ones to run. But the running only seems to inspire the blackbirds further. I often wonder what the blackbirds would do if the crows instead turned on them and attacked back. It reminds me of how one time my running from an angry dog only inspired it to become more vicious. I have read about a number of cases where begging a bank robber (transiently paranoid due to all the heightened tension and danger) to put down the gun he or she was holding to a victim's head and spare his or her life seemed to inflame him or her even more. So I thought that it might be better to take a chance on being strong and less masochistic, and order the bank robber to 'lay off and get a real job.' In my experience sometimes the most desirable therapeutic effect is produced on potentially or actually dangerous blackbirds, dogs, bank robbers, and psychiatric patients like me by being firm. So I would appreciate it if you would instead stop coddling me and stand your ground."

Like this patient, many paranoid individuals appreciate others' setting limits on them as an attempt to save them from themselves. I have seen a few potentially suicidal patients who, when told "you have a right to take your own life," view that as "here, let me help you do it," then react by killing themselves simply because they think that "no one cares." Sometimes we read of patients who, shortly after being sent home from the emergency room of a hospital after applying for and being refused hospitalization, go out and kill randomly. One such patient warned the emergency room personnel that he was about to become violent. In effect he was begging them to "stop me from killing." He felt angry and hurt because no one seemed to care enough to admit him to the hospital to help him control himself. Thus angered about being sent home, he went on a stabbing spree to take his disappointment and anger at his doctors out on strangers.

Once again, setting limits—and what often amounts to the same thing, exercising one's legitimate authority—must be done in a positive and, when done with friends and family, a loving, way. In setting limits on their children parents should reassure them that "I am not criticizing you, and I do respect you." Teachers should reassure their students that they are being taught, not hounded. Ministers should reassure their parishioners that "just because I focus on your liabilities does not mean that I believe you have no assets." Husbands should reassure their wives that you do as many things right as you do wrong, and that my bringing you up short about one thing or another does not mean that I do not love you. Bosses who fire people, especially people who are unstable, should make it a point to do so in as therapeutic a manner as possible. Citing specific impersonal reasons for the action taken can be helpful: for example, "I am firing you for what you did, or did not do, not for what you are, or were not." Bosses who fire people they suspect of being at all paranoid should make a special effort to be kind and even help them find a new job. Such humane treatment can make it less likely that an ex-employee will come back dressed in combat fatigues to "return the fire." As inhuman as it is, violence always has a human face. Behind many plots to take hostages or shoot up the school is a real man or woman whose anger is long in the making, and whose plot of revenge is against those who actually just did something, however trivial, to make them mad.

Even paranoid individuals tend to be most accepting of limitations and prohibitions when these are accompanied by rational explanations. Careful, rational explanations make limitations and prohibitions seem more reasonable and therefore less shame- and guilt-inducing. For example, an adviser should probably not tell a paranoid individual, "Listen to me, I know best," but instead say, "I am setting limits on you not to be parental but because in my best judgment that is the most effective way to help you stop being so self-destructive."

However, unilateral limit-setting without tenderness is sometimes indicated. People who are being stalked should never yield to the temptation to be flattered by all the attention. I have seen cases where secretly the stalker's victim enjoys being the center of attention and therefore subtly encourages the stalking. He or she makes all kinds of excuses not to intervene, like "This man has not yet done anything to harm me, so I won't go to the authorities." Denial ran rampant when a man who should know better saw a stalker as obsessed with, not delusional about, him, and tried reasoning with her as if she were misguided and inappropriately preoccupied instead of as if she were someone who had taken complete leave of her senses. In many such cases stern measures without backsliding are in order and should be taken and maintained from the start, such as going to the police and asking them to protect one's privacy and physical safety. The recognition that the stalker is a troubled individual should not tempt the victim to take pity and renounce all self-protective measures in favor of seeking help for the stalker. Getting him or her help is theoretically an admirable goal, but, practically speaking, the stalker too often takes that act of kindness and positivity in the wrong way, raising the stalker's hopes that his or her behavior will ultimately yield the desired results.

ACCOMMODATING

This said, whenever possible caretakers should try to accommodate to paranoid individuals by giving them what they legitimately want, need, and should have, even stretching a point and going that extra mile just to keep the peace.

A woman complained that her husband became furious and threatened to kill her when she told him that she wanted to expand her kitchen. He accused her of trying to steal his retirement money, of driving him into the poorhouse, and of attempting to deprive their grandchild of the college education she needed but that the grandchild's own mother, their daughter, could not afford. Several times the husband even pulled back his hand as if he were about to slap her. In her subsequent complaints about him she overlooked that he would not give her what she wanted because she would not give him what he wanted. He had practically begged her to sell an old piano to make room for a lounge chair he desperately needed so that he could put his feet up and sit back with his television set placed comfortably in his sight line. But she refused, complaining that a lounge chair would ruin the look of her living room.

Instead she made him lie on an uncomfortable couch and watch television off at an angle. When after some months of therapy she agreed to make room for him, he backed down and agreed to make room for her, that is, to let her have her kitchen.

In the workplace bosses often deal most effectively with their paranoid employees (all employees get paranoid of the boss, and the institution, at least temporarily and from time to time) by giving a little more, within appropriate limits, hoping that in response the employees will become less preoccupied with the bad deal most think they get from management, and instead settle down and ask only for what is reasonable.

Accommodating is clearly a valid emergency coping and calming method in a paranoid crisis, for example with a paranoid customer who is making unreasonable demands followed by threats when those are not met. However, while it can make for a useful emergency response it is not for everyone, and probably should be reserved for desperate situations. For there are clearly disadvantages to accommodating. While it buys some peace and can go at least part of the way toward building basic trust, many people feel that it is a form of appeasing and that appeasing makes them weak, passive, and dishonest. Also, accommodating involves forgoing self-defense and self-justification as well as relinquishing the pathological pleasure to be gained from being sadistic and the twin masochistic pleasures of getting the sympathy vote from friends and family and of wallowing in the suffering that goes hand in hand with proving to oneself once again that "I try and try, but nothing I do ever comes out right." For some, the most unacceptable thing about accommodating is that it involves suppressing one's native tendency to "be me," which for most people is difficult to do even when the goal is a nurturing "being us." Also, while accommodating can work temporarily to avoid provoking or to defuse a crisis, in the long run it often leaves the one doing the accommodating more vulnerable than before by inspiring an already paranoid individual to become more hurtful than formerly, reassured that more accommodation will be the only consequence he or she will have to face for being sadistic.

There are mass-scale psychological methods rooted in the principle of accommodating useful for managing widespread social dissatisfaction by making the dissatisfied customer always right. However, these methods are mainly useful for groups that have legitimate concerns that are being overlooked. Working with these groups and responding properly to their concerns can even help prevent social unrest, including riots. For example, a town that is displacing its poorer residents in order to develop luxury condominiums for outsiders must give something back to those from whom it is taking much away. It should offer not only monetary but also emotional support, not only assistance in relocating and adequate repayment for actual losses suffered but also sympathy for and understanding of the plight of the persons displaced. Sympathy and understanding humanize victims. They avoid adding insult to injury and legitimize instead of belittling and devaluing their complaints. Obviously these principles do not apply to terror groups that only claim that they want fairness in order to hide the base nature of their horrific unilateral intent.

HUMORING

Humoring is perhaps the single most useful approach for managing paranoid individuals effectively. One man discovered that he could not complain about anything work-related to his paranoid boss without the boss thinking that he was complaining about her. Also, if he did complain the boss saw to it that he had much to complain about. This man decided to humor her by not bringing up a pressing matter with her until he first determined that she was in a good mood. He made up his mind that he would rather wait up to a few weeks to broach a topic than to risk being greeted with an irrational temper tantrum along the lines of "Why are you bothering me with that stupid problem now; can't you see that I am busy?" On balance, he felt that humoring her this way was a good trade-off, because while he hated being so self-effacing and passive, in reality it cost him very little and paid him back handsomely in the long run.

Here are some clinical vignettes that illustrate the occasional virtue of humoring individuals who are paranoid:

An abused wife decided to deal with her abusive husband by putting up with his abuse and suffering in silence. She decided, and hers was a very personal decision, not right for everyone, that what self-realization and self-actualization she might have to relinquish by humoring him would be more than made up for by the resultant stability of her relationship. For example, she did not attend her son-in-law's graduation because her husband asked her not to go but to instead boycott the affair to offer him support. Even though her husband was boycotting the affair for irrational reasons (because he hated to see his son-in-law get a degree that he himself did not have), she went along with him to avoid making him feel that she was against him. As she put it, "It is either back him up, or he will give me a black eye." One day she was barbecuing chicken wings. The wings flared, and she burned herself slightly trying to put out the flames. Her husband became furious, saying, "I told you to buy them ready-made; why don't you ever listen to me?" Then he stormed out of the house and went drinking. She handled that situation by promising to reform, and, true to her word, the next time she had people over for chicken wings they were of the ready-made variety.

A couple's cat was losing her hair, and the owners were trying to find out exactly why. The husband blamed his cat's hair loss on his wife. He suggested, "The bathtub cleanser you are using is causing her to have that reaction." The wife became defensive and replied, "I don't use that; I use this, a much milder detergent that cannot possibly cause a cat to lose her hair." The husband doubted that, and accused her of either being unconcerned or of lying to him. Then he turned to the rest of the family and announced, almost proudly, "You see what I have to put up with at home?" A calming response on her part involved her saying, "I'll stop using that cleanser and buy another one. What's a little cleanser between two old buddies?"

A paranoid man became furious with his lover. In discussing Robert Frost, the first man said that in speaking of roads not taken the poet was simply describing a walk through a new, uncharted part of the woods. The lover sharply disagreed, saying, "Everyone knows that Frost was in fact commenting on the deep meaning of all journeys." The paranoid man, feeling that his lover was disagreeing with him just to be difficult and to upset him, made menacing gestures, as if he were about to strike out. The lover decided that the matter was of no real importance and that in this particular instance discretion was better than valor. He determined that, factoring in his lover's paranoia, he should keep his own opinions to himself because his only real choice was between analyzing Robert Frost's poetry the way he saw fit, and being alone, which was the last thing in the world that he wanted.

A paranoid man became furious because a neighbor had installed an ugly lawn decoration, a plastic wheelbarrow full of artificial flowers, right under the paranoid man's window. His wife said, "Forget about it." But the man responded, "Now I have two problems: his ugly lawn decoration and your refusing to see things my way." So he blew up and threatened to leave. His wife, identifying this as a serious emergency, offered an abject, if slightly less than sincere, apology, saying, "I was wrong. I took another look and it is truly ugly." As expected, her response soothed him and defused the crisis.

REASSURANCE

Reassurance, perhaps accompanied by apologies, is especially effective when also accompanied by specific evidence that offers the paranoid individual proof that he or she has no reason to be afraid or suspicious, and by a specific remedy suggested in place of a general "I'm sorry I hurt you" or "I'm sorry if I did anything wrong." The following is an example of an apology that offers first specific evidence, then a definite remedy. A nurse's husband accused her of having quickie affairs between work and home. First she heard him out without replying chapter and verse to his accusations. She reasoned that anything you say to someone who is acutely upset is likely to be inflammatory, if only because it makes it look as if you are not listening. She also said nothing because she reasoned, "I don't owe him an apology and I certainly don't owe him an explanation as to where I was yesterday." But on second thought she decided to say something. But she stifled the temptation to say, "You never believe me," and instead decided to give him that apology and explanation anyway to calm him down. So she said, "I'm sorry I was late getting home. Yes, officially I get out of work at 11:00 P.M. But I am a nurse, and a nurse has to do reports, and that often takes longer than expected. Next time I'll call you from the hospital when I am ready to leave. You will even be able to tell where I am because you will be able to hear all the hospital noises in the background."

Another wife accused of having noontime affairs replied to the accusation by saying, "I was at the hairdresser's; look here, see my new coiffure; talk to Joan, my stylist; she can back up my story." Her reply was demeaning to herself, but she felt that demeaning herself was worth it because it was both life-enhancing for her relationship and life-saving for her, maintaining as it did both her marriage and her physical safety.

Reassurance, already a kind of panacea for paranoid patients, becomes an even better remedy when one enlists the paranoid person's help in the reassurance process. For example, a woman replied to her husband when he accused her of being unfaithful to him, "I always want you to take comfort in the knowledge that you are the only one for me. Tell me how I can prove it, and that is what I will do." This technique parallels the automobile salesman's extremely effective "tell me what I can do to make this deal work for you" That approach counters the buyer's naturally occurring and understandably paranoid "he is trying to screw me" by making him or her a participant in, not a passive victim of, the reassurance process.

In a situation that illustrates the power of reassurance, at first a woman refused to reassure her suspicious husband that she wasn't being unfaithful. Instead she unhelpfully said, "I wish you didn't accuse me of doing things I didn't do. All that does is make me mad and make me want to do them." She had forgotten that a good general principle to follow is that the paranoid complaint "you are against me" is almost always a cover for the paranoid fear that "you must be against me because you are not for me." Ultimately she rescued the situation by taking what she just said back and instead telling her husband that he had no reason to think that she was up to anything sinister. This worked in part because it offered her husband affirmation along the lines of "she really does care how I feel," and that in turn helped him feel loved. Feeling loved, he became less defensive, and feeling less defensive he became less paranoid, and now even more open to accepting new reassurances.

Of course, there will be times when it is difficult or impossible to successfully reassure paranoid individuals that they are not being singled out for mistreatment. I once had a patient who felt that he was the focus of everything bad that happened in the world—that he was a kind of perpetual victim of misfortune. My office was situated on the first floor of a high-rise building. During one session a pipe burst on a higher floor and water rushed down the steps then seeped under my door and rose so high in the office that we had to clear out. I reassured him that he had nothing to do with this disaster, for it was just an accident that occurred at a time that he happened to be there. That held him until next week at the same time when, right in the middle of our next session, all the lights went out in my office because all the lights in the Northeast went out in a widespread blackout. Now it took weeks of effort to convince him that he had little or nothing to do with the bad things happening to him and to stem his growing fear that even I, as his therapist, could not protect him from disaster.

BEING HONEST

Caretakers should always be straight with paranoid individuals. While some holding back may be indicated, no one should ever tell even a white lie to someone who is paranoid, especially if it involves betraying a paranoid individual by doing things behind his or her back. In a cooperative building a sign went up on the bulletin board that volunteers were needed to serve on the cooperative board. A somewhat paranoid patient volunteered for the slot, only to be told that there was just one spot and two candidates for it—and that the choice between the two would be made by flipping a coin. Unwilling to compete, even in this impersonal manner, he graciously volunteered to drop out, only to later discover that the vacancy had long ago been filled with his rival and that the talk of a contest was just a way to manipulate him into giving up. He could never bring himself to trust anyone in the building's administration again.

CHAPTER 19

Things to Avoid Doing with Paranoid Individuals

In chapter 16 I listed some errors therapists should avoid making with paranoid patients. In chapter 18 I suggested some ways caretakers can help paranoid individuals while simultaneously enhancing their ability to cope with them and protecting themselves from being victimized by them. In this chapter, which overlaps with chapters 16 and 18, I suggest things caretakers should avoid doing with paranoid individuals. Since most of us are in fact at least mildly paranoid, this chapter can also serve as a compendium of social niceties and diplomatic behaviors likely to win the affection and respect of almost everyone in our lives, seriously paranoid or no.

EMBARRASS PARANOID INDIVIDUALS

Paranoid individuals are private people who keep secrets to maintain their self-esteem. Therefore they dislike probing questions, especially in areas where they are sensitive. For one thing, it is typical for paranoid individuals to not want to reveal their ages. Therefore, it was not a good idea for a hostess to publicly list the advantages of being a young 60 to a guest who claimed to be in his early fifties. It is rarely a good idea to probe into a paranoid individual's anger, especially when he or she comes from a violent family background. Those paranoid individuals with a history of excessive primal scene exposure and (what is often part of the same picture) intense masturbation and incest guilt resent being asked about their sexuality due to being ashamed of their erotic fantasies and actual past sexual encounters. Those who are addicted to alcohol or painkillers (many are, and some are paranoid, or more paranoid, because of that addiction) like to keep their addictions secret, even from their doctors—one possible reason why a patient attacked me physically after he read his record and saw that I had written in it that I refused him more pain medication because I believed that he was malingering his pain in order to obtain regular prescriptions for OxyContin.

PUT PARANOID INDIVIDUALS ON THE SPOT

Paranoid individuals dislike being put on the spot, particularly when that involves being double-binded. A patient became violent when his boss double-binded him by telling him to do one thing, then telling him to do the opposite thing, then ordered him to follow her directions or else. As he complained, "She reminds me of my wife. If I tell her the truth she complains that I am being too painfully honest, but if I try to spare her the gory details she chastises me for being deceitful. Saying nothing isn't an option either, because then she complains that I never talk to her. I feel like killing her."

As an extreme example of putting paranoid individuals on the spot, one gay patient brought a paranoid pickup home, then locked the door behind him from the inside using a combination lock. Thinking himself clever, he joked, "That's so that you won't kill me, because if you kill me you will be unable to get away afterwards." Feeling trapped, the pickup panicked and threatened to kill the gay man anyway, unless he immediately opened the door and let him go. Making a pass at hitchhikers runs the risk of putting them on the spot. Since flight is too difficult, the only way that they can extricate themselves from a tight corner is by fight, that is, by beating up or killing the person who is cornering them.

CRITICIZE OR PUT PARANOID INDIVIDUALS DOWN

The high degree of sensitivity and the suspicious nature of paranoid individuals makes them prone to react strongly and negatively to being devalued in any way. Paranoid individuals predictably react badly to words or deeds that are, or that they perceive to be, humiliating and embarrassing. Paranoid men even more than other men react negatively to even mild putdowns by feeling castrated, or ball-busted, and paranoid women even more than other women react negatively to even mild putdowns by feeling that they are antifeminist tirades that are the rough equivalent of the familiarly and justifiably despised "a woman's place is in the home." Of course, it is not always possible to anticipate and avoid these reactions—with paranoid individuals or with anyone else. Once I merely mentioned to a paranoid man that I liked Edward Gibbon's *Decline and Fall of the Roman Empire*, only to be reminded that it was a phallocentric tract completely dismissed by all right-thinking people of today. Therefore, if you err and say something potentially abrasive to someone really sensitive, and you desire above all to keep the peace, it is generally a good idea to back off immediately. Be quick to assume some blame, even if it is not completely warranted, and apologize. Saying the equivalent of "you are right; I misspoke and hurt you, and I am sorry" generally calms the victim down because that is exactly what a paranoid individual wants to hear, and indeed has spent his or her life trying to evoke. On the other hand, saying "you misinterpreted what I said; stop being so paranoid" causes a paranoid individual to flare, because it is exactly what he or she is afraid of hearing and has spent all of his or her life trying to avoid being told. In like manner, saying "I'm sorry" to someone in road rage, admitting that you did something to make him or her feel diminished in some key way, usually dissipates his or her anger. In contrast, counterattacking such people for being hotheads or otherwise giving them the finger, figuratively if not literally, predictably inflames them and can create a dangerously escalating situation leading to the equivalent of a bar brawl. If someone at the gym tries to take a machine right out from under you, smile and yield instead of criticizing the person for being pushy and selfish, which can make an enemy out of and start a feud with someone you are likely to be working near for a long time.

Here are two anecdotes that illustrate how some individuals unwisely criticized and otherwise put paranoid individuals down:

A patient complained that his lover was stupid for trimming his favorite magnolia tree in the spring when the sap was running, instead of in the winter when the tree was hibernating. When he didn't back off, his lover hit him so hard that he detached his retina.

A fish and game warden in a state where fish and game wardens have certain police powers stopped a man who was speeding. Instead of abject apologies and a promise to reform, the man who was stopped countered, "Buddy, you are not a cop, so why do I have to listen to you? Besides, why are you wearing that funny camouflage outfit, and what's with that badge of yours on your waist when it should be on your chest? And anyway that skinhead haircut is really a turnoff." At this writing the man is fighting to avoid 21 days in jail for resisting arrest by a warden who (he subsequently discovered through personal research) had a need to feel just like a real cop, and therefore hated to have his position challenged and his true role in life dismantled by what he considered to be a big nobody's devaluing it as mere role-playing.

Dissing adolescents is particularly risky. A schoolteacher first humiliated a dreamy, sensitive adolescent for being feminine, second forced him to participate in baseball games, which he hated, and third laughed at him for throwing the ball like a woman. Fortunately for the rest of the school, the adolescent reacted with self-hatred, so that instead of becoming paranoid he became depressed, and instead of becoming violent to others he made a gestural suicide attempt. Fortunately, too, another teacher came to the rescue just in time by simply reminding the adolescent, "Not everyone is athletic. God gave you so many talents; you do not need that particular one." Parents and other caretakers should not fail to understand that their young and adolescent children are immature individuals who, being inexperienced, predictably go wrong from time to time, like to have others respect their integrity even when they have erred badly, and conversely respond very negatively to anything that they can interpret as being a blow to their egos.

It is an especially bad idea to put down any paranoid individual—child, adolescent, or adult—for something for which he or she is not to blame. A man and a woman went into an antique store and asked the owner if he were interested in buying some antique lamps from them. "How much do you want for them?" the owner asked. "We don't know, we will leave it up to you to determine a price," was their honest answer. The owner then said, about "others," in an accusatory voice, with referential implications that fooled no one, "You should know what you want for them. Some people act like they are trying to sell something when they really just want a free appraisal." The man had all he could do to keep from hitting the owner. Fortunately, instead of striking out, at the last minute the man chose to walk out in a rage. In a parallel situation a therapist, hearing that his patient had a problem neighbor, replied, "I wondered how long you would go without one of those," implying fault on the patient's part when it was really just a matter of bad luck in neighbors plaguing him once again.

Paranoid people are especially put off by prejudiced people who discriminate against them, particularly for things that are beyond their control, such as their ethnicity or social status. That helps explain why affirmative action is a dynamically sound remedy for prejudice and discrimination. It offers not merely equal opportunity but also a corrective measure of respect.

It is an equally bad idea to criticize paranoid individuals for things that they do right and well, not wrong or badly. A college student worked a whole year preparing the solo piano part to a large-scale work for piano and orchestra by an American composer, only to have the entire music department ignore the originality of his selection and the stellar nature of his performance and respond to the jazz aspects of the work by telling him not to play that stuff anymore and instead stick to the European classics. This was a highly paranoid man who as a consequence felt totally shattered, to the point that to this day he still feuds with his college symbolically (the only way he can) by sending back every communication he receives from them with the word *refused* scrawled in red ink all over it.

Criticizing indirectly by what you do not say—not speaking of what paranoid individuals did wrong but simply overlooking what they did right—can be equally devastating. A somewhat paranoid composer complained to me that a colleague never acknowledged that the composer had written a single note. The colleague did not criticize the composer openly. He simply did not react or respond when the composer mentioned work that he had previously done or was currently doing.

Paranoid individuals are as sensitive to nonverbal as they are to verbal criticism. They are highly threatened by such things as a frown on the face, a neighbor's taking an obvious turn off the road to avoid having to say hello to them, or a therapist's remoteness accompanied by his or her all-too-obvious eagerness to end the session, as manifest by his or her constantly looking at his or her watch.

As noted throughout, many paranoid individuals can accept overt criticism better than the subtle, passive-aggressive kind. When the criticism is overt, they at least know what they are dealing with. When the criticism is covert, the lack of clarity enhances the negative impact.

However, caretakers need to keep in mind that paranoid individuals often imagine passive-aggressive attacks when none are intended. A neighbor walking his dog ran into another neighbor only because the second man was delayed on his walk that day. The first man merely noted, "You're late today," only to have the second man feel that he was being criticized for not being on time. A friend asked a nonfiction writer if he were going to write a novel, only to have the second man bridle because he felt that all the nonfiction work he had done up to that point was being devalued. He read the statement not as the half-full "you can do even more," but as the half-empty "what you already did was not very good." A psychologist told a paranoid patient that the patient was responsible for most things that went wrong in his life and that therefore his fate was mostly in his own hands, and that his serious problems were almost always the result of his own doing. When he told this patient that "there is no such thing as a victim, only a volunteer," he was simply trying to reassure him that the patient had the power within himself to make changes that would improve his life. But the patient, thinking that he was being criticized for stupidly bringing his own demise on himself, quit therapy in a huff.

It follows that when speaking to paranoid individuals it is important to always be clear in order to avoid implying negativity. A friend or a family member should not query a paranoid woman, "Do you ever plan to get married?" without somehow making it clear (if that is the case) that he or she is not accusing her of being remote, withdrawn, a social misfit, or a lesbian. A friend or family member should not ask a paranoid gay man, "Are you the one who does the cooking?" without also making it clear (if indeed that is the case) that he or she is not accusing him of being feminine. A father should not ask a paranoid son if he knows all about the facts of life without also making it clear that he did not bring the topic up because he suspects that bad things are going on behind his back and closed doors and is out to extract a confession.

It is wise to avoid communications that invite two contradictory interpretations, one of which can be perceived as critical. Quite by chance a woman happened to mention that there was such a thing as a Yorkie rescue organization to her brother who, unbeknownst to her, had that very day been debating with himself whether to purchase a Yorkshire terrier. He commented, "I cannot believe that you said that." His comment could be interpreted in two ways. He meant "what a coincidence." She thought he was criticizing her for having said the wrong thing. So she stomped off, complaining that "I cannot say anything at all these days without being taken to task for it."

People who in spite of themselves are tempted to be critical of and feel the urge to put paranoid people down can help master their hurtful critical tendencies in three ways. First, they should try to understand why they are compelled to be as critical as they are. Are they seriously competitive individuals trying to vanquish all competitors because they view them, rightly or wrongly, as dangerous rivals poised to keep them from being number one at all times? As men do they equate hurting others with being masculine, or as women do they believe that self-affirmation can only be accomplished by deaffirming others, the only way they have to enhance their self-image? Second, they should make a conscious effort to do an about-face and show their appreciation for, or actually compliment, paranoid individuals for what they do well. Third, if they must criticize paranoid individuals they can at least do so constructively. They can simultaneously make it clear that they are discussing individual problems, not problem individuals, and convey sympathy and support by acknowledging that none of us is perfect and that the best of us go astray. A husband orders rib-eye steak for dinner. His wife intervenes, saying, "Don't eat that; you always eat something with too much fat." He replies, "You are always picking on me," then announces to the rest of the table, "I love her but she hates me." Next time she tries a different approach. He orders a rib-eye steak, and she, acknowledging that we all sometimes feel hopeless in the face of temptation, says, "It must be hard to resist something so delicious." He can understand and go along with that, so he responds by saying, "You are right, I am giving in when I should be strong," and shows her how immune to temptation he is—by ordering the chicken.

In conclusion, as Oldham and Morris (1995) put it when speaking of coping with paranoid people, "you have to love a Paranoid person completely. Any criticism or annoyance you express will hurt this person intolerably, and you will find yourself on the long list of people who have wronged him or her" (p. 179).

TREAT PARANOID INDIVIDUALS UNDIPLOMATICALLY

The reader will recall the man, first discussed in chapter 3, who, suspecting that there was more going on between his wife and a mutual friend than met the eye, sent the mutual friend a letter inquiring about the status of things. An undiplomatic response to the accusations that his friend was less than innocent of wrongdoing would have been confrontational: "What do you think is going on? Do you think I am plotting behind your back? Obviously, you are accusing me of doing something wrong, so just as obviously this is the end of our relationship, and good-bye." A more diplomatic response would have been, "Don't worry, all we talked about was getting together soon.

I was going to tell you about it right afterward, and ask you to come over by yourself the next time."

A man standing in a parking lot happened to be standing in a parking place another driver, a man driving an imposing SUV, wanted to pull into. The man started an argument by refusing to budge. In a parallel situation with a more favorable outcome, another man standing in a parking space that a SUV driver wanted indicated that he was aware that he was taking up the space the driver desired by diplomatically bowing, grinning widely, stepping aside, and waving the driver of the SUV on. Now the driver of the SUV laughed and said, referring to his SUV, "You better not tangle with me"—triumphing for the moment by reaffirming his power and intactness.

DEHUMANIZE PARANOID INDIVIDUALS

Caretakers should never treat paranoid individuals as anything less than the human beings they of course are. Like anyone else, paranoid individuals respond to positivity, empathy, concern, and forbearance, and in some ways they respond more favorably to these than many other people. The general public should not go along with the dehumanizing-in-the-extreme implication/ assertion often found in the scientific literature that all paranoid persons are completely irrational and unresponsive to reason, have symptoms that cannot be understood in human terms, and are too detached interpersonally to react positively to affirmation. I strongly believe that there is a great deal to talk about therapeutically with paranoid people, no matter how irrational they at first appear to be. For example, I feel that erotomanic delusions can almost always be understood and discussed in the context of a person's sexuality, and that litigious delusions can almost always be understood and discussed in the context of a person's vengefulness. Caretakers can often profitably engage the healthier, more insightful, more motivated, more intelligent paranoid individuals, even those with a delusional disorder, in a discussion of their emotional problems as long as they reason with them unemotionally and impersonally, and neither challenge them nor attempt to force them to confess and reform, but instead enlist them as co-adventurers in the twin processes of sorting things out and settling matters fairly and equitably.

GET SADOMASOCHISTICALLY INVOLVED WITH PARANOID INDIVIDUALS

Paranoid individuals are effectively sadists. They persecute others as much as they feel persecuted by them. Their delusions are in fact disguised attacks on those about whom they are delusional. Also, it is sadistic to empty oneself of self-blame by blaming others. Like many sadists, paranoid sadists predictably escalate when their victims appear to accept being abused, and deescalate when victims set limits on the amount of victimization that they are willing to tolerate. For example, a paranoid husband, falsely believing that his wife was cheating on him, told his wife, "I wish I never married you," and threatened to leave her. She begged him to stay, sending him the message that she accepted his behavior and that if she were troubled by anything it was the possibility that he might abandon her completely—that is, that his bad behavior toward her would stop. Expectedly, he interpreted her begging him to stay as permission to continue as before, and he ultimately escalated to the point that he hit her. She should have realized that, like many paranoid people, he became most delusional about people who gave him very little reason to be afraid of the consequences of incorporating them into his delusions.

Not unexpectedly, paranoid individuals are effectively masochists. Like other masochists, they readily, willingly, and even deliberately give sadists the opportunity to persecute them. For one thing, they give sadists an opening to be hurtful by seeking positivity from those who for reasons of their own tend to be most negative to them. For another, being paranoid seems to make one a natural target—by making one into a desirable and readily available scapegoat. Many people see paranoid individuals as having been put on Earth to enhance group solidarity by becoming the group's long-sought-for and sorely needed common enemy. This is partly because sadists, smelling blood, view the paranoid individual's hypersensitivity, suspiciousness, and fear that he or she is being victimized as an invitation to turn his or her paranoid fears into reality, to in effect give him or her something to be paranoid about. An operative principle here is that one should never give masochistic paranoid individuals what they seem to be asking for. Predictably, they won't want it once they get it, will have one more reason to see others as their enemies, and will switch over from masochism to sadism.

BETRAY PARANOID INDIVIDUALS

Whenever possible, and within reason, it is best to be honest and above-board at all times with people who are paranoid. It is particularly paranoia-genic to say bad things about potentially paranoid individuals behind their backs, then when these things, as is predictable, get back, attempt to deny that you said them or meant what you said. A patient complained about a neighbor to someone who knew them both. The person complained to shot back, "I refuse to get involved in your struggles with her"—saying this so spontaneously and effortlessly that it became immediately apparent to the patient that the other person had gotten there first and that the two had by now formed an alliance. The patient felt that the neighbor should have told her to her face what he said about her behind her back, then asked to hear her side of the story so that she could have an opportunity to defend herself. Failing that, the patient began to suspect that all her neighbors were in it together, and out to shame and discredit her.

BE UNFAIR TO PARANOID INDIVIDUALS

Paranoid individuals treated unfairly tend not to assume (as is usually correct) that the people who are treating them that way are routinely unfair, and to everybody. Rather they tend to conclude that others are screwing them personally. A worker went on an emotional rampage because his boss treated him unfairly without apologizing for having done so. Without saying that he was sorry for the inconvenience or offering him extra pay, his boss demanded that he stay overtime on the eve of a holiday weekend. Making matters worse was that the boss herself did not always show up for work, and when she did show up often came late, left early, and expected him to do her work for her. She also on a regular basis called up to say she would not be in because it was snowing and the roads were icy, then insisted that he come in to cover for her—so that she could avoid having to drive in blizzardlike conditions. The patient was right to complain, "I am busting my chops while she is goofing off. I wouldn't mind working so hard if I weren't the only one doing it." But he was wrong to assume that his boss had it in for him personally. In fact she was just a slave driver who treated everyone the way she treated him.

Of course it can be extremely destructive to single out a paranoid individual for mistreatment, especially after undervaluing the individual in comparison to a colleague. I know of some cases where paranoid individuals who complained about being given a talking to at work, or being fired from their jobs, would have accepted that, but tipped because everyone else was let off easy for the exact sort of behavior for which they were being called on the carpet.

ARGUE WITH PARANOID INDIVIDUALS

As Oldham and Morris (1995) put it, "to cope with a [paranoid] person, back off. Don't try to talk him or her out of any suspicions, or you will soon be seen as a co-conspirator yourself. Avoid confrontations and try to stay clear of arguments" (p. 179). As emphasized throughout, carelessly and callously challenging and confronting paranoid individuals' delusional ideas usually does more harm than good. In part, this is so because many paranoid individuals are, at least on some level, already sufficiently in tune with themselves to know that they are wrong and to feel ashamed of themselves. Besides, arguing with them is futile to the extent that their minds are already made up because they want and need their distortions. Also, arguing with them is futile because they are often at least partly right. Being guilty, stubborn, and partly right is a deadly combination that creates an impenetrable fanaticism that does not respond favorably to being contradicted. Some paranoid individuals will, when given an argument, apologize in a superficial manner in order to deflect criticism. Others, being fanatics, will instead intensify their delusional beliefs in protest—in order to feel intact and on top. A teenager decided that Hitler was his hero and that he wanted most of all to be one of his followers. Arguing with him about how Hitler hurt innocent people was futile and counter-productive. Instead he became even more Nazi-like to put his newly found persecutors, the ones who challenged him with their opposing views, in their place. Since Hitler was his hero, he dealt with being challenged by authority the same way Hitler seems to have dealt with his challengers—by persecuting them.

It is particularly helpful to not respond one-on-one, that is, antiphonally, to a paranoid individual's distortions about one's person. It may be difficult to avoid a knee-jerk self-defensive response to paranoid assertions, but it is the wise victim who remains passive and says nothing during an acute outburst, secure in the knowledge that sometimes distortions that are ignored just stop, and in the anticipation that paranoid anger often soon subsides on its own and even ends in a retraction based on more of the same guilt that provoked the temper tantrum in the first place. Besides, paranoid individuals, like most people, only become more argumentative when they sense that they are having an effect and getting a rise out of people. In contrast they tend to lose interest in arguing when others do not react immediately by becoming upset, but instead at least act uninvolved and disinterested. Agitated counter-accusations in response to a paranoid individual's angry defiance almost always justify the paranoid reaction after the fact.

There are much better responses to patients with delusional ideas than abject argumentative confrontation, and many of these were previously discussed. Some of these are cognitive approaches for reality testing delusional thinking; acknowledging that none of us is perfect given the complexity of human interactions, admitting that we all make mistakes and errors of judgment; and helpful expressions of compassion and sympathy that acknowledge that a paranoid individual must feel frightened and hopeless about sorting things out. A patient complained to her lover that he put something in her drink in order to take advantage of her sexually. When the lover said, "You are imagining things," she dug in and insisted that she was right and he was wrong, mainly to cope with the humiliation she felt when he in effect told her that she was a fool and ordered her to "cut it out." If he had said, "You must really feel bad that I don't love you enough to not do something like that," instead of entrenching, she might have backed off and said, "Well, perhaps I imagined it." Also helpful is a positive approach that emphasizes the advantages, financial and interpersonal, associated with becoming less fearful, and the advantages of not creating adversaries but of instead learning to become a fair-minded, even-tempered individual who interprets reality precisely, correctly, and benignly in order to keep the peace and maintain and repair old and develop new relationships.

BUY INTO A PARANOID INDIVIDUAL'S ILLOGIC

Paranoid individuals are often persuasive people who tempt others to buy into their distorted ideation, in particular their heartfelt and clever blaming.

Victims are especially at risk for feeling cowed when the paranoid individual's assertions are aligned with and hook into something the victim already feels uncertain or guilty about. A friend, already feeling somewhat guilty about his conservative views in a liberal neighborhood, told me how upset he was that after a patriotic outburst in which he suggested that we should all support our troops during wartime, an acquaintance, who saw Nazis everywhere, told him that his patriotism smacked of totalitarianism and that therefore he was a Hitler at heart. He then actually apologized for being a little dictator. I suggested that instead of feeling guilty he should have identified his guilty response as just what the other had ordered. Next he should have stopped brooding incessantly about his so-called wrong-thinking, stood his personal ground even though others disagreed with his position, and just dismissed the controversy entirely from his mind.

RISE TO A PARANOID INDIVIDUAL'S BAIT

Teachers need to recognize that their students regularly view them as parent substitutes and authority figures conveniently put on Earth for them to rebel against and overthrow. In a typical sequence, adolescents first provoke the teacher, and then when the teacher responds negatively to the provocation, they react, as planned all along, in a hostile manner that they can now view as completely justified. The teacher next refers the students to a guidance counselor, washing his or her hands of the matter. The students then become even more defensive. They expectedly complain that they were inappropriately punished and abandoned for having been bad and, instead of admitting that they have been disruptive, demand their civil rights to speak their minds because this is a free country. In such situations teachers should consider bypassing this entire interaction and instead, ignoring the heated particulars, sit down with the students and attempt to establish rapport, hoping to turn an adversarial relationship around to become a cooperative venture, where the best interests of all concerned, not the student's resentment or the teacher's hurt feelings, remain in the forefront. Such an approach can avoid turning the students into resentful, disruptive outcasts or bullies. While this "we are allies" approach might not work perfectly, it will at least send the message that "after all, I think you are a sensible worthy person and I am at least trying to treat you that way." This welcome gesture may alone be enough to interrupt a vicious cycle of provocation and punishment on all sides.

USE OR TAKE ADVANTAGE OF PARANOID INDIVIDUALS FINANCIALLY OR SEXUALLY

Paranoid individuals already feel that other people are not to be trusted. Giving them a real reason to distrust only confirms their suspicions and invites retaliation.

HESITATE TO ASK FOR HELP WHEN FACED WITH A POTENTIALLY ASSAULTIVE PARANOID INDIVIDUAL

Potential victims should never hesitate to summon help out of concern that that might make an enemy. More likely the failure to act will inspire attack by broadcasting vulnerability. When working in a psychiatric emergency room, I found that even the most dangerous paranoid individuals could often be subdued without any, or with less, medicine by the use of a show of force. What usually worked was approaching the patient with an attendant or, better still, with a therapeutic phalanx meant to cow the patient into submission. This information accords well with the everyday observation that when jogging in the park at night it is often a good idea to do so with a companion, and with my observation detailed above that the best way to manage the sadistic element of paranoia is to avoid acting vulnerable like a masochist.

A final caveat is that caretakers, no matter how considerate they are, should not expect that every paranoid individual will respond in a positive way to their well-meaning interventions. It is not always possible to treat paranoid individuals right. Caretakers should try their best without necessarily expecting immediate or full success. They should not be too hard on themselves should they fail completely. They should even consider getting out of a relationship with a paranoid person when nothing seems to help. Parallel to the spread of knowledge about the wisdom of getting away from wife-beaters, people who are working for paranoid bosses and find that reasoning with them goes nowhere—as when the boss says, "I am the boss, and if you don't like it you can clear out,"—may be better off just quitting their jobs and leaving, and without ever looking back.

CHAPTER 20

Coping with One's Own Paranoia

Here are some specific ways that you, as a paranoid individual, can cope with your own paranoia, developing a less antagonistic identity and making yourself newly whole.

ENHANCE YOUR SELF-ACCEPTANCE

Paranoia is a negative attitude about others that originates in large measure in a negative attitude about oneself. If you are paranoid you no doubt believe that others do not accept you the same way, and for the same reasons, that you do not accept yourself, and that others criticize you the same way, and for the same reasons, that you criticize yourself. Typical reasons for not accepting, and for criticizing, yourself are homosexual tendencies you find forbidden, heterosexual wishes you believe to be shameful, and angry feelings you find personally unacceptable. It follows that one good corrective for being paranoid involves enhancing your self-acceptance by embracing your own (reasonable, mainstream) sexuality and gratifying it in healthy ways. Now, less guilty about your own homosexual wishes, you will be less likely to criticize yourself and others for being homosexual, and so less likely to develop delusional ideas such as the feeling that others are calling you queer or, with a combination of fear and hope, the belief that rays are penetrating your anus. Less guilty about your heterosexual wishes, you will be less apt to feel that others are staring at you because you are blushing—turning red and hot because you have shameful sexual thoughts—and less apt to be concerned that others are shunning you because you are sweating profusely or because you are emitting funny sexual hormonal smells. Another good corrective involves enhancing your self-acceptance by coming to grips with your own (rational) anger instead of condemning it, attempting to suppress it completely, and then attributing it to others, changing "I am angry with you" defensively to become "you are angry with me" and "punishing me for thinking evil things about, and planning to do bad things to, you."

You can also enhance your self-acceptance by correcting those self-directed cognitive errors that lead you to distort your self-image negatively. For example, you can correct the belief that you are all bad just because you are not all good, that is, just because you have a few undesirable personality traits and have actually done some things in your life that you rightfully regret.

You can enhance your self-acceptance by surrounding yourself with others who like and accept you. If you are not the sort of person who chooses complete or relatively complete isolation for yourself, you can develop a circle of honest friends and lovers who do not arouse your suspicion, noncritical friends and lovers who do not pick on and punish you, and steadfast friends and lovers who do not at a moment's notice threaten to or actually abandon you. You can avoid

- untrustworthy partners who cheat on you sexually then lie about it
- silent people—those who are obviously thinking a lot without saying precisely what they are thinking about, making you wonder exactly what they have in mind
- argumentative people who know it all and insist that you and everyone else buy into their (often unscientific) theories
- couples who, being at loggerheads with each other, predictably put you in the middle, making it inevitable that you will have to either side with one incurring the enmity of the other, or stop seeing them both

No doubt you, like most paranoid people, find that other paranoid individuals are apt to lower your self-esteem. That would include distanced individuals who are disinclined to look you in the eye, erotomanic individuals who complain that your modest sexual approaches are sexual harassment, and highly jealous individuals who accuse you of cheating, no matter how faithful you are and how many times you deny that you are looking elsewhere.

However, increased self-acceptance is not the right goal for you if you are one of those paranoid individuals who are in fact correctly blaming yourself for being a seriously evil person who has actually done some truly bad things in life. If this is you, you should blame yourself more, not less, and instead of viewing your low self-esteem as inappropriate and setting out to improve it psychologically, view it as appropriate and set out to correct the behavior that gives you true and proper reasons to dislike yourself.

Self-acceptance is also the wrong goal for you if you are a grandiose paranoid individual whose self-esteem is too high given who you actually are and your circumstances in life. If this is you, you should adjust your self-esteem to reflect an honest answer to the question "What is my true value, based on the sort of person I am, considering the talents I have, and taking into account the way that I treat other people?"

IMPROVE YOUR RELATIONSHIPS WITH OTHER PEOPLE

You as a paranoid individual should work directly on improving and maintaining your relationships with other people. You should become less antagonistic to other people, anticipating that in turn they will become less antagonistic to you. As a paranoid individual you owe it to yourself, and to the others in your life, to respect differences, leave room for diversity, and never define who is a bad person strictly according to your personal standard of what a good person consists of. You might need to stop thinking that you have the one and only truth, accept the possibility that others know something too, and pay attention to what they say. You probably also need to become more empathic toward others. As a more empathic individual you will better appreciate when you are making others suffer and stop doing that. As a simple example, you will measure what you say by what you anticipate your audience wants to hear and can comfortably take in. Long tirades or overinclusive tales with endless trivial details to shore up a shaky adversarial point are not for you. You should certainly start thinking less exclusively about your own anxiety and start thinking more about how others may feel about, and respond to, your tortured methods for making yourself feel better by torturing others and making them feel worse. Think about how you might feel should others blame and accuse you of something in order to absolve themselves of essentially the same thing.

You should differentiate constructive from destructive criticism, criticism that is fair from criticism that is unjust, and you should accept criticism that is constructive and just, and change accordingly and as soon as possible. You should never turn a compliment into a criticism, as did the man who, when complimented for being a good father, saw that as a criticism for lacking professional skills outside of the home. In short, you should respond to what others really mean and actually say, not to what you imagine they had in mind or think that they said. For example, a woman in her late sixties told her son-in-law that she had decided to return to work. He responded with a statement to the effect that, "Wow, that's great, I can't believe it." That is, he was expressing his admiration ("that's wonderful") for her ambition, stamina, tirelessness, and persistent and immutable work ethic. Unfortunately, she became furious because, as she saw it, he was expressing surprise that she could still do any work at all at her age. She reacted as if he had said, "Who thought at your age you had it in you? Who thought that a senior citizen like you could still be active at anything?"

You also probably need to become less critical of others. You should certainly avoid criticizing others for something in order to disavow a similar tendency in yourself and to inflate your own self-image. Never call someone a Nazi to proclaim how liberal you are, a homophobe to proclaim how simpatico you are, or a bigot to proclaim how you, unlike him or her, tolerate diversity perfectly.

An important part of improving and maintaining your relationships involves operating outside of the fringe. Be less eccentric. Keep your quack medical theories to yourself. Maybe metal bracelets do cure arthritis. On the other hand, maybe it's a placebo effect. A paranoid friend who was having problems meeting men asked me if it might help if she stopped talking about her interest in witchcraft on the first date. I agreed that it would be a good idea.

You should also refuse to buy into and propagate divisive social myths—those currently circulating, interpersonally negative, false beliefs that are a product of hatred and in turn promote hatred toward others. Examples include the belief that striving to do well academically is sissified; that the profit motive is inherently base and sinful; that homosexuality is on a par with incest, bigamy, polygamy, and bestiality (a postulate that simply ignores that homosexual partners are not the equivalent of mother and son, do not necessarily involve cuckolded spouses, and are certainly not animals); and that certain religious, ethnic, and racial groups are appropriately and adequately characterized, sweepingly and very negatively, as money grubbing, lazy and shiftless, or a threat to our economy.

In conclusion, the important operative principle is that if you treat others better, with a little more understanding and sensitivity, they will react to you more positively. Now they will treat you better, meaning that they will provoke you less. As a result you will have less reason to go through life feeling paranoid about what they have in mind and how they are using that to secretly plot against you.

MANAGE YOUR ANGER

As implied throughout, you as a paranoid individual can generally benefit from reducing your excessive and inappropriate anger toward yourself and others. Whenever possible you should avoid getting angry in the first place. There are a number of ways to accomplish that. One way is to stop looking for people who disappoint you just so that you can go through life as a masochist, suffering in the "I told you so" mode, and stop looking for people who upset you just so that you can go through life sadistically punishing others in the "eye-for-an-eye" mode. Another way involves reducing the excessive demands you make on people and on life in general and instead learning to expect only what you should have or that you have a reasonable chance of getting. Now you can avoid always being disappointed in what life and the people in it have to offer and avoid going through life in the "everyone screws me" mode. In this regard it helps to accept your ordinariness—to relinquish your need to be a grandiose perfectionist dissatisfied with being anything less than completely flawless. Stop seriously competing in those situations where, because you don't have what it takes, such as a certain talent, it is likely that you will lose. Instead of insisting that you be number one in all things at all times, accept the possibility that you will be second best at least in some things some of the time. Remember that because sooner or later everyone finds himself or herself in a one-down position, so can you, without that meaning that your true overall value is somehow diminished or your status in life completely negated.

You can also help keep yourself from getting angry in the first place by viewing situations and other people just as they are now, not through the distortive lens of your past experience. Just because you were abused or traumatized when you were young does not mean that fate is repeating itself now in the form of new experiences that resemble the old exactly. Instead, what may really be happening is that you view new benign as old traumatic situations. Now instead of complaining that every new encounter unleashes traumatic childhood memories, you can think about each adult situation afresh and evaluate each interpersonal interaction for itself, and on its own terms, as it is, not as you think that it should be.

You can also avoid getting angry in the first place by staying out of stressful situations where you feel, or are, especially vulnerable to becoming upset. As mentioned throughout, it is often a good idea to avoid passive-aggressive people who make you angry by their annoying ways, then, denying that that is what they did, leave you uncertain if, and mostly feeling that, you are the one at fault. Probably you should also avoid severely obsessive-compulsive people with annoying tic-like behaviors that drive you to distraction, like the teacher who ended every declarative statement with the question, "Is that right?" until one paranoid individual in the class switched out of the course because he felt that the teacher had deliberately set out to torture him personally.

For many people, taking care to avoid stress is the special watchword around Christmas and Easter, times when many individuals, religious or not, paranoid or no, seem to develop a holiday depression (which may really be a holiday paranoia). Around holiday times you should be especially careful of getting too involved with your family if that leaves you tired, disappointed, and enraged. In particular, avoid family members who cancel plans at the last minute due to whim and weather, leaving you feeling alone and rejected, and wondering what you did to deserve it. Meet your family obligations whenever possible, but never let overly scrupulous feelings of responsibility drive you to join holiday celebrations that require too great a self-sacrifice on your part.

Also, take special care during the winter to avoid developing a seasonal affective disorder that is in fact a seasonal paranoid disorder, representing as it does a paranoid response to the dark and the feelings of remoteness, loneliness, isolation, and intimations of death that darkness arouses in almost everybody.

Be very selective about the people you choose to get close to romantically. Some paranoid individuals should consider avoiding all romantic relationships, at least for the time being. That is the right advice for you if you simply cannot handle being disappointed by people you love, and perhaps love too well. If this is you, you have to be very careful not to fall in love with unavailable people such as those with avoidant personality disorders who lead you, as they lead everyone else, on, then drop you precipitously, doing that for personal reasons of their own, while blaming you for the bad outcome. That is the right advice for you if you are the sort of person who finds that lovers threaten your protective isolation to the point that you look for, and find, something to get angry about because you feel that they are clinging too hard to you and therefore that you just must shake them off. It is the right advice for you if you are so uncertain about your self-worth that you easily become jealous and react catastrophically if a lover appears to be ignoring and rejecting you even momentarily and in small ways. The operative principle here is that, while it is hard enough to maintain a relationship between two people when only one is difficult, it is almost impossible to keep one going when two difficult individuals are interacting with each other, each escalating the paranoia of the other.

If you have not been able to avoid getting angry you can at least learn ways to deal with your anger more effectively. Try to put yourself in the other person's place to see if there are more positive alternative explanations for what you feel convinced others have done to upset you. In one case a patient who put himself in his sister's place discovered that canceling one appointment after another was not her idea but her husband's, a man who jumped when his mother called, regardless of any prior commitments he had with anyone else. In cases where you cannot come up with alternative explanations/solutions, you can just try to be more charitable and forgiving. If that does not work, it might be best to simply respect the other person's limitations and restructure the relationship accordingly. For example, a patient invariably flew into a rage when his wife's sister was a few minutes late, correctly sensing that her lateness was a personal thing. I suggested that since she was unlikely to change that he only make a date to see her if she joined him in one of his ongoing activities. That way if she were late, it would not matter nearly so much.

If you are the sort of person who gets a little angry and then gets worked up over nothing, you should try to disrupt your chain thinking and escalating negative emotionality by taking time-outs from feeling enraged. That way you can interrupt self-created and self-sustaining crescendos of anger that cause you to lose control over your thoughts and actions, eventuating in a big blowup based on strong feelings that by now have become completely removed from the reality that originally provoked them.

Drinking to cope with anger is always a bad idea, especially when alcohol is used in combination with benzodiazepines. On the positive side, agents like alcohol and benzodiazepines individually or even together can have a temporary tranquilizing effect. But on the negative side they can contemporaneously remove inhibitions, create sensory deprivation, and produce a high degree of instinctual arousal—leading to escalating paranoid ideation.

Should you, as often happens, actually lose your temper in spite of yourself and despite all attempts at self-control, you can at least come up with better ways to deal with the anger you could not avoid feeling and expressing. You can soften your complaints/criticisms of others by making your angry points more gently. You can avoid personal slurs entirely or at the very least dilute them with simultaneously expressed self-criticisms such as "I wish I were the type of person who didn't get so inappropriately angry and critical" or "I wish I could be more charitable toward you." You can try to displace your anger from emotionally laden to neutral topics, changing, for example, personal slurs, nasty cracks, and taunts around to become comments of an impersonal nature. Name-calling of a general sort is actually less interpersonally disruptive than targeting another's flaws personally and specifically. Alternatively, you might be the sort of person who on balance can do better by expressing your anger not directly but laconically, that is, passive-aggressively. Though passive-aggression is pathological, in a way it is less so than raw, angry blow-ups, uproars, and overt displays of violence. While for most people passive-aggression is regressive, for many paranoid individuals passive-aggression is progressive.

When your anger is justified you should try to transform a generalized rage response into an honest, rational, reasonable, dispassionate, valid, concrete statement of issues worth pursuing in a constructive way. Instead of reacting globally to a troubling event in a basically perfectly acceptable relationship by saying, "Why should I bother with you; you are against me like everyone else," you can say specifically what it is that troubles you, for example, "Everyone I have ever known in my whole life has abandoned me, sooner or later, and so I need to be reassured that you are not going to do that to me too. What can you say and do to help me with that?" However, being honest and exact does not mean saying everything you think and feel. It is often enough to say what you are thinking, without, however, expressing what you are feeling—that is, it might be best to express your angry ideas dispassionately and without rancor, expressing the anger's ideational but not its emotional component.

A patient suspected that his lover was losing interest in him. The patient hesitated to discuss his fears because he blurred the distinction between discussion and upbraiding. He felt that expressing his thoughts was exactly the same thing as blowing up, and he was certain that blowing up would offend his lover and cause him to leave him. The solution was for him to say what bothered him exactly, but to say it unemotionally, without the angry, disappointed feelings that accompanied his negative thoughts.

A paranoid individual's date kept her waiting for over an hour. When he did finally arrive, he asked her, as if innocently, "Have I kept you waiting long? And are you upset about it?" Her reply was, "No, I have only been waiting a little while" and "I'm not upset because I am not in a rush." But she was being dishonest. In fact the whole time she had been waiting she had been stewing about being left hanging. Now she found that she could not enjoy the rest of the meal because of her deception. All she could think of was, "He has it in for me. He doesn't treat anyone else that way." Soon enough her negative feelings escalated from imagination to fantasy to complete conviction that her date did not come on time because he hated her. So after 15 or so minutes of this, she decided to tell him the truth. She decided to say exactly what was on her mind, but without getting angry. So she said, calmly and coolly, "Actually I was upset about your being late. I didn't want to say anything because I was afraid you would get mad at me." She felt better for telling him the truth, and she was proud of herself for putting him on notice that in the future his being late would be unacceptable. As it turned out this was a fortunate exchange. The friend came forth with explanations and apologies, relieving the tension and cementing the relationship.

A patient complained to me that her boss made her stay late without notice or extra pay and often for no valid reason. She was tired, frustrated, and furious. She saw her boss as her adversary, but then, projecting her anger onto him, feared that if she complained he would fire her. I suggested that she stay late without complaining if there was work to be done, while insisting on being paid for the overtime—either demanding overtime pay or demanding, and taking, compensatory time off. When she did that her anger, instead of ricocheting off her boss and bouncing back at her in the form of fears that he was persecuting her, disappeared into a new protocol for setting reasonable limits on him—part of her freshly created plan to deal with her anger not simply by getting it out but by resolving what was making her angry in the first place, and doing that in a direct, forthright, helpful, and corrective manner.

Finally, if you do get angry and become unpleasantly nasty in spite of all precautions taken, you should advise yourself to not overworry about it. Some people may not accept your difficult personality, but others will leave room for your being imperfect and stick by you. Keep in mind that others' basic feelings do not necessarily change from positive to negative as readily as you might fear. All is not necessarily lost just because you made one or a few injudicious remarks or had a bad blowup, as long as you have not become physically abusive (and sometimes not even then). Paranoid individuals who constantly fear the sudden and permanent demise of relationships just because they got angry one time should view their concerns not as realistic worries but as more of their characteristic alarmist fantasies.

In conclusion, on balance it is best to not get angry in the first place. If, however, you do get angry it is often better to keep your anger in than to get it out. Advantages of keeping anger in include justified pride in your ability to control yourself—that is, in your ability to disguise your negative emotions and avoid taking emotionally based action. Now you can keep from blaming yourself for getting angry. Now you will be less likely to develop low-self esteem over acting angry, and therefore less likely to defensively project your anger out to the point that you become even more paranoid than before. However, there are times and circumstances when you cannot help but get angry and when you just have to say something. At such times and under such circumstances, often what matters most is not so much what you say but how you say it. That can make the difference between a profitable discussion and just another bitter episode of explosive suspicion and mistrust.

LEARNING TO TRUST, LEARNING TO LOVE

As a paranoid individual you need to learn to trust. One way to learn to trust is to posit hypothetical situations, each with two alternative scenarios: the first reflecting your lack of basic trust, and the second, the one that you should live by, reflecting your newly found ability to become trusting. You might keep a journal of stimuli that actually disturbed you and your responses to them, so that you can later compare "what I thought, and was afraid, she said," to "here is what she actually said and probably meant." Put down every negative fantasy you might have about others on one side of the page and on the other side document alternative interpretations that reflect more positive realities. This exercise can help you recognize that others may be for you, not against you, and that in turn can help diminish your pessimistic "out-to-get-me" interpretations of others' intentions and behavior. As an example of a correctable misinterpretation, a man went to an artist's private home to buy a painting from her, and bought a much larger one than he had anticipated purchasing. When he met the artist some months later she, speaking to her husband, referred to his purchase as follows: "He wanted to buy a small one but wound up buying a big one." Only he heard, his guilty selfishness speaking, "He only wanted to pay for a small one so he worked on me until I gave him a big one for the same price." Keeping such a journal helps conquer the paranoid tendency to collect injustices, which of course only creates resentment, for which there is a price to pay. The journal, when studied coolly and dispassionately after the fact, can serve as a reality check that takes into account how you, as a paranoid individual, likely filter perceptions of others through a special personal scenario that by warping reality creates perceptual biases. Focus on the other side of your every story, asking yourself as you review your journal entries what someone else less paranoid would think and say. You should particularly look for oversimplifications that are the product of your having removed levels of complexity, particularly those other, less pessimistic possibilities that, when omitted, make your interpretation of other people's positions and events inaccurately and inflexibly narrow and one-sided, in a negative direction. You should be especially alert to how specifically you process information that contradicts your main thesis—what, in other words, you do with positive information that does not fit in with your negative oversimplifications.

Also, you should ask yourself whether, in addition to oversimplifying some things, you add unnecessary levels of complexity to other things by reading something alarming that is not there into a situation, then overreacting to your self-created prompt and losing positive focus. The latter process is exemplified by the patient who wrote in his journal, "I asked myself this morning why is my wife more dressed up on her way to work than usual and why this morning of all mornings did she put on that new shade of lipstick? Is she having an affair at the office?" On the other side of the journal the patient wrote, "No, I realized that I simply forgot that she is just attending a special conference with the owners of her company, and quite naturally she wanted to look her best."

A journal can also help you distinguish between really stressful, possibly dangerous situations and minor annoyances such as people cracking gum, playing hissing personal stereos, or talking loudly on cell phones in public places. That is, it can help you learn to distinguish things that are inherently only modestly bothersome from truly serious threats to your well-being. Far too many paranoid individuals feel that all dangers are created equal, so that a minor slight from the boss becomes the equivalent of being suddenly fired without preparation or notice or concern for how you are going to survive when unemployed. This flattening of the response curve—an inability to modulate the tone and amplitude of a response to make it fit the intensity, severity, significance, and importance of the stimulus—is one of the main things that leads you as a paranoid individual to perceive all danger as catastrophic. If this is you, your journal can help you avoid going through life as if it were flat out an entirely negative and always very dangerous experience, and can help you instead respond appropriately not only in kind but also in degree to what is actually happening.

LEARNING TO WORRY LESS

Paranoid individuals can profitably view and treat themselves as if they are compulsive worriers. Remember that you, as a paranoid individual, are likely to forget that you are a pessimist who, like all pessimists, sees only the worst-case scenario and believes that it actually represents reality. You likely react to trivial prompts as if they are momentous disasters, turning your minor obsessions into delusions as worry drives worry until concern becomes certainty. Instead, early on identify your tendency to overworry about every little thing, then start reserving your worries for the big things only. If necessary and whenever possible, either correct a real problem immediately, directly, and dispassionately, or try to simply ignore one that is insignificant. A good way to make corrections is to check in with the assumed source of your problem (the person you view as potentially victimizing you). Instead of imagining what is going on, ask him or her what is actually happening. Often forthright, simple, reassuring explanations will be forthcoming, and more likely than not calming. Or, check in with a trusted adviser, someone who knows enough to assess a situation for you in a way that may very well be reassuring and comforting.

SELF-ANALYZE YOUR PARANOID DEFENSES

An important preventive and corrective involves exploring your defensiveness and finding better, less defensive ways to deal with anxiety and guilt. Hopefully you retain the capacity for, and can benefit from, developing intellectual and emotional insight into your defensive projection—that process that disavows instead of solving a problem. I have been able to train some of my patients to identify how they extroject part of themselves from in to out, and then, becoming the object where once they were the subject, back again. That boomeranging of thought and feeling is not as elusive a process as you might at first think. Rather it has a very concrete representation in the mind that you can, with a little learning and practice, capture in graphic form in statu nascendi, that is, as it arises. Now you can catch yourself projecting and stop it or, when that is not possible, at least identify how irrational it is and refuse to let it guide you completely.

Also preventive and even somewhat curative are identifying, studying, and correcting your cognitive errors in preparation for thinking more logically and less emotionally. For example, many paranoid individuals can benefit from learning the role played in their antagonistic stances by some equals all and other forms of distortive oversimplified thinking. You might recognize that others are not necessarily criticizing you as a person (all) when they are merely complaining about one or more of your manifest behaviors (some). Discard passion in favor of rationality by relinquishing your tendency to divide the people in the world into protagonists and antagonists, creating high drama that has little basis in the lower things that constitute everyday reality. Identify and disallow catastrophic, chain, slippery slope, and "for want of a nail the ship was lost" thinking. For example, a neighbor asked me if she could store a large amount of food in my freezer because her freezer was full. Her freezer was full because she was a collector who hung on to years-old food the same way and for the same reasons that she hung on to years-old newspapers, the "you never know when you will want and need them" phenomenon. I agreed to let her use my freezer, but (correctly) anticipating escalating future requests, did so with silent reservations. Probably she sensed some hesitation in my voice. I did hesitate because I believed that the solution to the full freezer problem was to empty hers, not to fill mine up. So she wondered if I were angry with her (which I was a little bit, but it did not matter), and then escalated to how I did not like her, then to how no one liked her, and then to how everyone hated her.

ACCEPT INDICATED PHARMACOTHERAPY

Pharmacotherapy can help you feel better and accomplish many of your goals. It can reduce your anxiety, induce calm, and thereby improve your intrapersonal economy and your interpersonal relationships. Therefore you, as a paranoid individual, should accept medication if prescribed. However, while you should think twice about refusing pharmacotherapy that is indicated, you should insist on being given medication that is right for you. If you suspect that you are very paranoid and your doctor prescribes antidepressants alone for your presumed depression, instead of feeling reassured and flattered that your illness is not as bad as you feared, protest and complain, even though you risk being called paranoid (or more paranoid), and seek out a second opinion before you take medication that activates you to the point that you become really paranoid and start hallucinating or thinking violent thoughts. I will always remember the case of the paranoid psychoanalyst who was given antidepressants for all the wrong reasons. One day she was analyzing a friend. In the middle of the session, she got out of her chair, walked over to the side of the couch where he was lying, picked up his head in her hands, and, staring bullets at him, proclaimed, "I have about had it with you. I simply hate you too much to continue to treat you." Also be warned by an incident in which I was secondarily involved. I believe that my own analyst was a paranoid man whom I believe was being treated, probably incorrectly from what I gleaned from his responses to me, for depression. One day I said I thought that he did not like me. He agreed, and suggested that we stop therapy right now—in the middle of a session. (He charged me for the whole session, reasoning that I was paying not for his time but for his doing right by me.) Shortly afterward he called a colleague over, saying he didn't feel well and was very depressed. Then when the colleague turned away for a moment to call an ambulance, my ex-analyst jumped off the roof.

HIDE YOUR PARANOIA

Sometimes, no matter how motivated you are, it is not possible to be less paranoid than you already happen to be. When this is the case, you can at least settle for ameliorating the consequences of your paranoia by hiding it from the world. Try to train yourself to react with less of a paranoid knee-jerk response and instead attempt to distance yourself from your own gut reactions by inserting your observing ego between your emotional reflexive responses to others and any position you take and positional statement you make. After identifying what is delusional about your thinking, practice restraint by not acting on those thoughts. The operative principle here is that you can think it, but you mustn't say or do it. Perhaps you can take the next step and, going to the opposite extreme, become counterparanoid—forcing yourself to become the opposite of paranoid, as you rush headlong from anguish into calm, from suspiciousness to trust, and from fear into relaxed comfort. That is difficult to do for a number of reasons. Some of us balk at having to give up the rewards of being paranoid, such as the sadistic pleasures involved in hurting others and the masochistic pleasures of being mistreated by the great unjust and afterwards getting the sympathy vote. But as many of my patients have found, the rewards of forcing oneself to become counterparanoid are much greater than the satisfactions to be obtained from having more and more imaginary enemies.

Finally, on a positive note, as a paranoid individual you should cherish and maintain what is good about your paranoia. When a telemarketer calls to tell you that he or she is a financial wizard happy to help you manage all your money, or sell you a sure investment in natural gas futures, you should get more, not less, paranoid. You should call forth your good paranoia, become highly suspicious, get up on your high horse, think twice before getting involved, and just hang up the phone.

Bibliography

Akhtar, Salman. 1999. "Psychiatric Aspects of Terrorism: The Psychodynamic Dimension of Terrorism." *Psychiatric Annals* 26 (6): 350–55.

American Psychiatric Association. 1987. *Diagnostic and Statistical Manual of Mental Disorders.* Rev. 3rd ed. Washington, D.C.: American Psychiatric Association.

American Psychiatric Association. 1994. *Diagnostic and Statistical Manual of Mental Disorders.* 4th ed. Washington, D.C.: American Psychiatric Association.

Associated Press. 10 July 2003. New York.

Benjamin, Lorna Smith. 1996. *Interpersonal Diagnosis and Treatment of Personality Disorders.* New York: Guilford Press.

Bernstein, David P. 2002. "Cognitive Therapy of Personality Disorders in Patients with Histories of Emotional Abuse or Neglect." *Psychiatric Annals* 32 (10): 618–26.

Bone, Stanley, and John Oldham. 1994. "Paranoia: Historical Considerations." In *Paranoia, New Psychoanalytic Perspectives,* ed. John M. Oldham and Stanley Bone, 3–15. Madison, Conn.: International Universities Press.

Cooper, Arnold M. 1994. "Paranoia: A Part of Every Analysis." In *Paranoia, New Psychoanalytic Perspectives,* ed. John M. Oldham and Stanley Bone, 133–50. Madison, Conn.: International Universities Press.

Cornett, Carlton. 1993. "Preface." In *Affirmative Dynamic Psychotherapy with Gay Men,* ed. Carlton Cornett, ix–xvii. Northvale, N.J.: Jason Aronson.

Fawcett, Jan. 1999. "Psychiatric Aspects of Terrorism: Self-Justification and Terrorism." *Psychiatric Annals* 26 (6): 333.

Freud, Sigmund. 1957. "Psycho-Analytic Notes upon an Autobiographical Account of a Case of Paranoia (Dementia Paranoides)." In *Collected Papers.* Vol. 3. Translated by Alix and James Strachey. London: The Hogarth Press.

Fromm-Reichmann, Frieda. 1960. *Principles of Intensive Psychotherapy.* Chicago: University of Chicago Press.

Goldberg, Arnold. 1994. "Lovesickness." In *Paranoia, New Psychoanalytic Perspectives,* ed. John M. Oldham and Stanley Bone, 115–32. Madison, Conn.: International Universities Press.

Greenhouse, Linda. 2003. "Forcing Psychiatric Drugs on Defendants Is Weighed." *New York Times*, 4 March.

Haroun, Ansar M. 1999. "Psychiatric Aspects of Terrorism: Psychiatric Aspects of Terrorism." *Psychiatric Annals* 26 (6): 335–36.

Haroun, Ansar M., and Allen C. Snyder. 1999. "Psychiatric Aspects of Terrorism: The Terrorist in Court: Uses and Abuses of Psychiatry." *Psychiatric Annals* 26 (6): 357–61.

Holland, Bernard. 2003. "A Critic Reading His Critics." *New York Times*, 2 March.

Karg, Rhonda S., and Brad A. Alford. 1997. "Psychotic Disorders." In *Practicing Cognitive Therapy: A Guide to Interventions*, ed. Robert L. Leahy, 315–38. Northvale, N.J.: Jason Aronson.

Kernberg, Otto. 1994. "Leadership Styles and Organizational Paranoiagenesis." In *Paranoia, New Psychoanalytic Perspectives*, ed. John M. Oldham and Stanley Bone, 61–79. Madison, Conn.: International Universities Press.

———. 1985. Melanie Klein. In *Comprehensive Textbook of Psychiatry/IV*, ed. Harold I. Kaplan and Benjamin J. Sadock. Baltimore, Md.: Williams and Wilkins.

Kowszun, Graz, and Maeve Malley. 1996. "Alcohol and Substance Misuse." In *Pink Therapy: A Guide for Counsellors and Therapists Working with Lesbian, Gay and Bisexual Clients*, ed. Dominic Davies and Charles Neal, 170–87. Philadelphia: Open University Press.

Lehmann-Haupt, Christopher. 1999. "The Roots of Violence: A Frightening New Look." Book Review. *New York Times*, 27 September.

Levine, Sol. 1999. "Psychiatric Aspects of Terrorism: Youth in Terroristic Groups, Gangs, and Cults: The Allure, the Animus, and the Alienation." *Psychiatric Annals* 26 (6): 342–49.

Liberatore, Michael. 2003. "In the Rainbow Room. All Good Things . . ." *TriCityNews*, 27 March.

Millon, Theodore. 1981. *Disorders of Personality: DSM-III: Axis III*. New York: John Wiley and Sons.

Millon, Theodore. 1999. *Personality-Guided Therapy*. New York: John Wiley and Sons.

Millon, Theodore, and Roger D. Davis. 1996. *Disorders of Personality: DSM-IV and Beyond*. New York: John Wiley and Sons.

Munro, Alistair. 1999. *Delusional Disorder: Paranoia and Related Illnesses*. New York: Cambridge University Press.

News Report. 2002. Available on Internet.

Oldham, John, and Lois B. Morris. 1995. *The New Personality Self-Portrait*. New York: Bantam Books.

Oldham, John M., and Andrew E. Skodol. 1994. "Do Patients with Paranoid Personality Disorder Seek Psychoanalysis?" In *Paranoia, New Psychoanalytic Perspectives*, ed. John M. Oldham and Stanley Bone,. 151–66. Madison, Conn.: International Universities Press.

Potter-Efron, Pat, and Ron Potter-Efron. 1995. *Letting Go of Anger*. Oakland, Calif.: New Harbinger.

Reich, Wilhelm. 1949. *Character Analysis*. New York: Orgone Institute Press.

Review of *Living la Dolce Vita*, by Raeleen Mautner. Amazon.com. 8 April 2003.

Rhodes, Richard. 1999. "What Causes Brutality? The People Nurturing It." *New York Times*, 16 October.

Roth, Martin. 1989. "Delusional (Paranoid) Disorders." In *Treatments of Psychiatric Disorders*. Vol. 2, 1609–52. Washington, D.C.: The American Psychiatric Association.

Shapiro, David. 1994. "Paranoia from a Characterological Standpoint." In *Paranoia, New Psychoanalytic Perspectives*, ed. John M. Oldham and Stanley Bone, 49–57. Madison, Conn.: International Universities Press.

Sims, Andrew. 1988. "Delusions and Other Erroneous Ideas." In *Symptoms in the Mind: An Introduction to Descriptive Psychopathology*. London: Bailliere Tindall.

Slovenko, Ralph. 1985. "Law and Psychiatry." In *Comprehensive Textbook of Psychiatry IV*, ed. Harold I. Kaplan and Benjamin J. Sadock, 1960–90. Baltimore, Md.: Williams and Wilkins.

Sullivan, Harry S. 1953. *The Interpersonal Theory of Psychiatry*. New York: W. W. Norton.

Wettstein, Robert M. 1988. "Psychiatry and the Law." In *The American Psychiatric Press Textbook of Psychiatry*, ed. John A. Talbott, Robert E. Hales, and Stuart C. Yudofsky, 1059–84. Washington, D.C.: American Psychiatric Press.

Index

Road rage, 61, 87, 198–99, 215. *See also*
    Rage reaction
Role-playing, 155–56
Romantic relationships, 230

Sadism, 119, 192, 219–20
Sadomasochism: definition of, 24; in
    development of paranoid process,
    118–19; relationships based on,
    219–20; tendencies in paranoid
    individuals for, 48–51
Schadenfreude, 48, 136–37
Schematherapy, 157
Schizoid personality disorder, 26
Schizophrenia, 21, 171, 172
Schneiderian delusions, 22–23
Schumann, Robert, 193
Seasonal affective disorder, 229
Secondary delusions, 23–25
Secretiveness, 63, 82, 97
Seductiveness with paranoid
    individuals, 110, 184
Selective abstraction/attention, 135–37,
    154
Selective memory, 15
Self-acceptance and self-awareness, 13,
    180, 225–27
Self-analysis suggestions for paranoid
    individuals, 235–36
Self-control and self-protection, 14, 82,
    155
Self-esteem, 31–32, 55, 161, 226–27
Semidelusional thought, 8
Seminormal individuals, 74
Sense of humor, prognosis with, 193
Sense of self, 180
Sensitivity toward others, 228
Sensory deprivation and cognitive
    errors, 133
Sensory illusions, 39
Sexual exploitation of paranoid
    individuals, 223
Sexuality: acceptance of, 225;
    repression of and paranoia, 122–23;
    in therapy, 148
Shared delusions: as paranoia of
    everyday life, 75–76; religious
    influence and, 129; in seminormal

individuals, 74; sociocultural
    influences and, 129
Shared paranoia, 155
Silent treatment, 157
Social anxiety, 167
Social context illumination, 148
Social myths, 66, 228
Social phobias, 165, 168, 180, 201
Society: paranoid individuals and, 90;
    role in causing paranoia, 105–6; view
    of mental illness, 99–102
Sociocultural influences and shared
    delusions, 129
Somatic delusions: blaming and, 124;
    definition of, 17; description of,
    28–29; existential component of,
    129; Munchausen's disorder and, 29
Somatization in paranoid personality
    disorder, 49–50
Speech, 6–9, 202–3
Splitting process and selective
    abstraction/attention, 136
Spontaneity, 163
Standard delusions, 78
Standards for legal incompetency, 94
Stockholm syndrome, 35
Stubbornness, prognosis with, 192
Subjugated paranoia, 35
Subjugation, delusional, 35
Sublimation of anger: in
    psychodynamic/interpersonal
    approaches, 148
Submissiveness: and calming paranoid
    individuals, 88
Suggestibility: as paranoia of everyday
    life, 74–75
Suicidal behavior, 96–97, 172
Superstitions: as paranoia of everyday
    life, 77
Supportiveness: caretakers and, 202–3
Surprise, 183, 202
Suspiciousness, 41–42, 74, 167
Sympathetic discharge, excessive, 4
Symptom activation and delusional
    disorder, 121
"Symptom disorder," 74. *See also*
    Seminormal individuals
Symptoms of paranoia, 117–20, 123–29

About the Author

MARTIN KANTOR is a psychiatrist who has been in private practice in Boston and New York City. He served as Assistant Clinical Professor of Psychiatry at Mount Sinai Medical School and Clinical Assistant Professor of Psychiatry at the University of Medicine and Dentistry of New Jersey, New Jersey Medical School. Dr. Kantor is the author of 12 previous books, including *Distancing: Avoidant Personality Disorder, Revised and Expanded* (Praeger, 2003), *Passive Aggression: A Guide for the Therapist, the Patient, and the Victim* (Praeger, 2002), *Treating Emotional Disorders in Gay Men* (Praeger, 1999), and *Homophobia* (Praeger, 1998).